WHO ENTERS POLITICS AND WHY?

Basic Human Values in the UK Parliament

James Weinberg

BRISTOL
UNIVERSITY
PRESS

First published in Great Britain in 2020 by

Bristol University Press
University of Bristol
1-9 Old Park Hill
Bristol
BS2 8BB
UK
t: +44 (0)117 954 5940
e: bup-info@bristol.ac.uk

Details of international sales and distribution partners are available at
bristoluniversitypress.co.uk

British Library Cataloguing in Publication Data
A catalogue record for this book is available from the British Library

ISBN 978-1-5292-0916-7 hardcover
ISBN 978-1-5292-0918-1 ePub
ISBN 978-1-5292-0917-4 ePdf

Cover design by blu inc, Bristol
Front cover image: Alamy

This book is dedicated to those men and women who, outside the limelight of the media, are quietly and steadfastly trying to make a difference in this world every single day.

Contents

List of Figures and Tables   vi
Note on the Author   viii
Acknowledgements   ix

1 Why Do We Hate Politicians?   1

2 Psychological Scrutiny: Who Enters Politics and Why?   25

3 All the Same! Demographic Homogeneity and Careerism   53

4 Basic Values and Partisanship   79

5 Parliamentary Behaviour: Personal Choices, Political Results   107

6 Perfect Politicians? Voting Preferences in the United Kingdom 145

Notes   167

Appendix A: Twenty Item Portrait Values Questionnaire (TwIVI)   173
Appendix B: Confirmatory factor analysis of survey data on   175
            the basic values of politicians (UK Members of
            Parliament, $N = 168$)
Appendix C: External correlations across samples   177
Appendix D: Conjoint experiment of candidate preferences by   179
            partisanship

References   183
Index   217

List of Figures and Tables

Figures

2.1	Distributions of participants' basic values (centred scores)	32
2.2	Basic values and 'in-role' success	39
2.3	Comprehensive model of candidate emergence	43
2.4	Basic values and candidate emergence in the UK	45
3.1	Basic values by gender and status	60
3.2	Basic values by ethnicity and status	66
3.3	MPs' higher order basic values by occupational background ($N = 168$)	73
3.4	The basic values of career politicians	75
4.1	Basic values by partisanship	85
4.2	Correlations between MPs' basic values and their economic ideology	90
4.3	Correlations between MPs' basic values and their social ideology	91
4.4	Basic values by partisanship and status using ESS 8	96
4.5	Basic values by partisanship and status using ESS 7	99
4.6	Basic values and vote patterns in the 2015 General Election	104
5.1	An integrated model of parliamentary political behaviour (IMPPB)	117
5.2	EDM sponsorship as a function of MPs' power values	136
5.3	Submission of written questions as a function of MPs' security values	139
5.4	Basic values and select committee membership	142
6.1	Random iteration of a conjoint experiment testing personalized candidate selection	152
6.2	Conjoint analysis of candidate preferences in the UK	155

Tables

1.1	Descriptive data (including the House of Commons as of the 2017 General Election)	17
1.2	Profile of interviewees	18
1.3	Semi-structured interview plan (exemplar questions)	20
2.1	Value hierarchies based on sample means (most important to least important)	31
2.2	Independent samples t-test (centred mean scores)	35
3.1	Independent samples t-tests of basic values by gender and status (centred mean scores)	59
3.2	Independent samples t-tests of basic values by ethnicity and status (centred mean scores)	67
3.3	Members of Parliament by previous occupation ($N = 168$)	73
4.1	Independent samples t-test of basic values by partisanship and status (centred mean scores)	97
4.2	Independent samples t-test of basic values between MPs and non-voters in the 2015 UK General Election	105
5.1	Overview of prominent paradigms in parliamentary studies	112
5.2	Summary of three high-profile votes in the UK House of Commons	121
5.3	Correlations between MPs' basic values and their voting records	122
5.4	Predictors of voting 'for' the Marriage (Same Sex Couples) Act 2013	124
5.5	Predictors of voting 'for' UK Air Strikes against ISIL in Syria (2015)	127
5.6	Predictors of voting 'for' the European Union (Notification of Withdrawal) Bill 2017	131
5.7	Correlations between MPs' basic values and moderate/low-cost parliamentary behaviours	134
6.1	Value hierarchies for 'real' and 'ideal' MPs based on sample means (most important to least important)	158

Note on the Author

James Weinberg is a lecturer in Political Behaviour at the University of Sheffield, where he currently holds a three-year Leverhulme Fellowship to investigate how politicians govern in an age of distrust. His research interests span the fields of political psychology and youth politics, and his research on topics such as citizenship education in England and the psychology of political success has been published in leading journals including the *British Journal of Political Science*, *British Journal of Politics and International Relations*, the *Journal of Education Policy* and *Parliamentary Affairs*. In January 2019, James received the Walter Bagehot prize from the UK Political Studies Association (PSA) for the best doctoral research in the fields of government and public policy completed in 2018. James also holds the University of Sheffield's 2018 Chancellor's Medal, which was awarded to him for 'outstanding contributions to the Faculty of Social Sciences' and 'impressive achievements in government and parliamentary circles'. In May 2020, James was elected to the Executive Committee of the PSA. Prior to that, James co-founded the Political Psychology specialist group of the PSA with a view to growing a network of like-minded scholars in the UK who are interested in the psychology of politics and the politics of psychology. The group continues to flourish and welcomes new academic and non-academic members alike. James completed his PhD in Politics at the University of Sheffield, his MA in Political Science at the University of Manchester, and his BA in History at the University of Oxford. James started his career as a qualified secondary school teacher in West London.

Acknowledgements

The first specific mention must go to my family for their empathy and, in particular, their ability to listen to my banal diatribes about the state of contemporary politics (in the broadest possible sense) on any given day. I must thank my mother for providing me with a healthy dose of realism; my father for reminding me that we work to live and not vice versa; my sister for offering timely distractions; and my grandparents for their unwavering belief in my ability to 'get the job done'.

I also owe a debt of gratitude to Dr Todd Hartman and Professor Matthew Flinders, who supervised the PhD from which the idea for this book first arose. As a supervisor, mentor and subsequently a colleague, Todd has given me his time, attention and expertise with unwavering selflessness. I publish this book in full knowledge that he provided me with the skills needed to match my ambition. Matt has also been an incredible patron to me in recent years, opening doors and opportunities where there seemingly were none. More importantly, he taught me the importance of looking beyond the academic bubble and working with the public interest in mind. In other words, he has restored my faith in the ability of academics to 'make a difference'. Whatever the future holds, I will continue to count Matt and Todd as dear colleagues and friends.

I have been extremely lucky to enter a number of collegiate 'families' in my academic career to date and this has made the lonely moments of academic research much more bearable. To all my colleagues at the Sir Bernard Crick Centre, past and present (Kate Dommett, Marc Geddes, Matt Wood, Alex Meakin, Brenton Prosser, Holly Ryan, Leanne Cotter, Pat Seyd, Alexandra Anderson, Nikki Soo), I would like to say thank you for your friendship, guidance and your time. In particular I say a special thanks to Indra Mangule, who has at various times over the past five years shared an office as well as a house with me, and all without despairing at my terrible sense of humour.

I would like to thank all of the friends and colleagues I have made through the Political Studies Association, whether that be on the early career network committee, the committed team in head office, trustees past and present, or members of the Political Psychology and Young People's Politics specialist groups. Likewise, I am hugely grateful to members of the PACE peer review group – Jack Corbett in particular – for inviting me to join your meetings and to share my latest work. Your feedback has been invaluable in developing both the ideas in this book and future research plans arising from it.

I also extend a sincere thanks to all of the friends and colleagues I made in Australia during my visiting scholarship at the University of Sydney in 2017, which I completed in the midst of conducting the research for this book. Thanks go, in particular, to John Keane for his inspirational approach to good scholarship, public engagement and hearty intellectual discussion; to Simon Tormey for giving me so much of his time and wisdom during the 2017 Australian Political Studies Association conference in Melbourne; and to Keshia Jacotine for her ongoing friendship and transglobal deliveries of caramel Tim Tams. In a similar vein I would like to thank Martin Rosema for teaching me the true meaning of getting the most out of a conference and for inviting me to present some of the findings from this book at the 2018 Politicologenetmaal at Leiden University.

Lastly, I want to express sincere appreciation to every Member of Parliament, councillor and unsuccessful political candidate who agreed to participate in this research project. Your dedication to democracy, whatever your personal opinions, has been truly admirable and reassuring to observe.

Why Do We Hate Politicians?

'[Successful politicians are] … People with ability. People with ambition. People who are connected.'

Labour Party MP (Interviewee 8)

Long before the election of Donald Trump, the UK's referendum on membership of the European Union, the rise of populism across Europe, or the UK expenses scandal in 2009, the late Anthony King (1981) wrote of the biggest divide in British politics as that between Britain's whole political class and the great majority of the British people. The 'anti-politics' phenomenon is now well documented in Britain: low levels of party membership and diminishing partisanship per se, poor electoral turnout, badly performing governments and failures of accountability, and plummeting trust in political elites have all been common research foci and the subjects of academic as well as journalistic debate (Hay, 2007; Norris, 2011; Flinders, 2012). Yet the literature seeking to explain and understand this crisis of democracy focuses almost singularly on *popular* notions of what politics is and how it *should* work. By contrast, political science has failed to engage sufficiently with those who actually occupy political office: who they are, why they do it, or what they think and feel about a job that few of us would ever care to contemplate. Where existing research does focus on politicians, it has largely iterated an uncomfortable narrative of public hostility and alienation (Stoker et al, 2016; Clarke et al, 2018); it has explored how elected representatives are expected to behave (Carman, 2006; Bengtsson and Wass, 2010; André and Depauw, 2017); and it has developed our understanding of what politicians 'do' from analyses of parliamentary records and processes (Hix et al, 2007; Saalfeld, 2011; Geddes, 2020).

At the same time, survey data continue to reveal remarkable levels of public distrust, political apathy, political inefficacy and democratic despondency that crystallize around popular judgements about those who actually govern.[1] The Hansard Society's 2019 audit of political engagement in the UK concluded: '[o]pinions of the systems of governing are at their lowest point in the 15-year Audit series – worse now than in the aftermath of the MPs' expenses scandal' (p 3). The audit, which is carried out annually by Ipsos MORI with a face-to-face nationally representative quota sample of the British public, goes on to report that more people in Britain think the problem lies with the people in politics than the system; people have more faith in the military and judges to act in the public interest than politicians; more than 50% of people don't think that the main parties and politicians care about them; and despite the ongoing ramifications of Brexit, people still think that more major decisions should be put to the people than are currently (Hansard Society, 2019, pp 10–17). All this points to profound public dissatisfaction with the way politics is done and, more precisely, the people who are tasked with 'representing' them.

It is in this context that this book explores original data on the personalities of British politicians, specifically 168 Members of Parliament (MPs), in order to draw unique insights about who enters politics and why, how they represent 'us' once they get there, and whether public antipathy towards politicians is justified. In this respect, this book is distinctive in its approach to familiar issues predominant in academic, popular and journalistic press on anti-politics: to paraphrase Isabel Hardman's (2018) book, (why) do we get the 'wrong politicians'? The substantive findings presented in this book do, therefore, tell a human story that has appeal beyond the ivory towers of academia. Quantitative analyses of survey data are coupled with rich insights from interviews with current and former MPs who have held some of the highest political offices in the UK. These data are evaluated in themed chapters to tackle three interrelated 'problems' that academics, practitioners and the public will, it is hoped, find equally captivating:

Problem 1: Who enters politics and how are they different to the general public?
Problem 2: Do politicians' personality characteristics matter for their behaviour once they are elected to parliament?
Problem 3: Do voters really get the 'wrong' politicians?

In tackling these problems, this book traverses the interdisciplinary boundaries of political science and psychology. New data on the personalities of politicians in the UK, and MPs in particular, represent the centrifugal force of this book and the springboard from which an innovative and analytical dive is taken into related areas of academic research and public interest. These include, for example, the role of personality characteristics vis-à-vis candidate emergence and political ambition, parliamentary representation and legislative behaviour, and public voting preferences.

Whilst the empirics in this chapter and the rest of the book are based on data from just one particular geographic context, there are also a number of reasons why the UK presents an ideal case study. Firstly, the UK has long been overlooked as a locus for research in the fields of political psychology and personality studies (in politics) in particular. Specialist groups for academics working on political psychology in the UK's prestigious learned societies for politics and psychology (the UK Political Studies Association and the British Psychological Society) were only founded in 2016 and 2019 respectively. The potential to push new academic boundaries is, then, tremendous. Practically, the UK legislature is also the second largest in the world after China. With 650 elected members of the House of Commons representing a population that is smaller than most comparable democracies, the UK legislature provides a somewhat inflated target population of parliamentary politicians to study. Equally, the Westminster parliamentary system, its procedures and practices (legislative, party political, and even its professionalization of political office) have been replicated widely around the world. These practices and procedures ultimately define many of the pull factors that might facilitate or encourage candidate emergence and, in turn, candidate success. It is therefore anticipated that the findings presented throughout this book will be of interest to a global readership of academics, students, practitioners and citizens.

The scale and ambition of this project require considerable preface in terms of empirical, methodological and conceptual clarity. Therefore, this opening chapter is used to (a) highlight the premium that has been placed on politicians' personalities by the popular as well as academic press (thus clarifying the broader fillip for this book, the three 'problems' highlighted above, as well as its public appeal), (b) introduce basic human values as the measure of personality chosen for this study from within a broader literature on personality and politics, (c) clarify the data and empirics underpinning the content of subsequent chapters, and (d) outline the contribution of each chapter in the rest of this book.

Politicians and anti-politics: a human story?

Before examining politicians' personalities per se or even the effects of personality on politicians' behaviour, it is worth considering why the psychology of politicians has become such a trope in contemporary discourse. Put another way, why do we care so much about the personality characteristics of our representatives and does it actually matter? To answer this question – and thus provide a backdrop to the efforts of this book – is to engage with the nuanced arguments of well-developed academic scholarship on the anti-politics phenomenon in the UK and beyond. This literature distils broadly into two dominant explanations of democratic decline (for an extended review, see Corbett, 2015). The first is a 'gap' account of political malaise and the demonization of politicians based on a divergence of citizen expectations and politicians' performance. The second is a 'trap' account, in which politicians are caught between contradictory demands inherent in democratic publics and representative politics.

To take the first of these dominant approaches – the 'gap' account – is to distinguish between two further schools of thought. On the one hand a demand-side explanation, energetically pursued by Matthew Flinders (2012; see also Hatier, 2012), works backwards from public disengagement to a certain moral panic about the quality of our representatives. In this view, public apathy is underwritten by a lack of political education and thus an inflated impression of what is deliverable in democratic politics. On the other hand, a supply-side explanation (see, in particular, Stoker, 2006; Hay, 2007; Hay and Stoker, 2009) blames professional politicians and neoliberal reform agendas for their complacency in fuelling anti-political sentiment. The latter explanation sits nicely with those who welcome the threat of anti-politics as a chance to rejuvenate democracy through new forms of popular deliberation and participation (eg Dryzek, 2000; Evans et al, 2013). Whilst these explanations might contend with one another, there are distinct similarities. Above all, and of particular relevance for this book, both accounts come back to the people doing politics: one to defend politicians from the expectation of being superhuman and the other to criticize them for a range of human vices.

The evidence for these explanations is compelling whichever way it is interpreted. In their application of Kahneman's (2011) philosophy of fast and slow thinking, Stoker and colleagues (2016) show, for example, that the public's intuitive thinking about politicians is highly negative, cynical and characterized by a vernacular of disillusionment. Focus group participants provided 209 word associations for politicians, of which only seven were positive. Among the most common answers were terms like 'self-interested', 'self-regarding', 'unprincipled', 'ambitious' (Stoker et al, 2016, p 8). Such responses not only supplement the quantitative evidence gathered by larger surveys of the public, but they indicate the psychological narrative underpinning public disapprobation for those who govern. This argument is given even more weight by Clarke and colleagues' (2018) recent study of Mass Observation data from 1937 onwards.[2] Their analysis shows (unsurprizingly) that criticisms of politicians have always been prevalent, but (more surprizingly) specific notions of 'the good politician' have moved away from an emphasis on competence and towards one on trust, authenticity and warmth (that is, evaluations have become far more emotional, interpersonal and psychologically charged). Clarke and colleagues (2018) argue that politicians' personal qualities have thus become the heuristic by which everyday judgements about the activities and performance of political institutions and systems are also formed. Yet like the majority of the literature introduced here, the authors focus entirely on the public and their attitudes towards politicians without bringing the latter into the debate. Nor do they demonstrate the content and importance of the public's psychological claims for voting behaviour or anti-politics more broadly.

Allen and Birch (2015a, p 402) take this line of inquiry much further in their specific study of ethics and integrity in UK politics. Administering large-N surveys to the British public either side of the MPs' expenses scandal in 2009, the authors find a significant negative relationship between public confidence in politicians' personality characteristics, such as honesty, and more diffuse dissatisfaction in politics. As confidence in politicians' personal qualities increased, so too the gap between respondents' ideal beliefs about the process of representative democracy and their perceptions of the status quo decreased. As a causal relationship, it would appear sensible to believe that citizens who trust their politicians to be honest and interested in popular opinion will also be more satisfied with the operation of democratic politics. The obvious parallel imperative here – to study the psychological 'truths' about our politicians – is also iterated explicitly by Peter Allen's (2018) book on the political class and *Why It Matters Who Our Politicians Are*. Allen carefully unpicks the case for the prosecution against our contemporary politicians and, in line with previous studies, he repeatedly returns to popular abstractions about the self-interest and dishonesty of elected representatives. Indicative of institutional and sociological explanations of elite recruitment (see Bell, 2017), Allen treats these psychological criticisms as symptoms rather than causes of a detrimental homogeneity among political elites driven by inequalities in class, wealth, education and problems with the UK's majoritarian electoral system. These are important avenues of investigation, but they do not necessarily test the verity of psychological claims about politicians or the ways in which such individual-level characteristics might affect the ways they approach politics as a vocation. As Allen (2018, p 31) admits, '[t]here is little reliable evidence as to the content of politicians' attitudes'.

It is striking that such critiques of politicians and their motives, let alone their involvement in major policy decisions, are at direct odds with the beliefs and experiences of politicians as presented in a relatively small pool of political studies research (eg Reeher, 2006; Tiernan and Weller, 2010) and in academic texts or biographies by former politicians (eg Volgy, 2001; Ignatieff, 2013). This is a practical defence of politicians that has been specifically advanced in recent years by Jack Corbett (2015). According to Corbett (2015, pp 473–80), the disjuncture between evidence from politicians and public evaluations thereof points to four central defences. Firstly, the number of inter-confirmatory qualitative studies of politicians' ideological beliefs (eg Weller and Gratten, 1981; Tiernan and Weller, 2010), as well as various typologies of politicians (eg Searing, 1994; Navarro, 2009), suggests a level of heterogeneity that does not feature in the literature on political 'careerism' and the moral depravity of the political class. Secondly, self-report and interview data on politicians from numerous democratic systems conveys a common commitment to serve others and achieve goals directed at a 'better' future (eg Reeher, 2006). Thirdly, accounts of political life are replete with references to extreme time commitments, daily conflict, poor health and tense family relations (eg Volgy, 2001; Ignatieff, 2013). This is a sentiment echoed by Flinders and colleagues (2018) in their pioneering framework of stressors on politicians' mental health and wellbeing. It is put somewhat more succinctly by Rhodes' (2011, p 161) study of British government: 'The key task of the departmental court is to cope.' The final argument in Corbett's (2015) defence mirrors what John Keane (2009, p 51) calls 'the ubiquity of perplexity' in his *Life and Death of Democracy*. While the public criticizes politicians for procrastination and grandstanding, politicians themselves describe political life as beset by endless contingencies (see also Evans et al, 2013; Naím, 2013).

Although the literature cited above is largely based on subjective, secondary analysis, these arguments are compelling for the way in which they distil 'gap' accounts of anti-politics to common causes. In delineating the disconnect between emic and etic perceptions of politics, these claims also neatly bridge the conceptual divide between 'gap' and 'trap' views of anti-politics. For example, Corbett's (2015, p 473) concluding defence of politicians is that 'real *people* are neither saints nor sinners ... the demonization of politicians partly reflects our own discomfort with their function in a democratic system and our unwillingness to undertake the job ourselves'. Corbett touches on the essence of the 'trap': that politicians have always been plagued by their need to 'wear masks' (Runciman, 2008) and compromise on their own goals and those of others (Crick, 1962). Whilst the 'gap' view helps us to understand much of what has changed in democratic politics, from the role of the media to the rise of neoliberal reform agendas, the 'trap' account clarifies a number of constants.

To meet the contradictory demands of their publics, and to take leadership positions in a system supposedly committed to popular sovereignty, 'trap' accounts of anti-politics argue that politicians must be both leaders and followers, principled and pragmatic, ordinary and exceptional (Medvic, 2013). For example, principle and pragmatism do not necessarily contradict one another, but in the realm of democratic party politics one will commonly negate the other. Acting on deeply held principles is noble and sustaining those values in politics is even more admirable, but when politicians remain dogmatic in their adherence to a set of principles they are decried as harbingers of stalemate and political stagnation. Should politicians divert from principle too easily to reach a compromise, they are cast as unreliable and opportunistic. As Kane and Patapan (2012, p 44) argue: '[the electors] want somebody who will do their bidding, listen to them, and not break promises, yet they will hold in contempt the leader who merely follows the polls, has no "vision", and refuses to make tough, unpopular decisions'. Thus the trap is laid. Far from being overtly political, each of these paradoxes reflects a popular preoccupation with process space – how and by whom representation is enacted – and thus a focus on the personal qualities of those people doing politics.

The 'trap' account also reflects, to some extent, disaggregated popular conceptions of what 'good' representation actually means (Carman, 2003, 2006), as well as the contested psychological contract underpinning the notion of representation in and of itself. At the simplest level, representation implies the notion of one person (a citizen) authorizing another (a representative) to act on their behalf. As Jürgen Habermas (1996, pp 462–515) made explicitly clear, this human contract is a crucial condition for understanding representation as a facilitative institution for democracy, for the people's sovereignty, and it demands proper respect and attention. As a process, this simple definition also conveys the sense of unitary will that is conceived in the act of representation: this is a unitary will that does not necessarily pre-exist but is formed in the representative and as such demands an enormous amount of individual-to-individual trust (for early philosophical discussions of this tension, see Kant, 1991). Representation necessarily transfers power from the principal to the agent and disassociates democratic liberty from the direct authorization of will. In doing so, it places a performative emphasis on the role of the representative to (a) discern and secure the 'common good', or (b) to enter into an enduring process of contestation on behalf of certain factional interests. The implications and nuances of this debate will be returned to later in this book, but for now it suffices to highlight this theoretical fillip for the focus upon the *psychological characteristics* and probity of those who govern that is seen in scholarship and debate about contemporary anti-politics.

There are a number of conclusions that the reader might intuit from this discussion and the literature reviewed above. From a demand–side perspective, the reliance of the public on subjective process–space evaluations about politicians might confirm a deficit of informed popular engagement with politics. By contrast, the same evidence might be interpreted from a supply–side perspective as proof that the 'wrong' people are governing the country in the 'wrong' interests. The point to make here (and the purpose of this opening gambit) is that either interpretation involves a significant preoccupation with the psychology of politicians, but that preoccupation has not been acknowledged explicitly by the existing canon of research into UK politics or explored using the correct methods and data. This book seeks to do just that. The imperative of this research is, to an extent, two-fold. On the one hand, a range of threats to representative democracy demanding original research into the psychology of politicians have already been outlined. On the other hand this book attempts to answer that promise of political science to cultivate the public understanding of politics through engaged and relevant scholarship. By contrast, the dominant narrative of recent decades has been one of rational choice critiques of politicians and indulgent apocalyptic strap lines, so that 'political scientists have contributed significantly to the demonization of politics. [T]hey trained us, in effect, to be cynical. And in that respect at least, we have been excellent students' (Hay, 2009, p 587). Adding faux credence to a political witch hunt, the literature talks of political misconduct as if it is inevitable and in so doing convinces its readership that 'one might be forgiven for thinking that the ABCs of British politics are arrests, bribery and cheating' (Bowler and Karp, 2004, p 274). These examples are typical of a political science academy that has been complacent and complicit in the moral degradation of politics and political office, inadvertently fuelling the anti-politics it now seeks to explain. Yet far from acting as an apologist for politicians, this book represents the evidence-based, theory-driven insights of a concerned consumer of politics and a critical student of political science who seeks to develop empirical responses to rote claims. To this purpose, the conceptual wisdom of both political science and psychology are drawn upon to answer big questions about who enters politics and why, how they represent us once they get there, and whether public antipathy towards *all* politicians is justified.

Political psychology and the 'value of values'

This book aims to speak broadly to a gap in the research on democratic legitimacy and governance by exploring the fundamental motivations that inform the (self-)selection and behaviour of elected politicians. In order to achieve this, a great deal can be gained by approaching the study of politics, politicians and even political institutions from an interdisciplinary perspective. This book draws on political psychology, and in particular the subfield of personality studies, to argue and demonstrate that politics as a series of social structures, institutions and processes can only be properly understood when researchers rigorously evaluate how they are interpreted and reacted to, in context, by relevant actors (see also Schmidt, 2008; Bell, 2012). While the anti-politics literature has burgeoned with a common interest in the people doing politics, so too the extant research base on the role of personality in politics has gathered pace in recent years (Dietrich et al, 2012; Caprara and Silvester, 2018). Studies around the world – mostly in the US – have examined the links between personality and political ideology (eg Lewis and Bates, 2011; Fatke, 2016), political attitudes (eg Jonason, 2014), political participation (Vecchione and Caprara, 2009) and voting behaviours (eg Bakker et al, 2016). However, studies of personality in leadership (see Zaccaro, 2007) and, moreover, studies that examine basic human values (more to come on these) in politics are even scanter (see Vecchione et al, 2015). Within this smaller literature, studies that gather representative self-report data on politicians' personalities are particularly scarce (see Wyatt and Silvester, 2018; Weinberg, 2019).

The use of the term 'personality' in psychological studies is itself extremely broad and multifaceted, going beyond the narrow psychopathological differences that have preoccupied previous political science studies of politicians (see Caprara and Silvester, 2018). This clinical conception of personality ignores social cognitive approaches that make personality, in Henry Murray's (1968) words, 'the most comprehensive term we have in psychology'. However, it is especially important that academic studies crossing these disciplinary boundaries are precise about the terms they employ in order to avoid distorting or manipulating concepts in their application to new cases, what Sartori (1970) incisively critiqued as *conceptual stretching*. This book adopts a three-tier classification of personality. At the broad level of self-regulation, it agrees with Caprara and Vecchione (2013, p 24) that personality is a 'dynamic system of psychological structures and processes that mediates the relationship between the individual and the environment and accounts for what that person is and may become'. Beneath this complex system exists synergistic relations between various subsystems – cognitive and affective – that construct and communicate an individual's personal identity (Caprara and Cervone, 2000). Thirdly, the focus is narrowed onto values, and specifically the theory of Basic Human Values developed by Shalom Schwartz (1994), as the core of personal identity (see also Hitlin, 2003). In adopting a social cognitive approach, this argument stops short of genetics and accepts a dialogic understanding of the ways in which environments condition the functioning of personality as well as the ways in which the personalities of active agents influence the choice of, and change to, those environments.[3]

Readers versed in psychology and studies of personality may, however, be familiar with the Big Five measure of human traits, which is the most commonly researched foundation for personality studies to date (for a review, see Mondak, 2010). This taxonomy includes five basic traits: Extraversion (sociability, vigour, dynamism), Agreeableness (honesty, sincerity, loyalty), Neuroticism (impulsiveness, emotional stability), Conscientiousness (diligence, precision, reliability), and Openness to Experience (imagination, creativity, innovation). In political psychology, traits have been used to explain behavioural phenomena as diverse as vote choices (Caprara et al, 1999; Schoen and Schumann, 2007), party affiliation (Gerber et al, 2010), ideological self-placement (Jost, 2006), candidate preferences (Barbaranelli et al, 2007) and public policy preferences (Riemann et al, 1993). In recent years, a small pool of scholars has even been able to obtain self-report statistics on the Big 5 of politicians in a number of countries around the world (Caprara et al, 2010; Best, 2011; Hanania, 2017; Nørgaard and Klemmensen, 2018). These studies will be critical reference points in later chapters of this book.

In contrast to personality traits, basic values operate as a motivational feature of personality that pertain 'both [to] the nature of goals pursued by individuals and the ways in which these are pursued' (Caprara and Silvester, 2018, p 473). It is in this context that personality research in psychology continues to advance an integrative view of the individual that gives greater attention to values alongside traits as key functional bases of an individual's personality (see, for example, Cervone, 2005; McAdams and Pals, 2006; Barenbaum and Winter, 2008). There is now significant evidence to suggest that values and traits capture distinct yet complementary data about personality (Saroglou and Munoz-Garcia, 2008; Caprara et al, 2012; Parks-Leduc et al, 2015). For example, Caprara and colleagues (2006) found that basic values account for more variance in voting than traits, and that demographic variables such as education, location and income have no additional impact after values and traits have been included in regression analyses. Research has also shown that basic values mediate the effect of traits (Caprara et al, 2009), thus indicating the latter's causal importance in behavioural analysis, whilst people also tend to find their own values more desirable than their traits and express less of a wish to change them (Roccas et al, 2014). As such, '[v]alues are a central personality construct and the importance of studying them has been well established' (Sandy et al, 2017, p 1).

According to Schwartz (1992), basic values can be summarized as cognitive representations of sought-after, trans-situational targets that act as guiding principles in people's lives. They are underpinned by five key conceptualizations (Schwartz, 2006):

- values are beliefs inextricably linked to subjectivity or emotion;
- values are motivational insofar as they prescribe desirable end states of attainment;
- values are abstract and transcend specific actions or situations in a way that norms and attitudes, tied to certain actions, objects or scenarios, cannot;
- values provide individuals with criteria by which to evaluate other people, policies and their transitory environment;
- values share a relationship of compatibility, unlike norms and attitudes, that allows people to place them in a hierarchical order of priority.

The Schwartz (1992, 2006) theory of basic values produces ten values that are deemed universally valid, and which typically sit interdependently within a circumplex space. These ten values are ordered on this circle as Power, Achievement, Hedonism, Stimulation, Self-Direction, Universalism, Benevolence, Tradition, Conformity, Security, Power. These ten basic values then sit within four so-called 'higher-order' values on two orthogonals: Self-Enhancement values (Power, Achievement) oppose Self-Transcendence values (Benevolence, Universalism), and Conservation values (Security,

Conformity, Tradition) oppose Openness to Change values (Hedonism, Stimulation, Self-Direction). Openness to Change values emphasize receptivity to change as well as independent thought, feeling and action, whereas Conservation values motivate submissive self-restriction, a desire to maintain stability and the preservation of traditional ideas, practices and customs. Self-Transcendence values essentially encourage the acceptance of others as equals and place importance on regard for others' welfare, while Self-Enhancement values give weight to the pursuit of personal success and dominance over material and human resources. The closer values are situated to one another within the circle, the greater the level of compatibility between their motivations and by implication it becomes more probable that they can be achieved or expressed through the same sentiments and actions. As values increase in distance around the circle, the greater the level of conflict between them and the more likely it is that the actions and attitudes used to express them will diverge. These interdependencies have been demonstrated in different cultures and contexts using data visualization techniques and analyses such as multidimensional scaling (Döring et al, 2015; Borg et al, 2017).[4]

The content and structure of the Schwartz theory of basic values has been tested and reaffirmed across different sociodemographic and cultural contexts in a long list of studies worldwide (see Cieciuch et al, 2013, p 1216). According to Borg (2019, p 336), '[t]hese theorems have been replicated so many times in so many countries and cultures that they can almost be considered psychological laws' (see also Bardi and Schwartz, 2001; Schwartz and Boehnke, 2004; Bilsky et al, 2011).[5] According to Sagiv and Roccas (2017), the properties of basic values also provide a number of advantages for social science research. For example, all values in the theory are inherently desirable and reflect important or worthy goals for people. The inherent desirability of basic values makes them uniquely powerful as a motivator of behaviour and, consequently, incredibly useful as a way for social scientists to explain situated agency (Roccas et al, 2014). Instead of understanding basic values as distinct personality features like traits, it is their relational rather than sum importance that matters most. This provides greater explanatory purchase when examining agency in ambiguous contexts such as elite politics. Basic values also provide social justification for choices and behaviour in a way that traits, attitudes and intelligence do not (Sagiv and Roccas, 2017, p 5). Basic values are used to convey legitimacy on behaviours and can, given their trans-situational quality, be used to justify two normatively opposing choices in relation to one problem (eg Kurz et al, 2010). In seeking to explain why politicians act in contradictory ways, how they seek to justify their decisions to electors, or even how they reconcile personal beliefs with partisan actions, basic values carry enormous analytical purchase.

Data and methods

In order to fulfil the promise of this book, thus providing original yet rigorous insights about the personalities of politicians, requires a level of data collection that is not readily seen in modern political science or psychology. Of course there is no doubt that the existing literature on British politicians and MPs in particular – both academic and (auto)biographical – provides a rich harvest of insights into the world of electoral representation (Radice et al, 1990; Searing, 1994; Rush, 2001; Cowley, 2002; Childs, 2004; Rush and Giddings, 2011). In recent years, quantitative analyses of parliamentary behaviour have also pushed this field forward by analyzing, inter alia, patterns in MPs' speech, voting records and written questions to discern particular representative styles or manifestations of electoral pressures and principal–agent linkages (eg Childs and Withey, 2004; Saalfeld and Bischof, 2013; Koplinskaya, 2017). However, empirical studies that collect data from MPs themselves are overwhelmingly qualitative, small-n and ultimately few and far between (see Rosenblatt, 2006). Therefore, whilst the following discussion of data and methods may seem onerous, this extended outline is purposefully intended as a blueprint of sorts for future scholars who seek to navigate the tricky terrain of studying politicians – and specifically the basic values of politicians – in the UK and elsewhere.

Existing research on MPs in the UK has tended to avoid broaching highly sensitive topics such as personality, which necessarily invoke ethical dilemmas regarding participant recruitment and highly politicized fears of confidentiality. Research in the UK is not unique in this respect. The psychological assessment of political elites worldwide, especially in terms of personality theory and research, is heavily grounded in case studies done at a distance using psycholinguistics, content analysis, observation and remote interviews (for a review, see Post, 2003; Barenbaum and Winter, 2008). At the same time, good research practice requires ethical recruitment of participants that includes informed consent (Kelley et al, 2003; Vellinga et al, 2011). In that context, even medical studies of psychological phenomena in the general public – relying on 'opt-in' survey participation – suffer from notoriously low response rates of 20–40% (for a review, see Nelson et al, 2002; Hunt et al, 2013).

The challenges outlined above are exacerbated in studies of political elites where (a) no code of best practice exists that combines both maximal response rates and ethical recruitment, and (b) the response rates for political research have already dwindled significantly. In 1972 and 1973, Donald Searing (1994) interviewed 521 MPs (83% of the House of Commons) and achieved a 79% response rate to his follow-up questionnaire. In their study of the 1992–1997 and 1997–2001 Parliaments, Rush and Giddings (2011) secured response rates of 61% and 52%. In 2010/11, the Hansard Society could only secure a response rate of 25% in its study of new MPs ($n = 57/232$) who entered the House of Commons after the 2010 General Election (Fox and Korris, 2012). This is in spite of the fact that the Hansard Society operates with a respected reputation in Parliament, the support of political parties, and uses a well-resourced research team in terms of finance, access and time. In their 2012 study of MPs, Campbell and Lovenduski (2015) employed the paid services of a corporate research consultancy firm, ComRes, to recruit 156 parliamentarians (24% of sitting MPs). Not only are such methods expensive but Campbell and Lovenduski were unable to recruit frontbench politicians, thus introducing significant response bias and limiting the statistical power of their results. Without taking similar approaches, they suggest '[i]t is highly unlikely that such a high response rate is now achievable' (Campbell and Lovenduski, 2015, p 695).

Survey data

To address these difficulties, the findings presented in this book are based, primarily, on a three-phase tailored design study (Dillman et al, 2014) of MPs' basic values that ran from 1 November 2016 to 1 June 2017. This involved a customized survey procedure in which mixed modes of data collection were utilized in a scientific manner to reduce the four sources of error (coverage, sampling, non-response and measurement). Of particular concern for this research design was non-response error; regardless of response rate – which is often overestimated as an indicator of non-response bias – it was important that the final dataset did not over- or underestimate the prevalence of certain basic values in the MP population. All 650 sitting MPs were thus approached sequentially via post, email and phone, as well as through advocates recruited in the participation process.[6] In doing so, the data collection process focused on building a positive social exchange relationship with the target population, using strategic methods that are founded on theories of cognitive dissonance, reasoned action, leverage and cost–benefit analysis (Friedman, 1953; Stafford, 2008). For example, every email or letter to participants was personalized to address the MP by name; surveys were also accompanied by hand-written compliment slips; multiple points of contact were provided to add legitimacy to the exercise, promises of anonymity reduced the risks of participation; pre-paid return envelopes reduced the cost of participation; high-profile academic endorsements were included for added assurances of quality; and the public good attached to the research was outlined to reinforce the importance of participation. This three-wave data collection process was repeated twice, followed by a single wave of targeted email correspondence to recently retired MPs who were still active in Parliament as members of the House of Lords. This was done for two reasons: to bolster the sample size and to ensure maximum diversity of occupational experience. This produced a broadly representative sample of 106 MPs (85 sitting, 21 former).

The primary survey itself was designed in two main sections with a total of 30 questions. The first section included a version of the Portrait Values Questionnaire (PVQ) used to measure participants' basic values, whilst the second section asked MPs to answer questions about their economic and social ideology, attitudes to representation, as well as a range of demographic and socioeconomic characteristics. The PVQ emphasizes context-free thinking and contains short verbal portraits of individuals, gender-matched with the respondent. For each portrait, participants respond to the question 'How much like you is this person?' using a six-point Likert scale that ranges from 'very much like me' to 'not like me at all'. The shortened measure used in this research project – the Twenty Item Values Inventory (TwIVI) – contains two portraits for each of the ten motivationally distinct types of value (Appendix A). The TwIVI can be completed in less than five minutes and has already proven capable of fully recapturing the psychometric properties of longer measures in large-N comparative populations (Sandy et al, 2017).[7]

In 2018/19, an identical measure of basic values was also included in a longer survey project conducted with all political candidates who had stood in local (council) elections and national (Westminster Parliament) elections between May 2010 and May 2019, and who made their contact details available to the Electoral Commission at the time of standing.[8] This survey was part of a larger project on the policy attitudes and mental wellbeing of politicians, but it produced an additional dataset for this book on the basic values of local politicians (415 elected councillors) as well as a further 62 elected MPs (and 503 unsuccessful parliamentary and council candidates). Comparative data on the basic values of the general public in Britain were also extracted from the eighth round of the European Social Survey (ESS, 2016).[9] All of the data reported above are used throughout this book to conduct statistical analyses of how elected politicians in the UK Parliament compare, psychologically, to politicians at other tiers of governance as well as those they govern.[10] Descriptive statistics for the target and sample populations are reported in Table 1.1.

For each basic value, participants' scores were centred on their mean rating of all items on the scale in order to correct for individual differences in the scale use. Even without this scale correction, Schwartz and colleagues (1997) found that only 3–7% of the variance in results from value questionnaires taken by diverse samples could be explained by substantive social desirability bias (measured using the Marlow–Crowne index).[11] Cronbach alpha reliability coefficients for the four higher order values in the sample of MPs collected here are 0.718 for Conservation, 0.666 for Self-Transcendence, 0.824 for Openness to Change and 0.870 for Self-Enhancement (alphas for the ten individual basic values range from 0.443 for Security to 0.880 for Achievement with seven values scoring greater than 0.6).[12] Confirmatory factor analysis was also used to assess the validity of the data: the measurement model (standardized results reported in Appendix B) shows that these items measure the latent value constructs accurately. Nearly all factor loadings between the questionnaire items and the latent values are above 0.5 and every factor loading except one is statistically significant at $p < 0.05$ or $p < 0.01$.

Interview data

Mixed methods research has become increasingly fashionable in social science over the last two decades, reflecting a diverse and innovative combination of quantitative and qualitative methods in a way that transcends the rigidity of epistemological traditions (for a discussion, see Ragin, 2008). This study employs semi-structured interviews with MPs to drill down into the quantitative analyses presented throughout this book, and thus adds a layer of thick description to this study of personality in UK parliamentary politics. Importantly, interviews are used in a complementary rather than confirmatory fashion. There is a dubious heritage of mixed methods studies that have sought to verify findings using data derived from different sources (Pager and Quillian, 2005; Miller and Gatta, 2006). Again, by contrast, profit is found in the capacity of different types of data to measure the same phenomena in a way that compensates for the limitations of others. As such, this

Table 1.1: Descriptive data (including the House of Commons as of the 2017 General Election)

	MPs (N = 168)	House of Commons (N = 650)	Councillors (N = 415)	ESS (eighth round) (N = 1,557)
Gender:				
Male:	64%	68%	62%	45%
Female:	36%	32%	38%	55%
Age: (mean)	54	51	56	51
Length of Service, years: (mean)	9.6	9.4	Unknown	N/A
Party:*	40%	40%	32%	32%
Labour:	28%	49%	17%	35%
Conservative:	14%	2%	30%	8%
Liberal Democrat:	8%	5%	< 1%	3%
SNP:	10%	4.3%	20%	22%
Other:				
Frontbench (Over career)	19% (63%)	42%**	N/A	N/A

* ESS scores relate to votes cast in the 2015 General Election.

**Based on the four most represented parties in Westminster at the time of sampling.

book joins a long list of studies that have used participant observation, interviews or other qualitative methods as an additional tool through which to explain, interpret or add nuance to the results of surveys (eg Obstfeld, 2005; Small, 2009).

Given the difficulty of obtaining elite interviews (see also Huggins, 2014), this book ultimately relies on a self-selecting subsample of survey participants. At each stage of the tailored design method (discussed above), participants were given the option to volunteer for a follow-up interview. In total, 24 MPs (23% of the primary sample) agreed to be interviewed; in line with the contingent nature of elite interviews, a further seven of these MPs either cancelled their interview at the last minute or failed to respond to further email correspondence in order to arrange the interview in the first place. This left 17 participants (11 sitting MPs and 6 former MPs now sitting in the House of Lords) who were willing to conduct in-depth interviews. As a self-selecting sample, there is an overrepresentation of older, Labour Party MPs. However, the sample is diverse in terms of gender, tenure in elected office and experience of different occupational responsibilities (Table 1.2).

Table 1.2: Profile of interviewees

	Gender	Age	Party	Tenure (years)	Prior career in politics	Frontbench (at any point in career)	Select committee membership (at any point in career)
1	Male	60–69	LAB	15+	Yes	Yes	Yes
2	Female	60–69	Other	10–15	No	No	No
3	Male	60–69	LAB	<5	Yes	No	No
4	Male	60–69	Other	10–15	No	Yes	Yes
5	Female	50–59	LAB	10–15	Yes	Yes	Yes
6	Male	60–69	LAB	15+	Yes	Yes	Yes
7	Female	30–39	SNP	<5	Yes	No	Yes
8	Female	40–49	LAB	5–10	Yes	No	Yes
9	Male	60–69	CON	<5	No	No	No
10	Male	70–79	LIB DEM	15+	No	No	Yes
11	Male	70–79	LIB DEM	15+	Yes	Yes	Yes
12	Male	70–79	LAB	10–15	Yes	No	Yes
13	Male	50–59	LIB DEM	15+	Yes	No	Yes
14	Female	60–69	LAB	10–15	No	Yes	No
15	Male	70–79	LAB	15+	Yes	Yes	Yes
16	Male	60–69	LAB	5–10	Yes	Yes	No
17	Male	40–49	CON	10–15	No	No	Yes

Note: In order to maintain the anonymity of participants, the age and tenure of respondents have been grouped. Party labels are only provided for respondents in the four most populated political parties in the UK Parliament.

A semi-structured interview design carries a number of advantages in that it (a) allowed the interviews to relate directly to the research questions guiding this study and the results of the survey analysis; (b) provided a structure in which a large amount of relevant information could be obtained within a time-pressured interview environment; and (c) gave the interviewer flexibility to change the order of questions and offer bespoke follow-up questions. Given the personalized nature of each interview and the type of data already collected, interviews were conducted with a passive professionalism. Following the advice of Ruth Blakeley (2012), the utmost care was given to maintaining positive or neutral facial expressions and body language, hiding frustration and/or disapproval, and remaining wary of the fine line between pushing an interviewee further and besmirching their opinion. In this manner trust was built with the interviewee, who could answer honestly without fear of personal or professional judgement.

Questions were grouped around three themes that directly relate to the key research foci in this study (Table 1.3). The first set of questions on personalization within Parliament sought specifically to test the boundary between MPs' conscious and unconscious perceptions of their own values and the personal motivations they and their colleagues bring to the job. The second block of questions focused primarily on identifying behavioural constraints and enablers in Parliament in order to (a) understand how consciously MPs act upon or suppress personal motivations in their job, and (b) add nuance to the causal mechanisms (or lack thereof) revealed between MPs' basic values and a range of parliamentary behaviours in the quantitative analyses reported in this book. The final set of questions tested participants' awareness of how much they believe they are understood by the electorate, on a personal level, and how much importance they attribute to this (mis)understanding. In each case, questions were personalized according to prior responses in the survey phase of data collection and additional research carried out about the background of the participant prior to the interview.

Interviews lasted an average of 30 minutes; the longest went on for over an hour and the shortest finished after 17 minutes. Given the different occupational demands on each participant, there was significant variation in how much time each MP was willing or able to give to the interview. All of the interviews were conducted in person at the Palace of Westminster, although individual participants expressed different preferences about where in the Palace they would

Table 1.3: Semi-structured interview plan (exemplar questions)

Block 1: Personality	Block 2: Behaviour	Block 3: Public attitudes
If you were to describe yourself in three words, what would they be and how have those characteristics helped you in politics?	To what extent do you feel that you act according to your own motivations as an elected politician on a daily basis?	Do you think that the public perception of politicians is accurate? Why/Why not?
There is a dominant media narrative that paints politicians as greedy and self-interested. What do you think of those accusations?	How do you find the Palace of Westminster as a working environment?	Has public/media approbation of politicians had any impact on you personally?
In your professional experience, is there a certain type of person who enters elite politics? And do you think there are any personal similarities between those who rise to the frontbench?	Are there any aspects of your role as an elected representative that you feel you *can/cannot* be yourself?	Are you satisfied with your performance as an MP? Why/Why not?
Do you agree or disagree with the majority of your colleagues' opinions?	What do you perceive to be your priority as an elected representative?	If we stopped one of your constituents on the street, how do you think they might describe you in three words?
	How do your prior beliefs about elite politics compare to your experience of elected office?	Is it important, in your opinion, that the public *like* MPs?
	Have you achieved what you set out to achieve as an elected politician? Why/Why not?	What is the biggest reason, in your opinion, for popular disengagement from politics?

like to meet. Whilst some were happy to conduct the interview publicly in the atrium of Portcullis House, others insisted on meeting in their private office. Three MPs would only be interviewed at more discreet locations in Millbank House, away from the eyes and ears of their colleagues. From an anecdotal perspective, these requests reflected not only the highly sensitive nature of the discussions but also the varying experiences and personal characteristics of those being interviewed.

Overview of the book

This book speaks primarily to academics interested in the study of politicians and parliament in the United Kingdom, as well as those engaged in the fields of political psychology, political leadership and political behaviour worldwide who seek to understand the psychological underpinnings of representative democracy. To the extent that this book also revolves around issues of popular disengagement from politics catalysed by the 'quality' of our representatives, it should be of interest to anyone studying or researching anti-politics and democratic malaise. At a practical level, this book speaks directly to party selectorates who must design and implement candidate selection mechanisms as well as direct party campaigns, and above all to politicians who may be interested to know more about each other and just how similar they are to their colleagues beyond party labels. At the same time, four 'Brexit years' at the time of writing have recast a spotlight on public perceptions of, and trust in, politicians in the UK. The intensity of this public discourse has not been matched since the expenses scandal in 2009/10. Given that this book helps to unpick many of the assumptions about politicians replete in this discourse, and in turn challenges difficult questions that the media only speculates about, this book will likely appeal to a wide range of public audiences who are either cynically or optimistically enthused by politics.

Using a rich array of survey and interview data collected directly from UK politicians, the remainder of this book tackles the pertinent 'problems' listed at the start of this chapter. Chapter 2 builds on the contextual groundwork presented in this introduction to address the first of these questions. In particular, it uses data on the basic values of elected MPs, local councillors, unsuccessful political candidates and the public to interrogate 'who' occupies elected office in the Palace of Westminster and 'why' they choose to do it. Theoretical arguments are matched by quantitative and qualitative analyses that reveal, for example, a significant difference between the personality characteristics of the governors and the governed. In particular, these results indicate that elected representatives are more motivated by equality, social justice and caring for others (Self-Transcendence values). However, the results also indicate that MPs are more motivated than the public to control resources and be in charge of others (Power values), and that these differences are exaggerated among those MPs with frontbench experience. These results lead into a focused discussion of political success and ambition, and data are operationalized to show that personality characteristics like basic values may predict candidate emergence as well as the in-role career advancement of elected politicians.

Chapter 3 develops the results presented in Chapter 2 to add more depth and nuance to our understanding of the overarching 'problem' of how different MPs are, psychologically, to those they represent. The chapter is organized into two substantive sections. The first section interrogates the model of candidate emergence presented in Chapter 2 in more detail, focusing in particular on the effects of gender and ethnicity upon the basic values of both MPs and the public. Normatively, the sociodemographic similarity of our politicians and their physical dissimilarity to the majority of the population has become symbolic of a democratic deficit in the UK and abroad. This chapter shows that the differences between MPs' basic values by gender and ethnicity are actually smaller than those between MPs and corresponding sociodemographic groups in the general public, thus opening another (psychological) dimension to debates about descriptive and substantive representation. The second half of the chapter tackles another psychological criticism of politicians: careerism. The accusation proceeds that the UK Parliament is now occupied solely by those who have made politics a career and have no prior professional experience outside of politics. The corollary of that statement is that such a development is negative for the state of politics and society more broadly. However, what exactly this means, both individually and in relation to the rest of the population, is rather opaque. To answer this question, the basic values of MPs are compared according to their occupational backgrounds, and in particular those who have and have not previously worked in political professions. The results show that there are some descriptive differences between these MPs, but they are relatively small and none reach statistical significance. These indicative results are used to argue that the link between professionalization and 'bad politicians' may be a construction of the popular imagination and careless media reporting that serves no useful purpose in contemporary politics.

Chapter 4 focuses on the interaction between partisanship and basic values in British politics. This section analyses data on basic values to (a) understand psychological differences between MPs from different political parties, and (b) delineate psychological representative links between MPs and their party's voters. Survey data are used here to develop a compelling narrative of 'psychological sorting' in Parliament along partisan lines that has implications for why and how partisans (otherwise competitors for votes and promotions) cooperate to achieve common goals. In particular, Labour and Conservative Party MPs demonstrate clear differences in their basic values, but the picture is far more nuanced when comparing MPs in each party to their voters. Analyses reported in this chapter show (a) partisanship and basic values share a strong relationship at all levels, (b) differences in basic values between partisan elites are greater than those between partisans in the public, and (c) psychological congruence between leaders and followers occurs to a much greater extent on the Right of British politics than the Left. These findings lead into broader discussions of MP–voter congruency and, in particular, the successes and failures of the Labour Party in recent decades.

Chapter 5 addresses the second overarching 'problem' of this book: how do we assess the agency of those individuals elected to represent our collective interests. This chapter synthesizes the conceptual wisdom and empirical findings of existing research into the UK Parliament with the theoretical foundations of psychological studies to offer an integrated model of parliamentary political behaviour (IMPPB). The IMPPB unites research on ideology, party socialization and institutional choice to offer a new blueprint for analyzing politicians' parliamentary behaviours. It is used in this chapter to offer a more holistic understanding of how we, as academics or critical citizens, might interpret and assess MPs' parliamentary behaviours. Data on MPs' basic values are then coupled with Hansard records to assess the extent of MPs' political agency in a range of contexts of varying institutional constraint. The results show, in particular, that (a) elected representatives make important decisions based upon their own personality characteristics, and that (b) this effect operates in flux with informal pressures exerted by external role alters and internal party structures. In sum, agency matters far more in UK parliamentary politics than the extant literature has assumed and the preliminary findings in this chapter are used to outline a new research agenda for studies of parliamentary behaviour.

Chapter 6 extrapolates to the macro-level issues of representation and anti-politics governing the third and final 'problem' organizing this book: do voters get the 'wrong' politicians? The central argument in this chapter reduces to the existence of an unhealthy premium on the individual in contemporary democratic politics, both in terms of the ways representatives understand and execute their professional function and how/why voters become disillusioned regardless of their political choices. The opening section of this chapter develops this argument by engaging specifically with an existing literature on the personalization of politics in the media and the ways in which anti-political sentiments revolving around politicians' psychological flaws have been exacerbated. These assumptions are then tested by analyzing data from an original conjoint experiment conducted with a representative sample of 1,637 British citizens in October 2017. The data are operationalized to reveal the relative importance of personality characteristics – specifically basic values – to public voting habits and, at a further level, the types of people most desired in national politics. These data show that in experimental scenarios where voters do not know the partisanship of a candidate, personality outweighs other political and socioeconomic variables as a voting heuristic. Compared with data from 168 MPs, these results also indicate that at the aggregate level there is less of a disjuncture than assumed between the personalities the public *want* in national politics and the personalities they *get*.

Psychological Scrutiny: Who Enters Politics and Why?

'There are 650 people in Parliament and so with any group of 650, there is good and bad. There are people in Parliament I wouldn't trust as far as I could throw them and there are people in Parliament I would trust with my life.'

Conservative Party MP (Interviewee 17)

Members of Parliament are unique among elite groups for their capacity to affect substantial political outcomes with far-reaching consequences locally, nationally and internationally. Even backbench MPs, who are often callously cast as party political lobby fodder, play an important role in moulding crucial policy decisions, in assuming the most influential roles in the state (either as a pool of potential recruits for the executive or by granting and withdrawing support for the government of the day), and in helping to design and reform the institutional nature of the state (see also Best and Vogel, 2018). However, existing studies of the UK Parliament and other legislatures around the world have only given limited attention to the individual, psychological characteristics of those actors who hold elected office and exercise these powers. Chapter 1 argued at some length that it is these 'questions of character' that actually underpin much of the anti-political sentiment, and thus democratic malaise, that academics and journalists have spent so much time discussing in recent years or even decades. As Allen and Cairney (2015, p 6) conclude, 'many of the complaints put at the door of the 'political class' relate to Westminster politics and those with governing power or influence'. In attempting to fill this gap in our understanding of politicians, and in the public understanding of politics more broadly, this chapter analyses the Basic Human Values (Schwartz, 1992) of those individuals 'in the arena'; as Theodore Roosevelt (1910) famously put it, those 'who err, who come short again and again ... but who do actually strive to do the deeds'.

Before turning to examine the basic values of our elected representatives, it is worth reiterating why exactly it matters who our politicians are. Contra to the broader questions of anti-politics discussed in Chapter 1, the focus here is on the concept and institutions of democratic representation and, more precisely, the transfer of power from principal to agent that it entails. As with Montesquieu's (2002) long-lived distinction between the nature and principle of government, modern elections in the UK and elsewhere decide 'who' has power in the political system (its nature) but not that specific commitment that allows it to persist (its principle). A relatively recent constructivist turn in this debate goes even further in suggesting that democratic representatives are not simply responsive to the will of the people, but make present those people they represent through a series of individual 'representative claims' (eg Saward, 2006, 2010; Näsström, 2015). Whilst the notion of representative 'claim-making' may give rise to a broader palette of public opinions and marginal interests in formal political debate, it also assumes that representative claims will necessarily be democratic. As Hannah Pitkin (2004, p 339) argues, any schema that decouples representation from the legitimacy granted by formal elections risks a system in which representatives 'act not as agents of the people but simply instead of them'. For those of us who have been and remain concerned by the degenerative slide to 'mainstream populism' seen in western democracies (eg Mény and Surel, 2002; Jagers and Walgrave, 2007; Dean and Maiguascha, 2020) and the dog-whistle politics of those making representative claims that undermine democratic values (invocations about immigrants or EU bureaucrats during the 2016 EU referendum campaign in the UK being a case in point), there seems to be an academic imperative to understand the motivations and machinations of those who formally represent and thus make representative claims in that capacity.

It is precisely for this reason that democratic formalists such as Hans Kelsen (1999) have long argued that the political binding of elections is simply not enough to ensure that representatives both reflect the will of the people and are 'responsible' to their electors. Whilst political binding introduces a host of ethical and normative questions, Kelsen argues that the moral duty inherent in representation requires an imperative mandate secured by law. For Kelsen (1999, p 292) '[l]egal independence of the elected from the electors is incompatible with legal representation'. The UK does not constrain its representatives with an imperative mandate, although the Recall of MPs Act 2015 (effective as of March 2016) has introduced rules by which an MP can lose their seat in Parliament subject to a successful petition signed by at least 10% of constituents (The Electoral Commission, 2016). In reality the Recall of MPs Act 2015 is a limited rebalancing of democratic power towards the principal within the institution of representation. Petitions can only be triggered by the Speaker of the House on the occasion that an MP should receive a custodial sentence, falsify allowances under the Parliamentary Standards Act 2009, or find themselves barred from the House of Commons for more than 14 calendar days per year. Parliamentary elections therefore remain the institutional site of popular will, vested in representatives who, in the absence of an imperative mandate, must ultimately be judged on the merits of their values, opinions and ideological discourse – what Kelsen refers to as 'political fictions' (Kelsen, 1992). The emphasis of the debate thus switches from the institutional mechanisms by which democracy is enacted to the psychological characteristics of the people who are deemed eligible to act in our best interests.

It is argued that these processes create a politics of personality, both in terms of how people characterize their democratic choices and in terms of how they evaluate the performance of democratic governments. For similar reasons, Sofia Näsström (2015, p 4) suggests that elections, as an arena for perverted ideological competition about what is right for 'we, the people', have become 'a democratic straightjacket'. If elections induce a regular competition about 'who' is fit to instantiate popular power, then the health of democracy simultaneously rests on the personal qualities of those representatives who assume that power: representation becomes less a process of authorization by voters so much as a constant judgement about the character of laws and lawmakers. Where representatives are found wanting in their democratic capacity, the sovereign people can either disengage with politics, thus threatening the very system of government, or harness negative power to censure representatives via extra-parliamentary processes and institutions that may be equally unhealthy (Rosanvallon, 2006; Keane, 2011). This is not surprizing when one considers the disjuncture found between citizens and elites when it comes to agreeing upon acceptable behaviour by elected representatives (Jackson and Smith, 1996; McAllister, 2000; Atkinson and Bierling, 2005). On one hand, parliamentary institutions focus on the legality of representative behaviour (for example, the work of the Independent Parliamentary Standards Authority (IPSA) in the UK), whereas the public understanding of ethical behaviour prioritizes ideological, discursive and personal integrity (Allen and Birch, 2015b, pp 62–88). In sum, critical citizens may be justifiably exercised by the moral rectitude of their politicians given (a) the overwhelming responsibility placed upon those individuals elected to office and (b) the negative potential of a system in which popular power is ceded to those same individuals.

These debates have for some time underpinned a parallel literature on the concept of political will. Though more theoretical than empirical, and less concerned with the psychology of politicians than the *politics* of their characters, researchers like Nicholas Allen (2010), Gabriela Thompson and colleagues (2018) and Edward Hall (2018) have all suggested that institutional tools for parliamentary oversight are necessary but not sufficient when it comes to holding governments to account or combating corruption. Thompson and colleagues (2018) in particular argue that political will, as a precursor to the political behaviour of legislators, results from a synthesis of motivations, volunteerism and culture. The quality of any activity in a legislature – and even more so in the case of oversight and scrutiny – starts with the motivations of those individuals who are tasked with populating it:

> By accepting that political will does not necessarily originate in a legislature's culture itself but rather from the motivation of the legislator to undertake oversight, it must be accepted that it is their identity that will greatly influence, not only the form which oversight takes, but also the extent to which it is championed and its potential for success. If this is so, it follows that there are certain characteristics that are desirable in these individuals. But how are these determined? (Thompson et al, 2018, p 7)

The answers to this elusive question have for some time been grounded in the concept of Public Service Motivation (PSM; Perry, 2000). Revolving around a general altruistic incentive found in employees of varying public-facing professions, PSM encompasses 'an individual's orientation to delivering services to people with a purpose to do good for others and society' (Perry and Hondeghem, 2008, p vii). In their study of comparative commonalities in PSM, Kim and Vandenabeele (2010) go further in suggesting that PSM is fundamentally about self-sacrifice and relies on distinct categories of value-based, instrumental and identification motivation at the individual level.

Ritz and colleagues' (2016) systematic review of the literature on PSM also demonstrates a large evidence base linking it to demographic variables such as age, socioeconomic variables such as religiosity, parental and organizational socialization, and political variables like ideology.

However, attempts to understand the psychological underpinnings of PSM are surprizingly underdeveloped. It is here that studies of personality – especially in politics – have enormous appraisive potential to help us understand the characteristics of public service officials such as politicians, and whether or not these characteristics and resultant motivations are consonant with the expectations of PSM. A handful of studies in political psychology have made headway in recent years by extracting and analyzing self-report data on the personality traits of politicians in the US, Canada, Germany, Italy and Denmark.

In his study of German legislators in the European, federal and state parliaments, Heinrich Best (2011) found that politicians scored higher than the German population for the personality traits Extraversion and Openness, but lower for Neuroticism, Agreeableness and Conscientiousness. Given that prior research into personality traits and politics shows a strong positive association between Openness and liberal social/moral attitudes (Gerber et al, 2010; Mondak, 2010), Best's study might indicate a reassuring psychological backdrop to the exercise of political will in the German legislature. These findings are replicated among municipal candidates in Canada (Scott and Medeiros, 2019). Italian politicians in Caprara and colleagues' (2010) study scored higher than the general population for Extraversion and lower in Neuroticism but, unlike their German counterparts, Italian politicians scored higher for Agreeableness and only female legislators scored higher for Openness. Comparable studies in the US have also shown, for example, that state legislators score higher for Conscientiousness, Agreeableness and Extraversion than the American population (Hanania, 2017), whilst Nørgaard and Klemmensen (2018) find that Danish MPs score higher for Extraversion, Emotional Stability (the inverse of Neuroticism), Conscientiousness and Agreeableness than their compatriots. Taken together, these studies testify to a process of psychological self-selection to elite politics in a number of western liberal democracies. In particular, politics as a vocation appears to attract people who are energetic, assertive and action-oriented (Extraversion). However, comparable insights into the personality of national UK politicians have, until now, been absent.

'Only in it for themselves!' How do politicians differ from the British public?

As discussed, the observable nature of democratic politics makes possible a host of hypothetical contestations about the personal characteristics required, expected or assumed of political elites. Having done the heavy lifting required to convince the reader (if indeed you needed convincing at all!) that this matters for how politics is conducted as well as how politicians and politics more broadly are perceived by the public, this chapter turns to explore unique data on the basic values of UK politicians. The analyses that follow focus primarily on UK MPs and how they compare to the British public at the aggregate level.

Original data on the basic values of local councillors are also incuded as an additional reference point (see Chapter 1 for a full discussion of the data used here). Whilst this book focuses upon the nature and conduct of national politics, councillors are by definition politicians in their own right. As David Wilson and Chris Game (2011, pp 265–81) have argued, councillors also carry out key 'political functions' such as making, scrutinizing and delivering public policy; they put themselves forward to exercise their political will on behalf of a 'constituency' of the British public, and like MPs they are largely unreflective of the general population in their demographic and socioeconomic characteristics. At the same time, it is possible that the psychology of politicians – and the personalities that are attracted to political office – might vary by tier of governance. To answer the question of 'who enters politics and why?' without also considering local politicians would, therefore, be an obvious own-goal.

Having calculated the average importance of each basic value to MPs and councillors, derived from their responses to the 20-item Portrait Values Questionnaire (see Chapter 1 for more detail), it is possible to compare their value hierarchies to those of the general population (calculated from data collected by the eighth round of the European Social Survey). This comparison provides initial support for the suggestion that personality influences selectivity in UK political recruitment. The average value hierarchies for MPs and the British public only overlap in three of ten positions, whilst councillors and the public only share one commonality (Table 2.1). For all three samples, Self-Transcendence values are extremely important motivational goals. For MPs and the public, Benevolence values, which relate to the preservation and support of those known personally, are scored as more important than Universalism values, which represent an understanding of and protection for the welfare of all people and the environment.

Across the remainder of these value hierarchies, there are a number of distinct differences. In particular, MPs give greater priority to Openness to Change values, whilst the public gives more importance to Conservation values. This would suggest that MPs are motivated more by the need for independent thought and action, and autonomy

Table 2.1: Value hierarchies based on sample means (most important to least important)

Members of Parliament	Councillors	General population
Benevolence	Universalism	Benevolence
Universalism	Self-Direction	Universalism
Self-Direction	Benevolence	Self-Direction
Stimulation	Stimulation	Security
Conformity	Hedonism	Tradition
Power	Conformity	Conformity
Security	Power	Hedonism
Hedonism	Security	Achievement
Achievement	Achievement	Stimulation
Tradition	Tradition	Power

Note: UK Members of Parliament ($N = 168$), local councillors ($N = 415$) and the British population ($N = 1,557$).

in exciting, novel or challenging circumstances (Self-Direction and Stimulation values), whereas the public are more likely to respect and commit to traditional customs or ideas and in turn restrain their action so as to maintain social expectations or norms (Security, Tradition and Conformity values). These results support the findings of previous studies that have demonstrated strong positive associations between levels of mass political activism and Self-Transcendence values as well as Openness to Change values, and negative associations with Conservation values (Schwartz et al, 2010; Pacheco and Owen, 2015; Vecchione et al, 2015). Whilst wary of generalizing these findings across cultures, one might infer that in order to be motivated strongly enough to work doggedly in a political party, to secure a candidacy, and to operate in an elected capacity, a person must not only care about improving the lot of those they work for (that is, Self-Transcendence values), but also be particularly motivated to defy expectations, confront the status quo and take personal risks in that process (that is, Openness to Change values).

These differences between the basic values of governor and governed are revealed in greater detail by a direct comparison of group means (Figure 2.1).[1] The results of a series of independent sample t-tests with Bonferroni corrections suggest that the basic values of MPs and the public differ to a high degree of statistical significance across seven out of ten of the lower order basic values (only comparisons

Figure 2.1: Distributions of participants' basic values (centred scores)

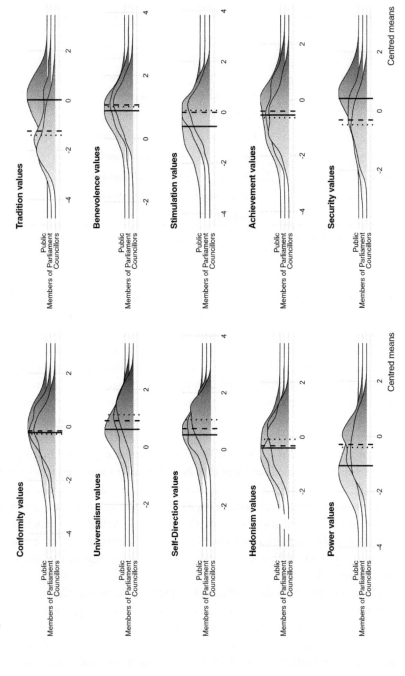

Note: UK Members of Parliament ($N = 168$, mean = dashed line), councillors ($N = 415$, mean = dotted line) and the general population ($N = 1,557$, mean = solid line).

for Conformity, Hedonism and Achievement values did not reach statistical significance). In contrast to those they govern, MPs appear to be significantly more driven by motivations to care for those around them and support those they know personally (higher scores for Benevolence values: t (1670) − 3.362, $p < 0.001$); they are significantly more driven by originality, creativity and autonomy (higher scores for Self-Direction values: t (1670) = 3.244, $p < 0.01$); and they are significantly less motivated to preserve traditions (Tradition values: t (1670) = −16.323, $p < 0.001$) or to secure stability in their own lives or society (Security values: t (1670) = −10.783, $p < 0.001$). The size of these differences and the test statistics, as well as levels of significance, point to specific personality factors in the selection and self-selection of UK MPs. In particular, higher scores for Benevolence, Universalism and Self-Direction indicate a greater commitment among MPs (than the public) to principles of freedom, social welfare and equality among citizens (for a discussion of theoretical and empirical linkages, see Caprara et al, 2006).

These quantitative results are supported by interview data. Although MPs might have a vested interest in self-reporting an inflated image of their own altruism, nearly every interviewee recognized that politicians of all partisan affiliations are driven, first and foremost, by a desire to help others and enact change. As one very experienced Conservative MP commented:

> 'I mean I've met literally thousands of politicians from all over the world in the course of my years [in politics]. They all believe that they're trying to do good and many of them are doing good and they're not in your party either, which is quite annoying. The idea of the self-seeking politician, it might have been true in Tammany Hall and in some of the murkier bits of the Italian political system, but overall people seek elected office to change things, particularly in the western democracies.' (Interviewee 9)

This observation was as common among interviewees with relatively little experience of elected office. One newly elected member of the Scottish National Party (SNP), who had been in office for less than 18 months at the time of the interview, said:

> 'I think probably some politicians are here to further their own personal life to get more money, to be more powerful, but a huge number of people from across the House, not

> just SNP members, Labour, Lib Dem, Tory members are actually here to try to make a positive difference to their communities. I could disagree with them on how to make that positive difference but that's actually their intention when they come here.' (Interviewee 7)

These comments are particularly interesting for two reasons. Firstly, they indicate that Self-Transcendence values (Benevolence and Universalism) are as clearly observable to those who have been socialized into elite politics for many years as for those who are new to Parliament. Secondly, these comments (especially that of interviewee 7) are indicative of the ways in which all participants articulated the principles of value instantiation – that is, the cognitive and social links between general categories of values and specific behavioural manifestations (this theory is developed in detail by Hanel et al, 2017). As such, interviewees were adamant that the majority of their colleagues came to Parliament with well-meaning intentions to change the lives of others for the better, but at the same time they often voiced disagreement with the policy or behavioural instantiations of those intentions. It is important to acknowledge, therefore, that the overall motivational goals of Self-Transcendence values may take a variety of behavioural forms in elite politics, dependent upon other variables (for example, age, gender, education) that may affect an individual's perception of the 'common good'. These differences will be explored later in this book.

The results presented in Figure 2.1 also illustrate stark differences between the basic values of elected councillors and the public. If anything, these differences are even more pronounced than between MPs and the public. Of the ten lower order value factors analysed here, councillors differ from the public to a high degree of statistical significance ($p < 0.001$) on all except Conformity and Achievement values. This is remarkably interesting in and of itself, as it suggests that fundamental psychological differences exist between those who enter politics and those who do not at more than one level of governance. As a vocation per se, politics appears to attract a rather unique group of people. At the same time, it does not appear that MPs and councillors are identical in their basic values. Independent sample t-tests between the two show (Table 2.2), for example, that councillors are more broad-minded and concerned with the welfare of all people and the environment (Universalism values); they are more driven by independent thought and action (Self-Direction values); they are less ambitious and desirous of personal success (Achievement values); but

Table 2.2: Independent samples t-test (centred mean scores)

Basic values	Estimate 1 (Councillors)	Estimate 2 (Members of Parliament)	Test statistic	Significance (*p* value)
Conformity	−0.275	−0.156	−1.391	0.165
Tradition	−1.398	−1.228	−1.650	0.099
Benevolence	1.012	1.066	−0.803	0.422
Universalism	1.123	0.916	2.515	0.012
Self-Direction	1.049	0.737	4.658	0.000
Stimulation	0.069	−0.006	0.945	0.345
Hedonism	−0.082	−0.323	2.944	0.003
Achievement	−0.639	−0.407	−2.574	0.010
Power	−0.394	−0.293	−1.151	0.250
Security	−0.465	−0.305	−1.866	0.063

Note: UK Members of Parliament ($N = 168$) and councillors ($N = 415$).

they attribute more importance to pleasure and enjoyment in life (Hedonism values). These differences do, to an extent, reflect contrasts in the nature of national politics (publicly salient, highly scrutinized by the media, tightly regimented by political parties and increasingly professionalized) and local politics (which tends to operate below the radar of public and media attention, is less dominated by the two main parties, and is, necessarily, more parochial in focus).

Dark intentions? Power values and in-role success

Although the findings discussed thus far have demonstrated a normatively positive image of MPs, who – contrary to media speculation – are more motivated by the welfare of others than themselves, the discerning reader will also notice that they are more motivated than the public to control resources and be in charge of others (Power values: t (1670) $= 10.937$, $p < 0.001$; Figure 2.1). In representative national samples around the world, Power values consistently receive the lowest average ratings (average 2.3) on the PVQ's Likert scale of 0 (Not like me at all) to 6 (Very much like me) (eg Bardi and Schwartz, 2001). This is likewise the case for the ESS sample used in this book (Table 2.1), in which Power values are rated as least important among all basic values for the British public. However, in this elite sample of MPs, Power values are rated as more important than Security, Achievement, Hedonism and Tradition values, and receive an average rating among participants of 3.6. A similar trend can be seen among councillors, who rate Power values higher than three other value factors.

A correlation of Power values and 'being a politician' (that is, MP or councillor) reveals a moderate positive relationship (r (2558) = 0.33, p < 0.001) that, taken together with the results above, adds weight to a previously anomalous association found in Vecchione and colleagues' (2015) comparative study of basic values and political activism across 28 countries and four continents. The authors unearthed positive associations between Power values and conventional activism (defined there as monetary donations to parties and contacting/working for a political organization) that have otherwise been unobserved in studies of basic values and expressive political participation (Piurko et al, 2011; Pacheco and Owen, 2015). It appears, however, that this finding is replicated in the UK when studying high-intensity forms of participation such as holding political office. Given the unparalleled access to personal and political resources and knowledge provided by elected office, these results also support some of the more cynical reservations discussed in Chapter 1: that politics necessarily attracts individuals who are more motivated by authority, social recognition and, importantly, control than those who elect them. It is crucial, however, to interpret this result holistically, given that basic values must be understood relationally rather than in isolation (Schwartz, 2014). In the elite samples, Power values remain subordinate to other Self-Transcendence and Openness to Change values. Whilst they may be more likely to influence MPs' decisions or behaviour than those of the public (links between basic values and behaviour will be discussed in more detail in Chapter 5), they remain less likely to be activated in decision-making scenarios, to guide perceptions and interpretations, or influence action-planning than, in particular, MPs' Benevolence and Universalism values.

Interview data provide two key complementary insights to this finding. Although interviewees talked of colleagues' motivations in terms readily relatable to Self-Transcendence values, they were also quick, for example, to argue that elite politics requires personality characteristics typical of Self-Enhancement values (Power and Achievement). One former Liberal Democrat frontbench MP even claimed "[t]here are quite a number – a disproportionate number – of aggressive people in politics, but I think politics is dominated by people who are, I would say, at least assertive" (Interviewee 13). Given that democratic politics in the UK is characterized by partisan competition and constant debate and deliberation between elected representatives, one could argue that MPs must necessarily come to the job with the confidence to put themselves forward and push their cause. As one Labour MP characterized it, "[y]ou have to have a personality that can project because people, and it sounds dreadful, but people need you to perform a bit. It's no good creeping into a room as a wallflower" (Interviewee 14). Whilst the majority of interviewees cast such characteristics as either necessary and/or desirable in elite politics, others were more candid about the prevalence of Self-Enhancement values among MPs and the accompanying self-interest that it entails:

> 'If you look at the people who succeeded in the Labour Party to get to the top, they were people who put ambition above anything and everything else – above family, above other social activities. They all, with the notable exceptions of Robin Cook and John Smith, I think, they all came down and lived in London. You had to be in the centre of things. You had to have ambition. You had to, to some extent, push people aside, even though they were your friends, and trample on them.' (Interviewee 12)

For a number of interviewees, Self-Enhancement values were activated when they joined the House of Commons or at some point during their career there. This is unusual given that extant research in political psychology – and psychological studies more broadly – testifies to the stability of people's basic values across time and situation, as well as people's conscious desire not to change their values in adulthood (Roccas et al, 2014). Nevertheless, a number of interviewees talked about an increase in their ambition and self-belief on becoming an MP. As one Liberal Democrat put it:

> 'I would say – and I think this is probably an important bit of your note on me – that I used to be actually very shy, and not terribly assertive, and didn't speak very much at meetings, but you gain confidence sometimes by engaging and sometimes being forced into the limelight.' (Interviewee 13)

There are two possible explanations for this. Either the immense stresses, challenges and unparalleled experiences of elected office are capable of generating value changes,[2] or the parliamentary environment is more immediately geared towards activating Self-Enhancement values in the first place. Correlations between MPs' Self-Enhancement values and tenure (length of service) are virtually non-existent and statistically insignificant in the elite sample used in this book. Therefore, the second explanation seems more plausible. Given that MPs attribute more importance to Power values than the general public in the samples used here, the principles of value activation (see Verplanken and Holland, 2002; Schwartz, 2005) suggest that those motivations will be more accessible to MPs (than the average member of the public) when placed in an immediate situation that activates them.

If this theoretical explanation is correct, then it is anticipated that the activation of Power values will be strongest among frontbench MPs. Being in a position of authority or responsibility in Parliament, especially a post in the executive, confers upon MPs incomparable influence over policy decisions. With this influence come innumerably more scenarios or opportunities (media interviews, public speaking requests, civil service portfolios, extended administrative support, access to classified information) that may activate Power values and associated motivations towards social status and prestige, control and dominance over people and resources. One interviewee, a former Secretary of State, articulated this when she recalled her time in office: "A certain amount of arrogance and self-belief, I suppose, that you have to have as a politician. In fact, if anything, I grew those. I grew the idea that I was quite good at it" (Interviewee 5). Likewise, it may be that the individuals who enter the UK Parliament with higher Power values in the first place are also those who are attracted to the upper echelons of the democratic hierarchy. As one former Labour frontbench politician sagely reflected: "[s]elf-belief, I think, is quite an important thing. If you want to advance in politics, you can't really afford to be self-deprecating, unless it's no more than an artifice" (Interviewee 16).

In order to explore the potential self-selection among those who do and do not pursue top parliamentary and governmental positions, a binary logistic regression is used here to test the predictive power of basic values upon in-role progression to the frontbench.[3] Participants from the initial, in-depth survey of MPs (see Chapter 1) are split between those MPs who held (or had ever held) frontbench positions in the House of Commons and those that had not (at the time of sampling). Frontbench experiences included Parliamentary Under-Secretary of State, Minister, Secretary of State, and Prime Minister. Parliamentary Private Secretaries were also included in this group. Although not technically a frontbench role, the position offers additional responsibility and proximity to decision makers, and often acts as a career stepping stone to higher office (Searing, 1994). In total,

63 participants reported frontbench experience at some point in their career and 43 reported that they had never held a frontbench position. Controls are included for MPs' age, gender and longevity in Parliament, and only six values are retained to maximize the statistical power of the equation. For ease of interpretation, all continuous variables in the model have been rescaled 0–1.

Average marginal effects (AME) for this analysis are illustrated in Figure 2.2 along with 95% confidence intervals. AME provide an average probability change in an outcome (being on the frontbench) for all participants when a regressor (basic values) increases by one unit. The results here show that an MP's longevity in office has a particularly strong and statistically significant effect upon their in-role progression. Those participants who had served in the UK Parliament the longest were, on average, 56% more likely to have held a frontbench position than those participants who had served for the least number of years (1–2 years at the time of sampling). This would suggest that service and

Figure 2.2: Basic values and 'in-role' success

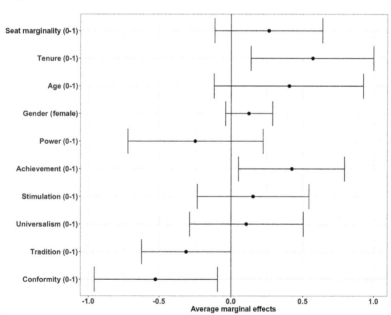

Note: Unstandardized regression coefficients, robust standard errors and p values: Conformity (−4.185(1.924), $p < 0.03$); Tradition (−2.484(1.348), $p < 0.065$); Universalism (0.858(1.616), $p < 0.595$); Stimulation (1.231(1.586), $p < 0.438$); Achievement (3.368(1.635), $p < 0.039$); Power (−1.981(1.945), $p < 0.308$); Gender: female (0.996(0.694), $p < 0.151$); Age (3.215(2.206), $p < 0.145$); Tenure in years (4.530(1.960), $p < 0.021$); Marginality: aggregate score of the election margin in each MP's seat at the last three general elections (2.092(1.582), $p < 0.186$). AIC = 95.034. UK Members of Parliament ($N = 106$).

experience are rewarded with promotion, and that the most effective way of succeeding in-role is simply to succeed at staying in office. At the same time, the results here indicate that one Self-Enhancement factor (Achievement values) exerts a strong and statistically significant effect upon in-role progression. MPs scoring highest for Achievement values were, on average, 42% more likely to hold a frontbench position than those participants scoring lowest for this value factor. The data would suggest, therefore, that those who rise to the top are far more ambitious, self-referential and desirous of influence than those who remain on the backbench. At the same time, the analysis also shows that Conformity values are a significant negative predictor of frontbench status. Those MPs scoring lowest for Conformity values in this sample were, on average, 53% less likely to have served on the frontbench during their career than those scoring highest on this value factor.

These findings say something interesting about the role of personality characteristics when it comes to political success in the UK Parliament and the psychological requirements of frontbench office in particular (for an extended discussion, see Weinberg, 2019). Holding leadership positions in a democracy necessarily demands a certain set of skills and characteristics that are associated with confronting others, arguing for and defending beliefs, leading others and, at the same time, manipulating or persuading them to behave for you in certain ways. MPs who score above average for Conservation values (such as Conformity) and thus attribute importance to authority, respect and moderation may naturally find it harder to succeed in this environment than those with above average scores for Achievement values who are ambitious for personal success. Asked if they could describe those MPs who succeeded in politics, Interviewee 6 responded: "People with ability. People with ambition. People who are connected." As powerful motivators of goal-oriented behaviour, it seems that Achievement values are as evident to MPs in the actions of their more 'successful' colleagues as Self-Transcendence values appear to be as motivators across the House. Answering the same question as above, another interviewee commented:

> '[A]mbition is a wonderful thing. They're all driven by extreme ambition; even in the Lords. And people, of course, who acquire ambition by the time they get to 50 or 60 can't give it up. How do you give up being what you are? It's habit.' (Interviewee 2)

Whilst voters may want MPs who are altruistic, authentic or loyal, party political gatekeepers may also see these characteristics as weaknesses in a contested and conflictual parliamentary environment where success depends on taking tough decisions, building compromizes and making sacrifices (Crick, 1962; Medvic, 2013). In the world of UK parliamentary politics, it appears that these considerations provide a psychological filter of sorts for those who do and do not rise to the top of the 'greasy pole'.

Basic values and candidate emergence

It is one thing to demonstrate psychological differences between politicians and the public, and between politicians at different tiers of UK politics, it is another to suggest that these differences actually lead these individuals to consider (and consequently enter) politics in the first place. This question of why individuals choose a political career, and what separates them from those who do not and never would, has troubled political scientists researching political ambition and recruitment for over 60 years. The rational choice paradigm that dominates this literature emanated, first and foremost, from Joseph Schlesinger's (1966) *Ambition and Politics*, which framed ambition as a response to opportunity structures in the political environment. Subsequent studies of the effects of, for example, term limits, legislative professionalization, party congruence with constituents, and party recruitment criteria and procedures have dominated a largely US-centric literature on political ambition (eg Kazee, 1994; Moncrief et al, 2001; Maestas et al, 2006). This research base builds from the premise that ambition itself is a fixed attribute of the individual that is expressed when citizens face favourable political opportunity structures (see Prinz, 1993). This theory has burnished a model for the micro-analysis of politicians' decisions inter alia to remain in their elected position (static ambition), to seek higher office (progressive ambition), or to step down/retire before an election (discrete ambition).

In treating political ambition and candidate emergence as the function of structural conditions in the political landscape, rational choice studies such as these limit themselves to highly particularistic explanations that do not account for individual differences between actors in the political arena. The rational choice paradigm put forward by Schlesinger and his disciples treats all (eligible) members of the public as equally desirous of candidacy should they be faced with the right political opportunity structure. Despite a nascent body of evidence to the contrary (Lawless and Fox, 2005, 2010), such a model does not account for the ways in which personal socialization experiences, attitudinal dispositions, or individual characteristics such as personality may discriminate between people's interest in running for office in the first place. Analyzing longitudinal data from the Citizen Political Ambition Panel Study in the US, Jennifer Lawless (2012, pp 37–48) found that more than 50% of participants had considered a political candidacy (what she terms 'nascent political ambition'). Those that did not, had not actively decided against a political career but rather it had never occurred to them. Lawless (2012, pp 192–3) found that a series of individual-level differences (as opposed to opportunity structures) had a significant effect on eligible candidates. For example, men were far more likely than women to consider running for office at all; racial and ethnic minorities were actually more likely to consider themselves qualified for office than their white counterparts; individuals from a 'political' and supportive family home were more likely to consider candidacy; and levels of political cynicism significantly reduced a person's ambition to run for political office (for a comprehensive summary of results, see Lawless, 2012, pp 192–3).

These results have been replicated in a survey of 10,000 citizens in England, Wales and Scotland (Allen and Cutts, 2018). Unlike the US study discussed above, Allen and Cutts (2018, pp 1–2) found that just 10% of participants had considered running for political office, and just 9% would consider running in the future. The implication is, necessarily, that aspirants to political office form a significant minority within the general population and arguably a much smaller pool than in the US if comparative data are accurate. Yet even among these 'aspirants', only 21% had taken steps towards becoming an MP (Allen and Cutts, 2018, p 2). These findings add retrospective nuance to Paul Whiteley and Pat Seyd's (2002) earlier panel study of Labour and Conservative party members. The authors tested four different models to explain such high-intensity participation as running for elected office: 'civic voluntarism' (including socioeconomic and resource variables), 'social-psychological' (including measures of personal efficacy, social norms or perceptions of attitudes towards parties and their members, and affective attachments to parties), 'rational choice' (including the perceived costs of participation, collective benefits associated with party policies, selective incentives or private returns from involvement, and ideological congruence), and 'general incentives' (combining the former two). They regress a series of scales for high-intensity participation on each of these models and find that, on average, the civic voluntarism model raises important findings but performs worse than the others, and that the

Figure 2.3: Comprehensive model of candidate emergence

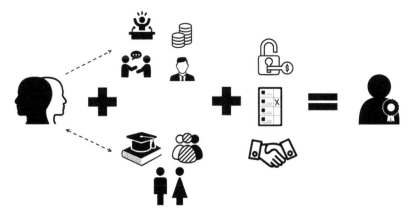

rational choice model performs much better when combined with the social–psychological model.

A pilot study of psychologically driven political ambition (Weinberg, 2020) builds on existing research by developing a more comprehensive model of candidate emergence (Figure 2.3). In this model, individual differences at the personal level, specifically personality differences, ultimately presage any cognisance of political opportunity structures and contribute to both nascent ambition to enter politics and ultimate success in the candidate emergence process. In proposing this model, comparative insights from social and organizational psychology are also drawn upon. For example, outside of politics, basic values have been researched in depth as antecedents of a range of organizational workplace phenomena, including organizational culture, socialization, employee performance, commitment and identification (for a review, see Bourne and Jenkins, 2013). These studies have shown that basic values can be highly predictive of career choice. For example, citizens high in Openness to Change values tend towards artistic and investigative professions (such as artist, musician, doctor, historian; Knafo and Sagiv, 2004), whilst those high in Conservation values favour conventional, programmatic occupations (administrative and hierarchical professions; Sagiv, 2002). Similarly, Self-Transcendence values have been strongly correlated with 'calling' professions with 'social' interest agendas, where the orientation of work is fulfilling socially valuable tasks (Gandal et al, 2005; Arieli et al, 2016). By contrast, Self-Enhancement values are positively associated with 'career' professions with 'enterprising' interest agendas, where the work involves managing subordinates towards a set of organizational or self-specific targets (Gandal et al, 2005; Sagiv, 2002). In terms of relating these findings to elected politics, there is a theoretical tension insofar as politics is a 'calling' profession where prosocial ethical behaviour – based on high Self-Transcendence orientations – is expected at the same time as intense conflict between tribal political parties and rigid hierarchies of power.

The model of candidate emergence presented in Figure 2.3 accounts for the role of personality (specifically basic values in this study) as the ultimate antecedent in the decision to run for political office. As such, political opportunity structures should not be taken as the catalysts of ambition, but rather the means by which individuals might service a variety of 'ambitions' that are grounded in individual differences. This model works with rather than against the existing evidence base, insofar as it acknowledges that personality characteristics are necessary but not sufficient to explain who makes it to Westminster. Put another way, it is anticipated that people do not appear in political roles randomly. As per Figure 2.3, they will require (a) a certain mixture of personality characteristics (basic values, personality traits and so on), (b) relevant professional skills and resources (skills of persuasion, articulation and criticality; knowledge of political systems; proximity to politics; financial security), (c) particular sociodemographics and socialization experiences (dependent upon gender, ethnicity, education, family dynamics, and cultural capital), and (d) favourable opportunity structures (such as institutionalized term limits, legislative professionalization including adequate pay and employee support, and transparent or at least accessible party selection procedures). The single-direction dotted line between personality and professional skills reflects the likelihood that individuals will be attracted to jobs that increase the possibility of pursuing motivational goals associated with their most important basic values. At the same time, the multidirectional line between personality and sociodemographics reflects the reciprocity between basic values and child/adolescent socialization experiences that are likely to be shaped by variables such as gender and ethnicity (Schwartz, 1992).

This model is tested below in a series of logistic regressions that combine data gathered from MPs, councillors and unsuccessful candidates with the ESS (eighth round) sample of the British public (AME for each regression are illustrated in Figure 2.4). Together, these datasets provide sufficient information to test the cumulative effect of personality (basic values), demographics (age and gender), socialization and professional skills (education and profession), and political opportunity structures (political experience). Prior involvement with politics – in the formal sense of working with, being an active member

Figure 2.4: Basic values and candidate emergence in the UK

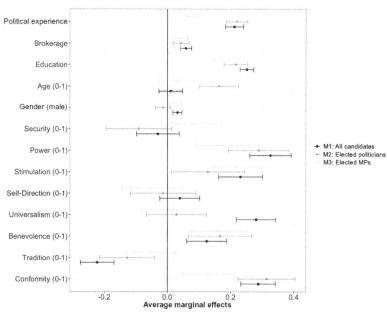

Note: M1 = candidates (N = 1,049), Cox & Snell R^2 = 0.677, AIC = 724.81, total N = 2,374. M2 = elected politicians (N = 584), Cox & Snell R^2 = 0.381, AIC = 1625.9, total N = 2,374. M3 = elected MPs (N = 168), Cox & Snell R^2 = 0.196, AIC = 1369.7, total N = 2,374.
95% confidence intervals for all estimates are shown by error bars.

of, or volunteering for political parties and trade unions – is used in these models as a proxy for the political opportunity structures faced by participants. Although prior experience may interact with other sociodemographic variables, it is assumed that (a) participants will be more likely to have accrued these experiences where opportunities to do so were transparent, and (b) that formal political participation will provide the contacts and knowledge necessary to secure a successful candidacy. To avoid the potential for multicollinearity that can occur when all ten interdependent value factors are included in regression equations, Achievement values and Hedonism values are excluded here a priori on the basis that they do not reveal any significant differences between MPs and the British public (see earlier analysis).[4]

From these analyses, it is possible to draw important preliminary conclusions about the role of personality characteristics such as basic values in fostering political ambition and candidate emergence. The results show that basic values are strong predictors of whether someone puts themselves forward as a candidate in a political election (M1) and whether someone actually becomes an elected councillor or MP

(M2). In the final model (whether someone becomes an elected MP), five basic values continue to exert strong predictive effects with high degrees of statistical significance (M3). These results hold even after controlling for a range of demographic and socioeconomic variables. Benevolence values appear to be particularly important. The AME in Figure 2.4 suggest that individuals who score highest for Benevolence values – and are by implication most motivated by caring for and supporting the welfare of others – are more likely to put themselves forward, and in turn enter politics, than individuals who score lowest for these values. The same is true of Stimulation values, indicating that those most motivated by excitement, novelty and challenge are more likely to harbour political ambition and enter elected office.

Tradition values, by contrast, are statistically significant negative predictors in M1 and M2. Those individuals who attribute most importance to these values, and by implication place importance on hierarchy, respect and commitment to accepted norms and customs, are less likely to consider a career in politics or indeed to be elected. In this study, those participants scoring highest on Tradition values were 22% less likely to have stood as candidates in a local or national election. Of all the basic values included in these models, however, Power values are the strongest predictors of candidate emergence. Compared to those participants scoring lowest for Power values across these samples, those individuals attributing most importance to them were, on average, 18% more likely to be elected MPs (M3), 29% more likely to be an elected councillor or MP (M2), and 33% more likely to put themselves forward as a candidate in a national or local election (M1). This suggests that candidate emergence in the UK, and hence political ambition, is underwritten by a psychological desire for social influence, authority and public recognition.

By contrast, demographic variables exert a surprisingly small effect on candidate emergence in these samples once all other controls have been added. The eldest participants were, on average, 16% more likely to be elected politicians (M2), but these effects dropped out in M1 and M3, indicating that age may not be a factor in the initial decision to run for office or a candidate's choice to run for (and ultimately enter) *national* office. The effects of gender are also muted: men were only 3% more likely, on average, to stand as candidates in an election (M1). Socialization variables (education and occupation) have a stronger predictive effect on candidate emergence. In the first instance, the highly educated (those with postgraduate qualifications) were, on average, 25% more likely to stand as candidates (M1) and 18% more likely to be elected MPs (M3) than those with no formal qualifications.

Individuals working in Brokerage professions (occupations such as Law, Finance and the Media that are conducive to professional skills and resources) were, on average, just 4–6% more likely to be a candidate, elected politician, or an elected MP but these effects hold consistent across all three models. As rational choice theorists would anticipate, the results reported here also show that individuals with prior experience of politics were, on average, 21% more likely to stand as a candidate and 8% more likely to go on to be an elected MP.

Given the dominance of political parties within UK politics, it is important to remember that political parties are also often arbiters of the opportunity structures available to individuals as well as certain sociodemographic groups. As such, they can 'pull' or encourage individuals into politics (see Durose et al, 2011). Although it has not been possible in this study, future research might examine how candidate emergence is impacted by, amongst other factors, the role of local party selectorates (who are often more regressive in their views on equality and diversity), the lack of diversity within the relatively small party memberships from which candidates are drawn (just 2% of the UK population), the presence or not of mentoring networks and support systems provided to potential candidates (the Labour Party's future candidates programme being a case in point), and the actual candidate selection process itself (all-women shortlists are one example of transformative change within the Labour Party that has increased women's representation in the UK House of Commons).

The results presented in these regression models are also testament to the hyper-selectivity of elite politics in the UK. Above all, these data show that basic values are – as in other occupational domains – highly predictive of career choice (Sagiv, 2002; Knafo and Sagiv, 2004; Bourne and Jenkins, 2013). On one hand, the strong associations found here between Openness to Change values and political office are indicative of the creative, problem-solving nature of the job, as opposed to more programmatic and risk-averse professions that tend to attract individuals high in Conservation values (Arieli and Tenne-Gazit, 2017). The predictive power of Stimulation values, in particular, suggests that this link may be more affect-oriented than cognitive (as associated with the explorative and investigative motivations of Self-Direction values); it is the desire for excitement, impulsiveness and diversity that attracts people to elite politics. On the other hand, these results also complement previous research demonstrating the link between Self-transcendence values and 'calling' professions (Gandal et al, 2005). It would appear that citizens attracted to political office have an intense calling orientation and see elected politics as a vehicle through which to fulfil socially valuable work and obtain some level of self-actualization. It is worth noting that both Benevolence and Universalism values are strong positive predictors of standing as a candidate (M1), but the effects of Universalism drop out in M2 and M3. This suggests that personality characteristics may matter more or less at different stages of the political career pipeline. Put another way, above-average motivations towards social justice, engagement with outgroups and social/environmental welfare (Universalism values) may predispose individuals to stand for office, but they do not necessarily help them to win an election.

A 'calling' orientation was also a common theme in the interview data. As Interviewee 7 commented, "[w]hen I left school, I had this plan that I wanted to help people and that was kind of my aim in life". For most interviewees, their decision to enter politics had been a value-laden one. There was, across nearly all interviewees, a sense of injustice or inequality that they perceived in the world around them and sought to correct through the political arena. One Labour MP expressed this sentiment in forceful terms:

> 'I don't remember ever deciding to [enter politics], it was more that it felt very natural to do it ... I think the world seemed an unfair place. I felt incredibly ... Nothing else interested me, really. I felt that that was so urgent. That it was what one should devote one's life to doing. That was kind of in my late teens. I just, I don't know, I suppose I was just awakened. I had no idea why anyone would do anything else.' (Interviewee 8)

However, the prosocial side of politics as a vocation is juxtaposed against politics as a tribal, competitive and (inside parliament) hierarchical occupation. It is possibly not surprising, therefore, that the results presented in Figure 2.4 show that individuals who attribute more importance to Power values are more likely to enter elite politics. This was captured neatly in the comments of one former Secretary of State:

> 'I am ambitious and, luckily, not too worried about showing it, which is always helpful, I think. [...] I'm strongly of the view that politics is a collective process. However, being an MP is one of the more individualistic things that I've ever done in my life. You need to have quite a strong sense of self-belief and ambition in order to survive and be successful.' (Interviewee 5)

If politics per se attracts people with a calling orientation, then parliamentary politics in the UK also attracts individuals with an above-average level of enterprising interest (see also Holland, 1997). Given that basic values have been found to predict employee performance as well as career choice (Arieli and Tenne-Gazit, 2017), it may be that individuals scoring highest for Self-Enhancement values are necessarily those most adapted to survive and succeed once they enter parliament.

Asked why they entered politics, interviewees also placed a great deal of emphasis on their education. In line with the results presented in Figure 2.4, interviewees were particularly insistent that university life had presented them with a gateway for politics. As a former frontbench MP reflected:

> 'I think I really started to get interested at university. I didn't get really involved in student politics but I know while I was at university, I remember, was the first time I actually went canvassing for the Labour Party in a general election.' (Interviewee 15)

Taken together, the quantitative and qualitative data presented here point to the powerful socializing effect of higher education on future politicians. This effect would seem to be as much about initiating individuals into political debate and thought as providing them with new opportunity structures to engage with formal institutions. The following interviewees typify this distinction:

> '[M]y political education really started at university. I went to university at a time of foment, when people said you don't come to university to get a degree and a good job, you come to university to change the world.' (Interviewee 1)

> 'I was at XXXX University and involved with student politics. I was President of the XXXX, the Student Representative Council, which is the Scottish equivalent, I suppose, of the Students' Union, and then became President of the XXXX. So, I was active in student politics, but I joined the Labour Party at the same time.' (Interviewee 12)

These interviews also revealed limitations with the statistical analysis. They highlighted variables that were neither measured nor considered in the survey data. In particular, interviewees talked about the importance of familial connections with politics and, above all, about luck. In the first instance, it was apparent to a number of interviewees that their political ambitions, or at least their readiness for political participation as an adult, had been burnished by familial networks.

> 'My idea of fun when I was a child was when election day came round, and I got to cycle backwards and forwards to the polling station and pick up the numbers, because my mum and dad were both actively involved as local councillors. So, I had a strong sense, from quite an early age, of debate and political process, and also, I suppose, was motivated by the idea that I could play a role in changing the way that things worked.' (Interviewee 5)

This adds weight to prior research indicating the link between interest in running for political office and parental socialization (Allen and Cutts, 2018). Given that basic values are at their most flexible in childhood, it is possible that they share a powerful interaction effect with early socialization into politics when it comes to predicting an individual's future political activism. What survey data and statistical analysis cannot account for, however, is the role played by luck. On top of the self-selection to elite politics demonstrated in this book, there is also a long list of potentially uncontrollable variables – for example, the inclinations and preferences of party selectorates and the wider electorate, or the performance of party leaders – that may help a candidate to reach office. Interviewee 6 reflects upon one such series of events:

> 'I looked at London, I was chair of the XXXX then, and I looked at the map of London, saw boundary changes: two old seats had been put together near where I lived, where I had some contacts. I put my hat in the ring with 60 other people and managed to use the lesson that I'd learnt from Margaret Hodge and beat the other 59 people and got selected as a candidate and ended up here.'

For others, their introduction to formal politics was far more coincidental and unplanned. Recalling a chance encounter with the Young Liberals in the basement bar of a hotel, one interviewee described the happenstance occasion that sparked their political career:

'One of the young persons walked towards me and he said, "Excuse me, we are the Young Liberals." No idea what the Young Liberals was, I said, "What's your problem?" He said, "We can't get on with our meeting because we haven't got a quorum." I said, "What's a quorum?" He said, "We need four or five people to make a quorum." I said, "What do I have to do?" He said, "You pay half a crown," that was two shilling six pence, "and you're a member." I said, "Great," paying two shilling six pence, something to chat about and that was my introduction to the Liberal Democrats.' (Interviewee 11)

The data presented here are rich in both the breadth and depth of the insights they provide about political ambition and candidate emergence. The quantitative data indicate that personality – here measured using the Schwartz taxonomy of basic values – can significantly discriminate between 'who' enters Parliament and the motivations that they bring to the job. Contra to previous studies of political ambition (Schlesinger, 1966; Lawless, 2012; Allen and Cutts, 2018), it is therefore suggested that structural and socialization variables, as well as political opportunity structures, do not inculcate political ambition but rather facilitate the expression of particular psychological motivations through the realm of politics. As such, future studies should examine political ambition and political recruitment within a far more holistic approach, one that recognizes the powerful explanatory purchase of the psychological dimensions of candidate emergence. As already intimated, there are also many more factors that need to be accounted for in future tests of this model: party political selection procedures and ethnicity/religion in particular.

3

All the Same! Demographic Homogeneity and Careerism

'[W]e're so keen to find fault – not just with our politicians but with our political system – that we very frequently forget, as citizens, that democracy is what we collectively make it. Casting stones at politicians, and diminishing the importance of the democracy in which we live, ultimately damages us all.'

Labour Party MP (Interviewee 16)

The personalities of politicians are playing an ever more prominent role in political leadership, debate and communication around the world. This was particularly stark in both the US presidential election of 2016 and the UK General Elections of 2017 and 2019. In 2017, for example, the media compared the main candidates for Prime Minister as much on psychological characteristics as physical ones; the 'robotic' yet 'decisive' Theresa May was contrasted with the 'principled' yet 'weak' Labour leader Jeremy Corbyn, and these terms stuck in the popular psyche (YouGov, 2017). At the same time, studies of elite personality in politics have been severely limited by at-a-distance methodologies and, in political science in particular, a reluctance to cross disciplinary boundaries (see Wyatt and Silvester, 2018). The previous chapter assessed the ways in which politicians, at an aggregate level, differ psychologically from those they govern. Data collected from 168 national MPs and 415 councillors show that politicians are unique in terms of their basic values; that these differences make an additional contribution to the effects of well-researched socioeconomic and demographic factors in determining who enters politics; and that basic values also distinguish between those MPs who reach the highest political offices and those who do not.

This chapter now builds on these findings to interrogate how such differences might or might not manifest at a subgroup level. To do this, the elite sample is split by gender and then ethnicity, and in each case MPs are compared to corresponding groups in the general population using the eighth round of the European Social Survey (2016). A series of factorial analysis of variance (ANOVA) models is used to assess the extent to which MPs are more or less similar to one another in their basic values than their 'descriptive' sub-populations. The final section of this chapter then focuses on a socioeconomic trope common in evaluations of politicians by examining the differences between career politicians and those without prior employment in politics. In each section of this chapter, the aim is to move beyond an existing research agenda on democratic deficits that is focused almost exclusively on the barriers to equal political participation or the benefits of descriptive representation (Rocha et al, 2010; Childs and Cowley, 2011; Uhlaner and Scola, 2016), and instead evaluate the psychological dimensions of these debates by analyzing the basic values of politicians and the public that elects them.

Preferable descriptive representatives

Many of the arguments against, presuppositions about, and epithets for politicians discussed in Chapter 1 have become – where they are not explicit about this – proxies for another long-standing malfunction of UK democracy: the sociodemographic similarity of our politicians and their dissimilarity to the majority of the population. Following the 2017 General Election, which took place in the midst of this research project, 68% of UK MPs were male, 92% of those elected were white (compared to 86% of the population), 82% were university graduates and 24% had attended Oxford or Cambridge, and just 7 of 650 MPs had previously worked in blue-collar manual professions (Audickas and Cracknell, 2018). That said, there is not necessarily a clean causal link between the demographic (dis)proportionality of parliaments and public disengagement with politics or even rising distrust of politicians. As Andrew Hindmoor (2017, p 7) points out, trust in politicians in the UK was actually higher in the 1950s but they were, as a group, less representative of society than they are today. At the same time, these statistics have provided fertile ground for a rich seam of research into the Westminster 'bubble' and the UK's *descriptive* democratic deficit.

Hanna Pitkin's (1967) seminal work in this field is clear: descriptive representatives ought to mirror the physical appearance and sociocultural experiences of their constituents. This interpretation of representation demands that parliaments accurately reflect the distribution of subgroups in a national population as pertaining to gender, social class, ethnicity, religion and sexuality: '[J]ust as portraits are seen as representative of the sitter, so parliaments are seen as representative if they reflect the composition of the society from which they are drawn' (Norris and Lovenduski 1995, p 373). As such, 'unrepresentative' institutions – in the descriptive sense – are illegitimate institutions. Jane Mansbridge (1999) argues that representatives with shared experiences of race, religion, gender, nationality, or even locality will ultimately make *better* MPs, and that a political class dominated by the same 'shared experiences' is not actually able to fulfil its democratic obligations. In sum, descriptive representation adds to the democratic legitimacy of political institutions. This is especially compelling when one considers that many of the barriers to equal opportunity and quality of life – for instance, low income and poor education – disproportionately intersect with particular racial, ethnic and gender groups (Verba et al, 1995; Conway, 2000; Atkeson, 2003; Banducci et al, 2004).

A raft of research on minority empowerment in the US has also shown that descriptive representation can increase voter registration, turnout, political interest and efficacy, as well as the informal participation of women, Latinos and African Americans (Burns et al, 2001; Griffin and Keene, 2006; Barreto, 2007). These results have been replicated in comparative contexts (Wolbrecht and Campbell, 2007; Karp and Banducci, 2008; Barnes and Burchard, 2013). In turn, the importance of this dyadic mapping of representation between citizen and legislator has been nuanced by scholars who are more interested in the collective representation of national institutions. For example, Atkeson and Carrillo (2007, p 94) find that 'collective female representation influences external efficacy in a positive way', whilst Rocha and colleagues (2010) find similar effects on the turnout of African Americans and Latinos. Put another way, the overall descriptive composition of a legislature has as much or more impact on the political efficacy of underrepresented groups than direct representation by someone of the same demographic group. Analyzing data from seven US elections to the state legislature, Uhlaner and Scola (2016) show that the mobilizing benefits of collective descriptive representation also vary intersectionally. Their results suggest that collective representation increases turnout among all previously excluded groups but, in particular, gender matters more for white women and race matters more for African American men and women (Uhlaner and Scola, 2016, pp 247–8). Such studies add greatly to our understanding of political empowerment via descriptive representation in national parliaments, insofar as the latter provide macro-level cues to minority groups who subsequently perceive intrinsic value to participation.

In contrast to this literature, this chapter is more interested in demand-side representation in the UK Parliament. Although the studies cited above justify descriptive representation in national parliaments on the basis of the participative benefits generated among minority groups, they do not interrogate the extent to which descriptive representatives actually share experiences, values or substantive interests with those represented. To support these claims requires political science to cross disciplinary boundaries in order to study differences and similarities between legislators and citizens that are not directly observable. Such considerations may not be relevant when focusing upon levels of trust, efficacy or participation among minority groups, but it is argued that they do matter in the search for what Suzanne Dovi (2002) calls 'preferable descriptive representatives'.

Dovi (2002, p 739) argues that proponents of self- and descriptive representation have underestimated the vertical divisions within groups that can make physical appearance misleading as a basis for increased substantive representation of the whole group. She calls, therefore, for more focus on preferable descriptive representatives who share the same experiences and thus the same values as the group, and in turn appreciate the diversity of opinion within it. Indeed, to strengthen the case for descriptive representation requires further research into the motivations, issue positions and personalities of representatives from different demographic and socioeconomic groups. In line with Dovi, it is therefore contended that (a) the potentiality of democratic representation is discernible when national institutions collectively represent the people; (b) political science has not given sufficient attention to the demand-side factors involved in the substantive representation of sectional interests; and (c) democratic legitimacy in terms of substantive policy responsiveness may rely on preferable descriptive representatives with shared psychological characteristics. This chapter explores the last of these claims by studying the basic values of elite politicians in the UK alongside those of their respective demographic and socioeconomic groups in the general populace. Within the limits of the data available and in order to offer comparative findings to the majority of work on descriptive representation, the focus here is in particular on gender, ethnicity and occupational groups. At the same time, it is recognized that other social groups such as LGBTQ+ or people with disabilities are underrepresented and historically disadvantaged, and future research should build on the findings presented below to encompass these groups as well.

Gender

In spite of improvements to the gender balance between men and women MPs in the UK Parliament in recent decades, women remain woefully underrepresented. As of the UK General Election in 2017, just 32% of MPs and only 29% of the House of Lords were women. After the 2019 General Election, the number of women in the House of Commons rose again to a new all-time high of 220 (34% of all MPs). Not only is such a statistic shocking in and of itself in this day and age, but it compares unfavourably with other supposedly progressive European democracies such as Sweden (47.3%), Spain (41.1%) and France (39.7%).[1] In the UK, there also remain distinct discrepancies between the major political parties. In the 2017 General Election, 45% of elected Labour MPs were women as opposed to just 21% of Conservative MPs. Both parties improved their gender balance at the 2019 General Election, although only Labour achieved parity (51% women MPs as opposed to 24% of elected Conservative MPs). This overall gender imbalance remains despite the efforts of key figures in *both* main parties as well as the Women's Equality Party, which was founded in 2015 and quickly expanded to a membership of 45,000 by the time of the 2016 London mayoral elections (Evans and Kenny, 2016). Yet when proposals to improve female representation – including regulations and sanctions for political parties – were brought before Parliament in September 2017, they were rejected by Theresa May's Conservative Government on the grounds that women's representation was 'an important aim' but did not warrant legislation (Elgot, 2017).

It is in this context that political parties remain the gatekeepers to gender equality in national politics in the UK. At the same time, government responses to proposals such as those seen in 2017 depoliticize the issue and place more emphasis on the demand side of the debate (that is, women themselves). Here a wealth of research shows that women are less inclined to put themselves forward for political office in the first place than men (Lawless and Fox, 2010). They are also less likely to perceive themselves as able or qualified to enter politics (Fox and Lawless, 2004); they have different attitudes towards competition than their male counterparts (Kanthak and Woon, 2015; Preece and Stoddard, 2015); they experience different norms of socialization that deter political ambition (Fox and Lawless, 2014); they face more complicated considerations about work–life balance than men (Silbermann, 2015); they must overcome institutional biases in political recruitment procedures (Karpowitz et al, 2017); and they generally have less confidence in their own abilities than male candidates (Preece, 2016). There are, then, myriad reasons why political ambition remains highly gendered in the UK and beyond.

In the context of this book, existing research on women in politics produces two antithetical possibilities. On the one hand, such entrenched informal and formal impediments to women's access to politics may deter and restrain the political ambition of those potential candidates who would make preferable descriptive representatives (that is, those women with the same values, experiences and issue orientations as the majority of the female population). On the other hand, the gradual and incremental increase in the number of women in politics, as well as the heightened sensitivity to gender imbalances created by movements like the Women's Equality Party, may have narrowed the gender gap in everyday political ambition. Research has shown, for example, that women are more politically active and more politically knowledgeable when they are represented by women, and that such effects are magnified for young women exposed to new female candidates (Fridkin and Kenney, 2014; Wolbrecht and Campbell, 2017). As Campbell and Wolbrecht (2006, p 233) conclude: 'the presence of visible female role models does in fact increase the propensity for girls to express an intention to be politically active'. It is possible, therefore, that women in politics today may be more representative of the general female population than ever before.

To explore the psychological dimensions of these arguments, a series of factorial ANOVA models is used to assess the extent to which men and women MPs might be more or less similar to one another in their basic values than their descriptive sub-populations. In these models, participants' higher order values are analysed using two between-participant factors of status (MP versus public) and gender (male versus female). Figure 3.1 shows the main effects of each factor and the interactions between them. Taken together, these models accounted for 21% (adjusted partial $\eta^2 = 0.209$) of the overall variance in the four higher order values within these pooled samples. These results show that when one ignores the presence of gender, MPs and the public differ considerably across all higher order values (as per Chapter 2). When one ignores whether a participant is an MP, gender also has a statistically significant effect on the variance of three of the higher order values. Put simply, men and women appear to differ in their basic values. Supporting prior analyses of men and women in 127 samples from around the world (Schwartz and Rubel, 2005), these data indicate that men in the UK attribute more importance to Self-Enhancement values in general, whilst women in the UK score higher for Self-transcendence values. Yet arguably of more interest and importance for this book, the interaction statistics in these models show that the effect of gender on basic values is different among MPs and among the general public for two higher order values (Self-Enhancement and Conservation values).

Additional t-tests add nuance to these results (Table 3.1). The data presented here show that men and women MPs exhibit inverted differences across a number of basic values by comparison with men and women in the general population. Women MPs are, for example, more ambitious to succeed and gain recognition (Self-Enhancement values) than male MPs, but also less likely to be submissive in their social/ professional relations or to prioritize traditions and security (Conservation values). Men and women in the general population differ across all four value factors to a high degree of statistical significance (Table 3.1). Unlike their parliamentary counterparts, women in the general population are less motivated than men by the need for creativity, autonomy, excitement and pleasure (Openness to Change values) and by the need for prestige, social status and demonstrating their competence (Self-Enhancement values). Yet as with women MPs, women in the general population sample *are* more motivated than men by understanding, appreciating and protecting others (Self-Transcendence values). The last of these findings complements prior research on the heightened psychological need for communal affiliation among women (Chodorow, 1990) and the impact of socialization variables in childhood upon women's basic values (Schwartz, 2005).

Table 3.1: Independent samples t-tests of basic values by gender and status (centred mean scores)

Mean differences				
Basic values	Public women versus *men*	MPs women versus *men*	MPs *men* versus public men	MPs *women* versus public women
Openness to Change	−0.09 ★★★	0.01	0.23 ★★★	0.33 ★★★
Self-Transcendence	0.16 ★★★	0.25 ★	0.27 ★★★	0.36 ★★★
Self-Enhancement	−0.17 ★★★	0.17	0.30 ★★★	0.64 ★★★
Conservation	0.08 ★★	−0.28 ★	−0.50 ★★★	−0.87 ★★★
N	831/674	59/107	107/674	59/831

Two-tailed significance: ★★★ $p < 0.001$, ★★ $p < 0.01$, ★ $p < 0.05$.

These findings are also extremely informative at a between–groups level: supplementary t–tests show that men and women MPs differ significantly in their basic values to their counterparts in the public on all four higher order value factors. The size of these differences in aggregate mean scores is, however, much larger between women MPs and women in the population than it is for men (as per Figure 3.1). This would suggest that male MPs are potentially more psychologically representative – in terms of basic values – of men in the general population than women MPs are of women. At the same time, these data show that the differences in basic values (by gender) are

Figure 3.1: Basic values by gender and status

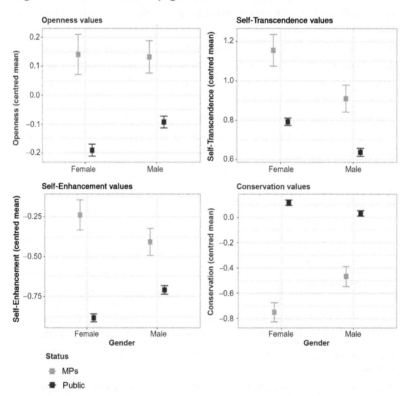

Note: Main effects of status: Openness to Change, $F(1, 1667) = 36.94$, $p < 0.001$; Self–Transcendence, $F(1, 1667) = 37.66$, $p < 0.001$; Self–Enhancement, $F(1, 1667) = 60.32$, $p < 0.001$; Conservation, $F(1, 1667) = 162.97$, $p < 0.001$). Main effects of gender: Openness to Change, $F(1, 1667) = 9.87$, $p < 0.001$; Self–Transcendence, $F(1, 1667) = 37.09$, $p < 0.01$; Self–Enhancement, $F(1, 1667) = 16.12$, $p < 0.001$; Conservation, $F(1, 1667) = 2.68$, $p < 0.102$). Significant interactions between gender and status: Self–Enhancement, $F(1, 1667) = 7.85$, $p < 0.01$; Conservation, $F(1, 1667) = 12.16$, $p < 0.001$). 95% confidence intervals for all estimates are shown by error bars.

greater between MPs and their corresponding cohorts in the public than within either group. This finding is significant given that anti-political narratives about politicians, as well as academic scholarship on democratic deficits, often collapses to complaints about failures of descriptive representation (in that politicians do not look like the people they represent) and failures of substantive representation (in that politicians are out of touch with popular interests) (Allen and Cairney, 2015).

It seems appropriate that these findings are placed within the context of Westminster's enduring gender imbalance. Although all-women shortlists and parliamentary reforms to working hours and childcare have greatly improved gender parity in the UK Parliament, the institutional fabric of formal and informal parliamentary politics remains overwhelmingly masculine (see Campbell et al, 2010). Not enough has been done, above all, to challenge an historical culture of male dominance and the corresponding exploitation of women MPs (Meakin, 2017). In a report on the representativeness of the House of Commons, the All-Party Parliamentary Group on Women in Parliament (2014, p 26) noted: 'You see pictures of men on the walls; you see statues of men lining the corridors; you see men everywhere.' It is in this context that the findings presented here might indicate the strength, or at least style, of character needed by successful women candidates. The data indicate that women MPs are not only governed by less concern for stable or harmonious social relations than their male colleagues, but they are also more confident when it comes to violating social expectations and norms. These characteristics are arguably highly apposite for anyone entering politics, but especially so for women, who require extraordinary resilience and ambition to overcome the effects of generalized political socialization patterns and to succeed in a highly gendered working environment.

Whilst it is clear that women MPs differ from their male colleagues and bring different basic values to their job, it is not clear that these values align with women in the general population. This would suggest that, from a psychological perspective, women are not descriptively represented in the UK Parliament and – given that basic values inform particular behaviours (eg Bardi and Schwartz, 2003) and political attitudes (eg Leimgruber, 2011) – the increasing number of women MPs in the UK Parliament may not be impacting as much as assumed on women's substantive representation. Such a claim requires more extensive research into individual patterns of behaviour, especially since it runs contrary to prior research showing distinct policy preferences among women legislators for issues concerning women's health, education, family care and gender equality (Dodson, 2006; Childs and Krook, 2008). However, the gender differences in policy preferences found in prior research may also be skewed due to the unequal success of parties on the Left in recruiting women candidates (see also Best and Vogel, 2018, p 351). Of the 59 elected women MPs recruited in this study, 30 were members of the Labour Party and only 14 were Conservatives. The unequal ratios of men:women within parliamentary parties may, given the differences in basic values presented above, inhibit the advances made in descriptive representation when it comes to the substantive representation of *all* women in Parliament.

In line with demand-side theories of political ambition, the results presented here also indicate that women who do successfully enter politics are more likely to share similar personality characteristics with men than their fellow women in the general population. In the first instance, this develops an important research agenda into politicized gender schema that directly rely on psychological assumptions about men and women in politics. Whilst women candidates are typically stereotyped as compassionate, consensual, passive and emotional, male candidates are perceived as rational, decisive, strong, intelligent and successful (eg Huddy and Terkildsen, 1993; Dolan, 2004). At the same time, advocates of representation theory have argued that voters choose between candidates who display 'desirable' character traits and competences for politics (Mansbridge, 2003). Regardless of the normative (un)desirability of the stereotypes outlined above, it is likely that these assumptions will influence voting calculations when it comes to choosing between men and women candidates, and potentially even more so in a majoritarian electoral system like that in the UK where candidates go head to head in each constituency. It is possible, therefore, that successful women candidates (such as participants in this study) not only navigate the gendered game of politics because their basic values are more aligned with those of their male colleagues than women in the general population, but also because they may signal those same characteristics to a voting public who are socialized to assign them more importance at the ballot box.

In exploring these findings, there is a strong consciousness that this research is not used to argue for undesirable constraints on the behaviour or beliefs of members of any historically underrepresented group. As Anne Phillips (1995, p 157) rightly argues, 'the presumption that all women or all black people share the same preferences and goals, ... is clearly – and dangerously – erroneous'. Rather, this research builds directly on Suzanne Dovi's (2002, p 738) call for preferable descriptive representatives who share mutual relationships and aims with dispossessed subgroups in the population. If women politicians are, as indicated here, more significantly outside the normal distribution for women in the population (psychologically) than their colleagues in historically dominant groups (that is, men), then Dovi's criteria for group representation raise important questions about the inequalities of political recruitment to the UK Parliament. This research does not in any way seek to undermine the advances made in gender equality in elite politics, but rather to highlight how much more needs to be done in this area of policy and scholarship. As discussed elsewhere (see, for example, Lovenduski, 2015), the blame here must lie with both the UK Parliament and political parties (as the organizations responsible for candidate selection and outreach) for not committing to supply-side reforms that improve institutional access and incentives for equal political participation by all members of underrepresented groups.

Ethnicity

The underrepresentation of ethnic minority groups in politics has been documented and scrutinized by a well-developed literature in the UK and beyond (Banducci et al, 2004; Bird et al, 2010; Stegmaier et al, 2013). Focusing on the nominal presence (or lack thereof) of black, Asian and minority ethnic (BAME) groups in UK politics, this literature has established that these subgroups in the general population are not descriptively represented in Parliament and that this is a direct consequence of a series of systemic barriers (Bloemraad and Schönwälder, 2013; Durose et al, 2013; Fisher et al, 2014). As with the descriptive underrepresentation of women in parliaments and legislatures, the saliency of this democratic deficit has been reflected in movements outside of academia as well. The Speaker's Conference report of 2008/09, produced by the then newly established All-Party Parliamentary Group for Fair Representation, pushed all political parties to commit to internal targets for greater ethnic diversity and increased support for BAME candidates (OBV, 2008, 2009). These commitments – however sporadically and differentially implemented between and within political parties (see Sobolewska, 2013) – have led to an improvement in descriptive BAME representation in the UK Parliament. At the 2017 General Election, 52 BAME candidates were returned, representing 8% of all MPs and an unprecedented high for a UK parliamentary election. After the 2019 General Election, this figure rose again to 65 BAME MPs (10% of the House of Commons). Whilst moving in the right direction, this figure still falls short of the 13.6% of UK citizens who self-identified as BAME in the 2016 Annual

Population Survey and the 14% of UK citizens identified as BAME in the last national census in 2011.

When it comes to understanding 'why' this democratic deficit exists, a number of persistent explanations emerge in extant research. The first relates to the relatively decentralized nature of candidate selection mechanisms in UK political parties. Partly as a result of the UK's electoral system, it is the local party that selects candidates and then leads on candidate campaigns (relying heavily on party members' voluntary involvement). For the three main parties at least (Labour, Conservatives and Liberal Democrats), there is the perceived risk of creating electorally detrimental antagonism with this support base by imposing centrally determined selection criteria or candidate lists. This was evident in the Conservative Party when Prime Minister David Cameron's 'A-List' of priority candidates (gender balanced and inclusive of BAME candidates) was slated by local Conservative Associations and eventually abandoned (Evans, 2008). As such, prejudiced party selectors can continue, where they exist, to perpetuate minority underrepresentation.

The second barrier relates to candidate supply. At the aggregate level, BAME groups command lower socioeconomic resources and are thus less able to meet the extreme monetary costs and time commitments involved in political candidature (Norris and Lovenduski, 1993; Li and Heath, 2010; Hardman, 2018). The third barrier is all about demand. Put simply, the received assumption among party selectorates has been that BAME candidates only win support in constituencies with higher BAME populations (Norris and Lovenduski, 1993). On the flip side, this erroneous logic also assumes that traditional Conservative seats will only vote for white middle class men (eg Carlin and Isaby, 2006) and that working class Labour voters will defect on the basis of feeling economically or socioculturally threatened by BAME candidates (Ford and Goodwin 2010; Biggs and Knauss, 2011). Almost 20 years ago, Saggar and Geddes (2000, p 27) argued that this presumption precipitates a ghettoization of minority participation in electoral politics. Related to the third, the fourth dominant barrier to BAME representation focuses on broader public opinion. In his study of ethnic minority MPs and BAME electoral success between 1992 and 2010, Patrick English (2019a, 2019b) finds (a) a significant negative relationship between rising anti-immigrant public opinion and the success or even presence of BAME MPs in selected regions of the UK, and (b) an in-role penalty for ethnic minority MPs, who are less likely than their white peers to access positions of power and influence.

The hurdles for aspiring BAME MPs in the UK are, then, considerable. As with women, the political opportunity structures to facilitate, enable or encourage political ambition are far more limited than those provided to their white, male colleagues, friends or fellow citizens. The candidate emergence model proposed in Chapter 2 suggested that political ambition is grounded in personality characteristics such as basic values that, in turn, cumulatively contribute to successful candidature in conjunction with political opportunity structures. In the case of underrepresented subgroups in the population, who exhibit similar levels of partisanship to white British citizens (see Heath et al, 2013) but face unfavourable opportunity structures, it is entirely possible that individual factors such as basic values actually play more of a role in successful candidacies. Future research should seek to replicate the tests of candidate emergence run in Chapter 2 to account for the contribution of ethnicity.

This chapter is, however, less interested in the *nominal* under-representation of BAME groups (and the structural causes thereof) and more concerned with whether or not existing BAME MPs are preferable descriptive representatives of the wider BAME community in the UK. At first glance, the 2010 Ethnic Minority British Election Study and subsequent quantitative studies of minority ethnic parliamentary representation suggest that the *substantive* representation of minority interests, or at least the public perception of it, has not kept pace with improvements to the descriptive presence of minority ethnic candidates and politicians (Heath et al, 2013; Saalfeld and Bischof, 2013; Koplinskaya, 2017). For example, Koplinskaya (2017) finds that whether or not UK MPs come from a minority background actually has limited impact as a predictor of whether they ask minority-specific written questions in Parliament by comparison to institutional predictors such as being in opposition. This is pertinent in the context of arguments made earlier vis-à-vis preferable descriptive representatives, since it raises important questions about the principal–agent relationship at the heart of democratic representation in the UK's Westminster system and, specifically, whether or not successful BAME candidates share the same goals and motivations – as well as expertise and insights on minority issues – as BAME voters.

As a preliminary foray into this research agenda, a series of ANOVA models are reported (Figure 3.2) that compare the higher order basic values of BAME politicians with their white British peers and respective subgroups in the general UK population. Given that only 3 of the 62 elected MPs who agreed to self-report their ethnicity in this study identified as BAME, they are combined in these analyses with a larger

Figure 3.2: Basic values by ethnicity and status

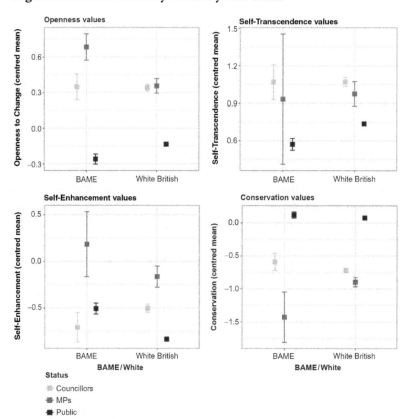

Note: Main effects of status: Openness to Change, F(1, 1959) = 265.62, $p < 0.001$; Self-Transcendence, F(1, 1959) = 118.36, $p < 0.001$; Self-Enhancement, F(1, 1959) = 73.59, $p < 0.001$; Conservation, F(1, 1959) = 615.85, $p < 0.001$). Main effects of ethnicity: Openness to Change, F(1, 1959) = 4.04, $p < 0.05$; Self-Transcendence, F(1, 1959) = 7.93, $p < 0.01$; Self-Enhancement, F(1, 1959) = 14.67, $p < 0.001$; Conservation, F(1, 1959) = 0.92, $p < 0.34$). Significant interactions between ethnicity and status: Self-Enhancement, F(1, 1959) = 9.96, $p < 0.01$. 95% confidence intervals for all estimates are shown by error bars.

sample of local councillors collected in the extended electronic survey (see Chapter 1). The results below therefore necessarily seek differences between the public and politicians per se, as opposed to simply MPs as in the analysis of gender earlier in this chapter. For the purpose of clarity, councillors and MPs are illustrated separately in Figure 3.2. As per Chapter 2, the main effects of status (politician or public) are once again highly significant in explaining the variance in all four higher order values in these samples. The main effects of ethnicity (BAME or White British) are weaker but still notable and statistically significant across all of these factors apart from Conservation values.

At the aggregate level, there is also a significant interaction between status and ethnicity for Self-Enhancement values. This implies that the variance in Self-Enhancement values in the sample populations is different between BAME and white British politicians than between their counterparts in the general population. Overall, these models account for an impressive 47% (adjusted partial $\eta^2 = 0.465$) of the total variance in the four higher order values within these pooled samples.

Based on these data, BAME and white British members of the public appear to differ in their basic values in a number of key ways: the former are, for example, less receptive to new ideas and place less importance on autonomous thoughts and actions (Openness to Change values); they are less concerned about the welfare of others (Self-Transcendence values); but they are more ambitious and place more importance on goals such as social status and prestige (Self-Enhancement values). When it comes to Conservation values, it seems that BAME and white British members of the UK public are equally oriented towards obedience and respect, social order and traditions. These results are supported by a series of split-group t-tests (Table 3.2). Far more important for the current discussion, however, is the fact that these differences in basic values do not replicate between BAME and white British politicians. Politicians barely differ in their basic values according to ethnicity and none of these differences reach statistical significance.[2]

Politicians appear to be unique in their basic value orientations by comparison to the general public, and these variations seem to

Table 3.2: Independent samples t-tests of basic values by ethnicity and status (centred mean scores)

Mean differences

Basic values	Public BAME versus White British	Politicians BAME versus White British	Politicians (BAME) versus public (BAME)	Politicians (White British) versus public (White British)
Openness to Change	−0.13 ★	0.04	0.64 ★★★	0.48 ★★★
Self-Transcendence	−0.16 ★★★	−0.01	0.48 ★★★	0.32 ★★★
Self-Enhancement	0.33 ★★★	−0.16	−0.11	0.38 ★★★
Conservation	0.04	0.07	−0.79 ★★★	−0.82 ★★★
N	130/1373	30/430	30/130	430/1373

Two-tailed significance: ★★★ $p < 0.001$, ★★ $p < 0.01$, ★ $p < 0.05$.

reproduce at the subgroup level between politicians and citizens of the same ethnicity. It is possible that the inclusion of councillors in these comparisons actually mutes the differences between BAME MPs and their descriptive subgroup in the population (see Figure 3.2). Such a claim obviously relies on future research with a larger sample of BAME MPs, but the results presented here remain interesting in and of themselves for what they say about the state of representation in the UK. At both the local and national level, there is a distinct lack of psychological congruency between politicians and the public, and between politicians of different ethnicities and their descriptive publics. Put another way, the public do not get 'preferable' descriptive representatives regardless of their ethnicity. Both BAME and white British politicians are significantly more open and receptive to change, and considerably less bound by order, security and self-discipline than their descriptive constituencies.

If ethnic minority (and majority) groups do not get preferable descriptive representatives – at least in terms of shared cognitive principles and trans-situational goals such as those captured by basic values – then the obvious question is 'why not?' Typically, basic values are adapted to an individual's life circumstances in childhood and adolescence (Schwartz, 1994, p 13). In most cases young people will heighten the importance they attribute to a value that is achievable and reduce the importance attributed to one that is frequently thwarted or clearly unattainable (Bardi and Schwartz, 2001, 2003). The reverse tends to be true only for values associated with material wellbeing and security; when these are difficult to attain, their relative importance to an individual increases (Schwartz, 2005, p 13). These 'determining' life circumstances will be, to a greater or lesser extent, shaped by a person's education, age, gender, ethnicity and other central characteristics that direct socialization and learning experiences in childhood. As such, these variables act as influential antecedents of differences between people's value hierarchies. They are also likely, therefore, to catalyse differences between the value hierarchies of people *within* any single descriptive group – hence the reciprocity between basic values and these factors in the candidate emergence model outlined in Chapter 2. In terms of making sense of the results presented above, it is suggested that we – referring here to the political class itself as well as academic commentators – may have grossly underestimated vertical divisions within demographic and socioeconomic groups. In analyzing and evaluating candidate emergence, political ambition or substantive representation, physical appearance appears to be a poor proxy for shared psychology (precipitated by shared experiences) between politicians and their descriptive subgroups in the general population.

With preliminary data in hand, a more refined research agenda on descriptive representation should not only study the participative benefits for citizens of descriptive legislatures, but also give greater scrutiny to those in the political arena *doing* the act of representation. Politicians constantly make representative claims about specific groups of citizens in which they not only identify or constitute the group's problems but also the political solutions that are needed. There is clearly not a linear conveyor belt between citizens and representatives in this scenario, and the extent to which representative claims are accurate will depend upon (a) a politician's perceptions of citizens' views and life experiences and (b) the pre-existing interests or opinions that shape politicians' decision making and political attitudes. Yet in this study of elite and mass basic values (the first in the UK), a distinct mismatch is found between the psychological backstops that women and BAME MPs (and politicians in general) bring to the act of representation and those of the public(s) they claim to represent. Future studies of this problem should seek to identify whether or not these psychological differences precipitate divergences in substantive policy opinions between descriptive representatives and subgroups in the public (regardless of whether these differences might be normatively positive or not).

These data also add to that collective voice of scholars in this space who advocate for a move away from numeric measurements of group representation (for a review, see Celis and Mügge, 2018). Once again, it should be stressed that this analysis is not intended to question the valuable and evident benefits to political participation that arise from an increase in descriptive representation. Rather, it is argued that academia also has a responsibility to move beyond a crude litmus test for political equality, whereby democracy 'works' when certain thresholds or critical masses are met. Indeed, a nascent body of academic work has claimed that the simplicity of the 'politics of presence' thesis elides far more complex yet pertinent debates about, for instance, women's influence in leadership positions (Dahlerup, 2006), the actual implementation of laws relating to women's interests (Mazur and Pollock, 2009), and the contested content of women's issues (Celis et al, 2014). Yet this research remains relatively staid in its conceptualization of how, and to what extent, debates in the UK Parliament (or any other) about equal pay, reproduction, or maternity leave are representative of *all* women. Utilizing unique data on the basic values of national politicians, a new avenue of investigation for this research arena is offered and it is demonstrated, specifically, that the motivational goals and interests of women and BAME members of the public do *not* align with those of their descriptive representatives in the UK Parliament.

Professional politicians and claims of 'careerism'

Discussions about the political class invariably extend to discussions about professional politicians (see Cairney, 2014). Whilst the previous two sections of this chapter focused on the basic values of demographic descriptive subgroups in the UK Parliament and the population, this section moves to focus on another recurrent, psychological criticism of politicians: careerism. The accusation proceeds that the UK Parliament and successive governments have been occupied solely by those who have made politics a career and have no alternative professional experience (for a review, see Borchert and Zeiss, 2003). The simple corollary of that statement is that such a development is negative for the state of politics and society more broadly.

In the 1990s, Sidney Verba and colleagues (1995) tried to counter this intuitive response to professionalization by arguing that it not only improved the quality of politics but that the experience of professional and managerial work (acquired in certain pre-political careers) actually developed a number of highly apposite political skills in aspiring candidates. Yet in democratic politics, there is a fear that with such professionalization comes greater independence for the political class and further detachment between the interests of those that govern and those that are governed. In the House of Commons in particular, the rise of the career politician and the associated professionalization of politics 'is much more ambiguous as it suggests a form of separation and careerism' (Wright, 2010). It is this issue of elite integration that has dominated the work of interested political scientists since the mid-twentieth century (eg Mills, 1956; Domhoff, 2005). It is important, however, to be clear about the empirical evidence supporting this interpretation of modern politics and the basis upon which a causal link between professionalization and careerism (as an abstract concept denoting certain psychological qualities) is justified.

To begin with, three broad contentions need to be addressed. In the first instance, there is a certain naivety to concerns about the rise of 'new' career politicians. The nineteenth century and early twentieth century were not halcyon days of amateur politicians living *for* politics, but were characterized by parliaments filled with wealthy aristocrats who acted relatively independently of their constituents' interests (Berrington, 1985; Crewe, 1985; Norton and Wood, 1993). With neither income nor career as a primary incentive, politicians were 'self-perpetuating aristocrats and gentry [who] regard[ed] service in Parliament and government as part of their inherited duties' (Riddell, 1993, p 266). Those MPs who now make politics their life's ambition tend to work harder than their predecessors and in a Parliament that is both more transparent and better organized to hold them and their colleagues to account (Norton, 2001; Benton and Russell, 2012).

The second dominant narrative raises concerns about the occupational homogeneity of modern politicians (eg Barber, 2014). This is a subject that has interested both the press media, who tell the story of a politics bereft of 'real people' (Kirkup, 2014; Lamont, 2014), and academics who have surveyed the increasingly professionalized, paid, and often unelected roles that MPs occupy before entering office (Cowley, 2012). Paul Cairney (2007, p 6) divides these 'politics facilitating' occupations into 'brokerage' jobs such as law, which are conducive to entering politics, and 'instrumental' jobs such as being a full-time councillor, party official or parliamentary staff, which are of direct aid to election. Cairney (2007) illustrates that the post-war trend among parliamentarians is heavily skewed in favour of those with instrumental backgrounds. Moreover, there is evidence to suggest that MPs with instrumental occupational backgrounds are more likely to be elected at a younger age than those without, to reach higher office once elected, and to receive promotions more quickly (Allen, 2013).

If we consider that politicians are advantaged by both their control over public resources and context-specific knowledge unavailable to non-elites, then the issue of occupational background becomes central in the recruitment process to parliamentary politics. Working for political parties in Parliament itself, or in a related organization, is likely to give aspirant MPs unrivalled knowledge about the formal and informal processes of elected politics and thus heighten their chances of success – both of entering parliament and of rising within it. This logic underlies the assumptions visualized in Chapter 2's candidate emergence model: successful candidature is a combination of individual-level psychological and demographic characteristics as well as resource-based professional skills and networks. If it is, at the same time, presumed that aspirant politicians are choosing certain instrumental occupations specifically as a stepping stone to elected office, then there is an additional element of occupational self-selection at work. However, there is a necessary *psychological* leap from this logic to assumptions about the substantive personality differences between these MPs and those from non-political backgrounds. Michael Rush (2001, p 112), for instance, regards career politicians as full-time MPs 'in both attitude and practice' but what exactly this means, both individually and in relation to the rest of the population, is rather opaque.

The third argument in the literature on careerism distinguishes between individual and institutional professionalization. Here it is useful to think of professionalization processes as measures of accountability and avenues of incentive. The former, such as the establishment of a behavioural code by the Committee on Standards in Public Life under the chairmanship of Lord Nolan, have laid down strict rules regarding parliamentary conduct and transparency in the House of Commons (Oliver, 1995; Rush, 1997). The latter, such as the introduction of MPs' salaries, select committees and devolution, have not only made politics sustainable as a career for those who may have been lured into other professions, but have also proliferated the number of prized positions (even the size of the political class itself) that those with ambitions for personal influence or power may pursue. For some, these reforms are characterized by an intention to make politics more professional precisely in order to facilitate the collective advancement of a closed system (eg Dodd, 1994). To an extent, and subject to the caveats presented in Chapter 2, the data already evaluated in this book – showing in particular that politicians per se are more motivated by prestige, personal leadership and resource dominance (Power values) than the general public – may support this inference.

At the same time, the regressions reported in Chapter 2 indicate a moderate association between brokerage professions (law, management consultancy, public relations, journalism and finance), as well as 'instrumental' political experience, and becoming an MP. How basic values are meted out between representatives with differing occupational backgrounds may, in turn, be a more appropriate measure of careerism as it is conceived above. Of those MPs who participated in this research, 44% had previously worked in brokerage professions and only 4% had worked in manual occupations (Table 3.3). Given that similar occupational groupings are used as proxy indicators of social grades (NRS, 2016), these results also support comparative research on (a) the amplifying effect of wealth upon political ambition (Allen and Cutts, 2018, p 3), and (b) the increasing exclusion of the working classes from elite politics (Evans and Tilley, 2015, 2017). However, there is a leap of abstract reasoning required to presume that these politics-oriented professions, and the conveyor belt between their offices and Westminster, necessarily produce MPs of such questionable moral fibre.

Table 3.3: Members of Parliament by previous occupation (*N* = 168)

Occupational group	Frequency	Percentage of sample
1. Brokerage (such as law, finance, consultancy, public relations, journalism)	72	44
2. Public sector professionals (such as secondary or higher education teaching, medicine or health care, public infrastructure design and management)	21	13
3. Manual (such as construction, engineering, amenities, transport)	6	4
4. Administrative (such as secretary, personal assistant)	5	3
5. 'Helping' Professions (such as emergency services, charity sector, the Church)	24	14
6. Political careers (such as civil service, local government, party official or Trade Union employee)	31	18
7. Refuse to answer	6	4

Figure 3.3: MPs' higher order basic values by occupational background (*N* = 168)

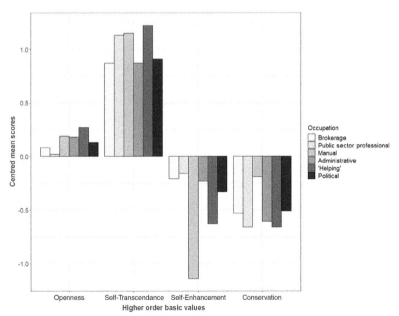

If MPs from brokerage backgrounds are, in fact, more self-interested and career oriented than their colleagues from 'real jobs' (see Lamont, 2014), then these differences should emerge in their basic values. Simple comparisons of MPs from brokerage and non-brokerage professions do reveal some variation (Figure 3.3). For example, MPs who have worked in brokerage occupations score slightly higher for Self-Enhancement values than those from other occupations, but no more so than those from public sector professions. They also score slightly higher for Conservation values and lower for Self-Transcendence values. However, a series of t-tests on these data indicate that these differences are not statistically significant in the current sample. If MPs are not matching up to public expectations for ethical integrity (see Allen and Birch, 2015a, 2015b), these data would suggest that it is not because of their occupational homogeneity. In fact, the relative importance of Self-transcendence values for MPs from all occupational backgrounds runs counterintuitive to the claim that elite politics is restricted to those *only* interested in the pursuit of wealth.

As discussed, scholars and journalists alike have shown equal if not greater concern about the rise of the career politician (Cowley, 2012; Allen, 2013). Indeed, Paul Cairney (2007) argues that the post-war period has seen a proliferation in the number of 'instrumental' jobs (from local councillor to party official, parliamentary staff to special adviser) that are of direct aid to election and, increasingly, occupy the majority of MPs' pre-parliamentary careers. In the present study, 80 out of 106 participants in the first survey of MPs had worked in politics at some point before entering Parliament (either before, after or alongside working in other professions). The current sample ranged in their prior experience of politics from 'none at all' to elected office in local or devolved governments, working as a party researcher, trade union official, special adviser and party campaign manager. However, t-tests revealed no statistically significant differences in basic values between those with and without pre-parliamentary political careers. The data also revealed no significant correlations between MPs' previous political experience and their basic values.

Adapting Cairney's (2007, p 6) categorization of politics-facilitating professions, participants from 'instrumental' careers were split further between 'elected' and 'non-elected' subtypes. It was anticipated that those who had pursued elected office elsewhere might share substantive psychological motivations (that is, to serve others through meaningful policy proposals or, alternatively, to dominate policy resources; see Chapter 2 for comparisons of MPs and councillors) that are not necessarily served in other 'political' careers. The differences in basic

Figure 3.4: The basic values of career politicians

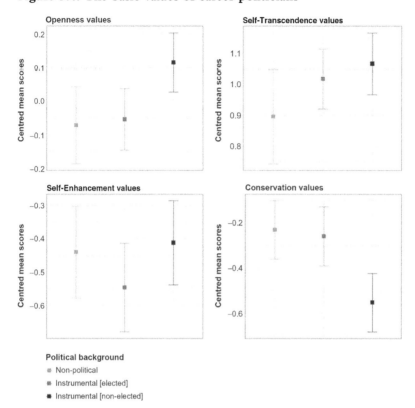

Note: MPs with no prior political experience (N = 26); MPs with prior experience of elected office in local or regional government (N = 43); MPs with prior experience of non-elected political jobs (N = 36). 95% confidence intervals for all estimates are shown by error bars.

values between these subgroups, though still not statistically significant, reveal two interesting variations between those with non-elected political experience and the rest (Figure 3.4). For example, the data indicate that non-elected instrumentals are moderately more likely to seek risks, challenges and to innovate (Openness to Change values), and to be less concerned with conforming to traditional ways of thinking or acting (Conservation values). This suggests that 'new' pre-political careers inside the Westminster bubble – those that are *of politics* but do not carry elected responsibility – are potentially producing a different kind of MP. Where possible, these trends warrant further research with larger samples.

The data presented here also contradict assumptions made in the anti-political narrative about the careerism of MPs who have only ever worked in politics. If these MPs are *more* desirous of personal gain, policy control, or wealth, this is not borne out in their basic values. If anything, they are just as committed to helping others and seeking equality for all groups (Self-Transcendence values) as their colleagues from 'normal' professions. Only two of the MPs interviewed for this study disagreed with the principle of professionalization and the idea, in particular, that MPs might only ever work in politics prior to election. These two MPs were adamant that non-political careers created more balanced representatives who were in tune with the zeitgeist of their electors.

> 'I sound like a fuddy-duddy now, but I think it's good to have done something else. To have what Denis Healey used to call a "hinterland" [...] I was a mental health social worker for six years sectioning people in my twenties, which is something else, I can tell you. Then I was on the staff in XXXX teaching various bits of social work and social policy, and law and stuff. It didn't actually change my political stance right [or] left, as it were, but it gave me a huge insight into [...] what my constituents are struggling with. So, when I got here, I think I was fully fledged.'
> (Interviewee 4)

By contrast, the idea of building a community connection via politics was a much more prevalent theme to emerge in interviews with MPs. For the majority, political jobs provided aspiring MPs with far greater exposure to people's needs (and how to help them) as well as the salient social, economic and political feelings of a time.

> 'I'm not sure, actually, because you've had a life in politics, meeting ordinary people through campaigning, fighting elections, working with experts in lots of different fields, makes you any less qualified to stand up in parliament and speak up on causes than if supposedly you've done something like, say, run one business for 20 years and then after 20 years of running a single business become an MP. It means as an MP you know an awful lot about that one business you've run, but not necessarily much else.'
> (Interviewee 13)

Contrary to accusations that career politicians might be out of touch, interviewees argued the exact opposite. For most, politics necessarily involved listening to people and getting to know their problems and their beliefs. Starting early was, therefore, not simply an advantage in terms of forging links with all types of people, but it also produced more competent representatives when those individuals finally stood for office. Interviewee 8 – who had been both a councillor and a political researcher prior to entering Parliament – talked passionately about the effective foundations provided by her previous employment:

> 'It all felt very familiar. Especially as well as being a researcher, being a councillor. It really helped, understanding how Whitehall worked, because you could make them work for you when you were trying to get stuff done as a constituency MP. You knew who to speak to, you knew how the processes worked. I think it saved me a lot of time as junior minister having been a special adviser, because I knew how to operate within that system [...] I think that was unbelievably helpful, just made me more effective.'

Taken together, the anecdotal evidence provided by interviewees and the quantitative data collected from all survey participants suggests that career politicians are *not* substantively different in terms of their basic values than MPs without prior political employment. Nor do those MPs from brokerage backgrounds in law, finance, consultancy and the media attribute significantly more importance to power and self-interest than MPs from other occupational backgrounds. It is important to be clear here about what these data can and cannot tell us. On one hand, it is not possible to discern why career politicians tend to get elected younger than their colleagues, progress more quickly in the role, and ultimately comprise a majority of the highest frontbench offices (see Allen, 2013). On the other hand, the results presented above *do* suggest that these phenomena are *not* based on the psychology of *career* politicians. These MPs do not show any remarkable peculiarities in their personality characteristics when compared to other successful candidates. Rather, they are as unique as every other MP by comparison to the population as a whole. It is argued, therefore, that these professions and experiences provide the resources, skillsets and networks to facilitate candidate emergence, but they do not explain the psychological imperatives behind nascent political ambition. As such – and as evidenced by the data above – they cannot provide an accurate shortcut for anti-political claims about our representatives. At a time when our politicians are critiqued as much on abstract notions of character as physical attributes such as the colour of their skin, age or gender, this is an important finding.

4

Basic Values and Partisanship

'[W]e have a role beyond making the machine here work better for everybody and that is, without being too grand about it, we have a national purpose being here. It is to make ourselves redundant.'

Anonymous MP (Interviewee 4)

Political parties carry out roles and functions that are pivotal to liberal democracies. In recent years political parties have, however, been the subject of intense criticism for catalyzing popular disengagement with politics and stoking unrest by capitalizing upon *some* citizens' political fears or intolerances. At the same time, a vernacular of 'cartel' parties current in political science connects the strategic organization and functioning of political parties with their apparent inability to mobilize citizens to participate in politics or trust in other political institutions (Mair, 2003; Hay, 2007; Katz and Mair, 2009). They are, then, as much a part of the anti-political tidal wave discussed in Chapter 1 as politicians themselves. Yet as Lisa Herman (2017, p 2) rightly points out, 'parties are criticized precisely because they are so important as agents in democratic government' (see also Kitschelt, 2006; Schattschneider, 2009). Political parties run campaigns and raise funds to do so, they provide manifestos of policy pledges capable of uniting disparate public interests, they turn electoral majorities into governing agendas and form the majorities in parliament capable of seeing those agendas through to fruition, and they hold governments to account whenever they do not win elections. The dominant literatures examining how and when parties fail at these democratic tasks tends to focus upon survey-based indicators of citizens' trust, partisan identification and party membership, and public opinion (eg Dalton and Wattenberg, 2000; Biezen and Poguntke, 2014). In contrast, it is argued that academe should pause to consider a potentially more interesting story about the root causes of partisanship and the psychological similarities or differences between politicians from different parties, and indeed between politicians and their voters, that might precipitate 'good' or' 'bad' democratic performance.

It is in this context that this book now turns to explore the relationship between basic values and partisanship in the UK in order to provide an additional answer to *who enters politics and how are they different to the general public?* The specific focus here is upon exploring the psychological factors underpinning partisanship and, in turn, how a more precise understanding of these determining factors at the micro and meso levels (both within and between party voters and representatives) might contribute to our collective understanding of three big sets of issues at the heart of contemporary politics in the UK and beyond. The first are issues of representation: do politicians share the value priorities (and thus motivational goals) of those citizens who vote for them and, ultimately, trust them with their democratic sovereignty? Aggregate comparisons conducted in earlier chapters would suggest not, but it is possible that psychological sorting occurs along partisan lines to mitigate these differences. The second set of issues relates directly to anti-politics: one dominant accusation explored in Chapter 1, for example, states that MPs are 'all the same'. This may prove true at a descriptive level in terms of sociodemographic characteristics, and indeed at a psychological level between elites and citizens from similar demographic groups (Chapter 3), but does it hold between elites and voters who self-identify within the same political bloc? The final issues are related to governance: democracy relies on the contention and contestation of a plurality of ideas about the 'common good' and what good government should look like. What we do not know is whether we have a parliament of representatives who are sufficiently different from one another to ensure this, or whether they are sufficiently similar to those in their own partisan bloc to provide strength and stability when in government or opposition. During the course of this chapter, data on the basic values of UK Members of Parliament are explored at a horizontal level to understand psychological differences between MPs from different political parties and vertically to delineate psychological representative links between MPs and voters.

Theories of partisanship

Understanding the determinants of partisanship among elites and voters matters at a number of levels. For parties themselves, it can help strategists to understand their core supporters and in turn help them to tailor manifestos and campaign adverts that appeal to voters in a differentiated manner. For students of liberal democracy, it can help to explain why people may disengage from formal politics and, in turn, how we might reinvigorate formal political participation. Whilst partisanship in the US has strengthened in recent decades in response to increasing polarization between the Republican and Democrat parties (Nicholson, 2012; Huddy et al, 2015; Abramowitz and Webster, 2016), the prevalence, origins and character of partisanship in Europe have remained much murkier and more contested (Dalton and Wattenberg, 2000; Johnston, 2006; Thomassen and Rosema, 2009). These debates have been driven, in part, by a gradual decline in party memberships and the (more recent) decline in vote shares for dominant parties at national and local elections.

In the UK, these statistics are particularly stark. As of August 2019, the Labour Party was the largest political party with just 485,000 members (Audickas et al, 2019). Taken together, membership of the Labour, Conservative and Liberal Democrat parties in 2019 accounted for just 1.7% of the entire electorate (Audickas et al, 2019). In the Conservative Party leadership election of that same year, just 92,000 votes from an unofficial party membership of 180,000 would elect Boris Johnson as the country's next Prime Minister. Of course, the notion of partisanship refers to a broader set of behaviours and individuals than those pertaining to official membership of a political party. Chapters 2 and 3 have already shown that politicians are psychologically unique by comparison to the British public, and it is possible that similar, diluted effects could be seen when comparing those who join political parties generally (and thus take a step towards high-intensity activism) and those who do not. Nonetheless, there remains strong evidence that partisanship and its effects persist among the general population in the UK and other complex multiparty systems (majoritarian and PR) across Europe (Holmberg, 2007; Bartle and Bellucci, 2009; Bankert et al, 2017; Huddy et al, 2018).

Prominent explanations of the nature and origins of partisanship in political science tend to fall within one of two accounts that are neatly captured by dual motivations theory (for a review, see Groenendyk, 2018). This theory identifies two pathways to partisan affiliation that have been researched in depth and are often pitted against one another. In the first of these pathways, partisanship comes from instrumental evaluations of the political environment. In other words, citizens are attracted to parties (and their policies as well as politicians) that best suit their personal and political preferences (eg Dalton and Weldon,

2007; Brader and Tucker, 2012). From an instrumental perspective, partisanship is grounded in a responsive and relatively well-informed degree of contemplation by citizens. Voting behaviours – taken as indicators of partisanship – therefore reflect citizens' agreement with a particular party manifesto and can be equally responsive to a party's policy successes, failures and the performance of its leaders. Diego Garzia (2013) provides strong supporting evidence for the instrumental model of partisanship in Germany, Italy, the Netherlands and the UK. Using instrumental variable analysis to decouple partisanship and leader effects on vote choice, Garzia (2013, p 181) finds that popular evaluations of party leaders predominate over social cleavages and prior voting habits when it comes to predicting electoral behaviour. Critics of the instrumental model argue, however, that empirical studies assume a false level of public deliberation – a type 1 error of sorts. For example, Adams and colleagues (2011) have shown that the general public is largely ignorant of changes in party platforms, whilst other studies have found only marginal changes in popular perceptions of political parties following comparatively major changes in their issue positions (Fernandez-Vazquez, 2014).

In the second pathway, partisanship is an expressive choice grounded in identity and therefore resistant to changes in party personnel or policy platforms (eg Mason, 2015; Huddy and Bankert, 2017). Drawing on social identity theory (Tajfel and Turner, 1979), expressive partisanship is a subjective feeling and/or cognition through which membership of the political party (as a real or imagined community) is internalized. Grounded in demographics and socialization experiences, the intensity of expressive partisanship will vary according to individual differences (Tajfel, 1981). Once an individual has identified with a group (or political party in this context), then they also become more energized to defend and promote the party by pursuing affiliated measures of security or prestige such as electoral dominance. In a recent study of political systems in Europe, including the UK, Huddy and colleagues (2018) find strong evidence of expressive partisanship among voters who, for example, engage more in motivated reasoning, display more animosity to out-groups, and exhibit defensive or positive emotions respectively when their party is threatened or reassured (see also Huddy, 2001).

Both the instrumental and expressive theories of partisanship are compelling and well researched, but they do not necessarily get to the heart of why someone joins, votes for, or runs for political office with a particular political party. In the instrumental account, voters are optimistically assumed to be Athenian democrats who are able and willing to navigate the complex terrain of modern politics, interrogate political options and reach fully informed political decisions. In contrast, expressive partisanship treats voters as motivated reasoners, but in many ways this theory simply outlines how partisanship is maintained once it is formed. This book joins political psychologists studying the role of personality in politics who argue, instead, that explanations of partisanship must account for the role of personality characteristics that define citizens' psychological needs or desires and direct their behavioural tendencies in varying domains such as politics (Jost et al, 2003, 2009; Mondak, 2010).

A raft of studies in recent years, conducted in different global contexts, has demonstrated the potential of personality studies to add to the explanatory purchase of canonical models of voting behaviour (Caprara et al, 2006; Vecchione et al, 2011; Bakker et al, 2016). In both US and European contexts, two of the Big 5 personality traits (Openness and Conscientiousness) have consistently differentiated between liberals or left-wing voters (who are more open-minded, autonomous and creative) and conservatives or right-wing voters (who are more conventional, reserved and organized) (Van Hiel et al, 2000; Barbaranelli et al, 2007; Schoen and Schumann, 2007; Gerber et al, 2010). A smaller pool of studies into basic values and partisanship has found similar results. In Israel and Italy, for example, voters for liberal parties attributed higher priority to Self-Transcendence values such as Universalism (Barnea and Schwartz, 1998; Caprara et al, 2006). In contrast, conservative voters scored higher for Conservation values. Findings also indicate that basic values explain more variation in voting habits than personality traits, whilst sociodemographic variables such as wealth and education have no additional predictive impact once values and traits have been considered (Caprara et al, 2009). The basic assumptions underlying these findings extend the instrumental model of partisanship, in particular, by linking citizens' vote choices with ideological portfolios that satisfy their psychological needs.

At a deeper theoretical level, the link between personality chara-cteristics and partisanship makes a great deal of intuitive sense. The success of a political party relies upon it fulfilling a democratic responsibility to mediate between citizens and the state by, ultimately, communicating a set of normative ideals and principles that justify the ways in which it would exercise power. These principles are normally anchored in distinct visions of an overarching common good that speaks to competing interpretations of elementary concepts such as equality, freedom or security (see also White and Ypi, 2016; Bonotti, 2017). Labour's commitment to 'the many, not the few' under its previous leader, Jeremy Corbyn, is a case in point. In fostering popular support, this process speaks to citizens' particularistic values, ideals and interests in a way that allows them to give psychological legitimacy to their choice of political party. Put another way, citizens mobilize their personality characteristics (traits or basic values) in weighing up the alternative aspirations of competing political programmes and then choosing which parties to support and which to oppose. Scholars working on moral foundations theory, Jonathan Haidt and colleagues in particular, have made similar claims: that the act of voting for a party is as much a psychological, moral commitment as a material or ideological one (see also Lakoff, 2004; Westen, 2007; Graham et al, 2009). The same contention arguably holds, at a greater magnitude, for those individuals who not only vote for a party but join it, campaign for it, and run for political office under its banner. To test the veracity of this claim, this chapter now compares the basic values of UK politicians from different political parties.

Elite differences in basic values

As outlined at the start of this chapter, political parties are uniquely important agents in the democratic process generally. Their control over parliamentary selection procedures makes them specifically important for MPs. The main question explored in this section – whether MPs from different political parties differ in fundamental personality characteristics like basic values – is then of special relevance to scholars interested in both the causes and symptoms of partisanship. The inaccessibility of political elites as well as the sensitive nature of psychological survey information on topics like personality have meant that the evidence base in this subfield is virtually non-existent. A small but scattered handful of studies in recent years have, however, successfully gathered data on the personality traits (as opposed to basic values) of politicians in comparative contexts.

In the US, there have been two studies in the last decade that have applied the Big 5 framework of personality traits to American legislators. Dietrich and colleagues (2012) studied 94 politicians from three states and found that only Conscientiousness differentiated between Democrats and Republicans to any degree of statistical significance. Similarly, Richard Hanania's (2017) larger study of 278 American state legislators found higher Openness and Agreeableness among Democrats and higher Conscientiousness among Republicans. Working in a different cultural context, these findings are replicated to some extent in Italy (Caprara et al, 2010) and Denmark (Nørgaard and Klemmensen, 2018). In Italy, right-wing politicians scored higher in Extraversion and Conscientiousness, whilst in Denmark left-wing politicians scored higher for Agreeableness. In Germany, Heinrich Best (2011) uncovered comparatively little variation in the personality traits of MPs from different parties, although he did find some polarity between the Neuroticism of post-communist MPs in the PDS (Party of Democratic Socialism) and MPs in the liberal FDP (Free Democratic Party) that he ascribes to specific cultural antagonisms. Taken together, these studies suggest that personality characteristics contribute to the political affiliation of politicians as well as voters. Given the strength of associations between people's personality traits and basic values (Parks-Leduc et al, 2015), it is highly likely that the latter might also discriminate between politicians from different political parties in the UK.

A comparison of UK MPs' basic values attests to the international findings reviewed above (see Figure 4.1). Although the numbers of MPs sampled from smaller parties makes statistical comparison difficult, the trends in the data reveal, for example, that Labour, SNP and Liberal Democrat MPs score considerably higher for Self-Transcendence values (Universalism and Benevolence) than their Conservative colleagues. These results reflect the ideological foundations of the UK's centre-left

Figure 4.1: Basic values by partisanship

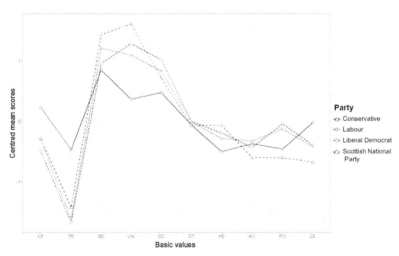

Note: CF – Conformity values; TR – Tradition values; BE – Benevolence values; UN – Universalism values; SD – Self-Direction values; ST – Stimulation values; HE – Hedonism values; AC – Achievement values; PO – Power values; SE – Security values. Labour MPs (N = 68), Conservative MPs (N = 45), Liberal Democrat MPs (N = 24), and Scottish National Party MPs (N = 14).

parties and, in particular, their strong advocacy of social welfare ideals such as 'a fair, free and open society, in which we seek to balance the fundamental values of liberty, equality and community' (Liberal Democrat Constitution, 2013). By contrast, Conservative MPs score higher for Conservation values (Conformity, Tradition and Security), again in line with the party's historic ideological roots in social and economic hierarchy (Dorey, 2011). These data reinforce a number of conclusions drawn in Chapter 2: that basic values may act as both an internal selection criterion for candidates, who are drawn to parties with a shared set of values, and as an external criterion by which party-specific selection mechanisms may favour or disfavour candidates in the recruitment process.

A series of t-tests comparing MPs from the UK's two largest parties – Labour and Conservative – reveal statistically significant differences across six of the ten lower order basic values illustrated in Figure 4.1. Only the differences between Stimulation, Achievement and Hedonism values in each group fail to reach statistical significance. For example, Labour Party MPs attribute greater importance to a broad world view based on equal access to social welfare and justice (Universalism values: $t(111) = 4.969$, $p < 0.001$), whilst also being more motivated by independent thought and action (Self-Direction values: $t(111) = 2.412$, $p < 0.05$). Conversely, Conservative MPs are more authoritarian, placing more importance on discipline, customs and traditions, personal and national security (Tradition values: $t(111) = 5.223$, $p < 0.001$; Security values: $t(111) = 2.037$, $p < 0.05$). These differences were also borne out by in-depth interviews with elite participants. In particular, it was clear for a number of MPs that their respective affiliations to political parties had been motivated by personal value judgements. One former Labour frontbench MP recalled:

> 'I got to know a South African student [at university] quite well. He was a black South African student who had come on a sort of scholarship. Just talking to him about the realities of apartheid really opened my eyes to some of what was going on in the world. I suppose I felt back then there were things that needed to change. Which party most fitted? It was Labour.' (Interviewee 15)

For these MPs, there was a tendency to talk of personal priorities, interests and motivations in party terms, and vice versa. Older interviewees, in particular, and those in the Labour Party especially, reflected very clearly on the values of their colleagues and the political manifestos that were produced from value calculations:

> 'Wealth is power. We see now what I was saying to you earlier, where the real power lies in the establishment, where the mega-corporations, the newspaper barons, the hedge fund managers, that's where all the power is. I think it's only radical parties, like the British Labour Party, the French Socialist Party, the German Social Democratic Party that ultimately can do something about it.' (Interviewee 12)

Other MPs were more pragmatic, acknowledging a diversity of opinion within each political party. However, even these interviewees were adamant about the moral or ideological differences between the two main parties and the need to join one side or the other of a dividing line:

> 'I think politics is about coalitions. In that each political party is a coalition and we live in a two-party country, pretty much, so you need to accept that and you know, work out which side you're on. And that there are good reasons for wanting your side to win.' (Interviewee 8)

Subject to further investigation, these results contradict much of the work done in recent decades on mass, catch-all (eg Kirchheimer, 1966) and cartel (Katz and Mair, 2009) theses of party competition. The arguments routinely stated – that ideological conflicts between parties have become little more than amorphous differences in Left–Right orientations – are not reflected in the basic values of MPs within UK parties. In particular, Richard Katz and Peter Mair's (2009, p 758) claim that 'party psychological identification' has declined does not hold at the elite level. In light of the findings in this book, future research might address these contradictions between observational conclusions and empirical data by focusing on (a) the possible dissonance between the beliefs of individual MPs and party manifestos; (b) the value trade-offs caused by professionalization processes (such as salaries), which may encourage MPs and parties to shy away from ideologically driven campaigns and focus on the 'reasonably anticipated minimum pay-off' (Katz and Mair, 2009, p 758); and (c) the centralization of party organizations that distances the leadership from those below and thus transforms party representation from an ideological loyalty to a contractual employment of sorts.

Ideology and basic values

Studies of partisanship in political science have tended to focus overwhelmingly on political values, commonly those '*ism*' ideologies such as egalitarianism, liberalism and so on, that are perceived to underpin political evaluations and behaviours such as voting for or joining a particular political party. However, these political values are highly contextual to the domain of politics and moreover contested between political contexts as well (see Feldman, 2003). Schwartz and colleagues (2010) contend that ideologies are actually expressions, particular to politics, of underlying basic values that direct behaviour in all areas of daily life. In prior research on the value convergence of party members, Caprara and colleagues (2006, p 2) go so far as to argue that basic values 'are the crucial grounding of ideology' (see also Leimgruber, 2011). Psychological studies of political elites have also used ideology as an additional proxy of partisanship. As a dependent variable (usually measured on a scale), ideology provides the added benefit of both complementing results taken from comparing party-rank variables and allowing researchers to look for variations between politicians *within* parties. In the US, for example, Hanania (2017) found significant correlations between legislators' ideological self-placement and the personality trait Openness, whilst Nørgaard and Klemmensen (2018) found similar correlations between ideology and Agreeableness among Danish MPs. In understanding the relationship between MPs' partisanship and psychological characteristics such as basic values, ideology is worthy of attention in this chapter.

Two-dimensional models of political orientation or ideology (such as liberal versus conservative) are easily aligned with the bipolar orthogonals of basic values theory. For example, a standard liberalism scale (charting issues of civil liberties and individual rights) mirrors the Openness to Change/Conservation dimension of basic values. Similarly, a socioeconomic scale concerning resource distribution and state intervention maps onto the Self-Transcendence/Self-Enhancement dimension. In making this connection between ideology and basic values, it is assumed that individuals are likely to be drawn to those political values, and in turn the parties or policies representing them, that promote and defend the personal values (and the associated motivational goals) that they cherish (Barnea and Schwartz, 1998; Schwartz et al, 2010). A number of empirical studies now support this bidimensional theory of basic values and political orientation (Caprara et al, 2006, 2010; Thorisdottir et al, 2007). For example, Piurko and colleagues (2011, p 554) use data from the ESS to show that basic values account for more variance in ideological self-placement than sociodemographic variables in 10 out of 11 'liberal' western countries.

It is equally possible that abstract personal beliefs or personality characteristics like basic values require political translation in order to have specific behavioural outcomes in the domain of politics. Van Deth (1995, p 6) argues that the personal 'values of individuals can be transformed into political orientations which have some impact on their behavioural intentions'. Not wanting to lose sight of what politics is and how it really works, it is accepted that behavioural choices – such as joining a political party and running as a candidate – may be traced back to basic values *through* salient political orientations or ideologies that allow a voter/citizen/politician to evaluate specific political issues in line with personal needs. To test this, the relationship between UK MPs' basic values and their political ideologies are examined (Figures 4.2 and 4.3).

MPs' ideology is measured here using two 11-point Left–Right scales, reflecting the heterogeneity of economic and social ideology (Feldman and Johnston, 2013). The decision to measure economic and social ideology separately builds on empirical research into the multidimensionality of ideological preferences across policy domains (Duckitt, 2001; Layman and Carsey, 2002; Treier and Hillygus, 2009), the variety of symbolic connotations attached to ideology (Ellis and Stimson, 2012), and the distinct meanings attached to a single liberal–conservative continuum by participants within and between research populations (Zumbrunnen and Gangl, 2008). As per other studies of politicians' personality characteristics (Caprara et al, 2010; Nørgaard and Klemmensen, 2018), the statistical power of the data is maximized here by grouping party representatives on the Left (68 Labour MPs, 24 Liberal Democrat MPs, and 1 Green MP) and Right (45 Conservative MPs and 1 UKIP MP).[1] As expected, MPs from left-wing parties or those on the left of centre score towards the bottom of the scale for both economic ideology (mean = 3.5, standard deviation = 1.6) and social ideology (mean = 2.3, standard deviation = 1.2). MPs from right-wing parties or those representing parties on the right of centre score much higher for both economic ideology (mean = 7.4, standard deviation = 1.4) and social ideology (mean = 5.4, standard deviation = 1.9).

Figure 4.2 illustrates the correlations between MPs' higher order basic values and their economic ideologies. Whereas previous studies of elite personality characteristics and ideology look at associations among all politicians, here a linear random slopes model for MPs in political parties on the Left and Right is overlaid to show the variations in these

Figure 4.2: Correlations between MPs' basic values and their economic ideology

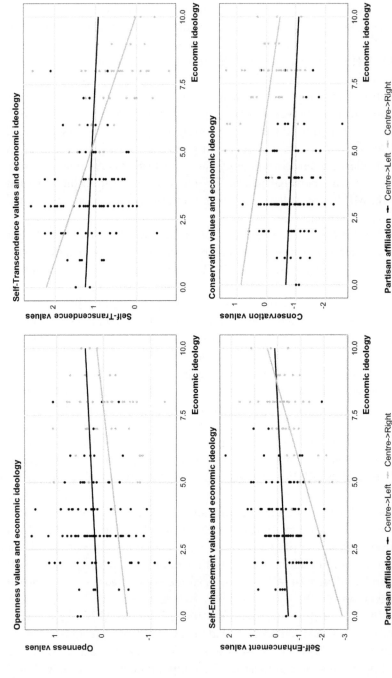

Note: Ideology runs Left–Right on an 11-point scale, based on responses to the following question: *In politics people sometimes talk of Left and Right. Where would you place yourself on the following scale for economic issues (where 0 = Left, 10 = Right)? N* = 168.

Figure 4.3: Correlations between MPs' basic values and their social ideology

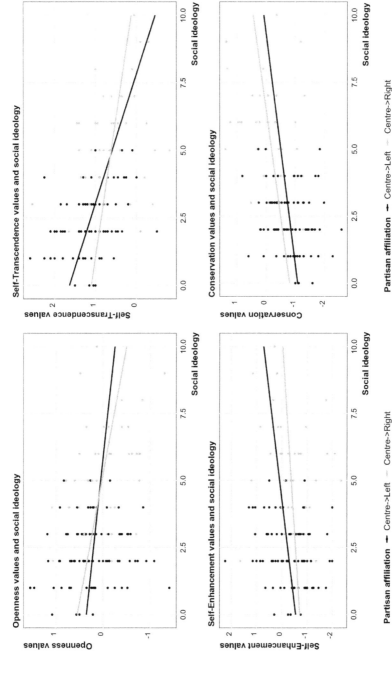

Note: Ideology runs Left–Right on an 11–point scale, based on responses to the following question: *In politics people sometimes talk of Left and Right. Where would you place yourself on the following scale for social issues (where 0 = Left, 10 = Right)?.*

relationships within party groupings.[2] In terms of economic ideology, weak and non-significant correlations are found with the higher order basic values of MPs on the Left. However, there are highly significant and moderately strong correlations between the economic ideologies of MPs on the Right and their Self-Transcendence ($r = -0.47$, $p < 0.001$) and Self-Enhancement values ($r = 0.56$, $p < 0.001$). Not only do these inverse correlations support the theoretical opposition of these value factors, but they suggest that these values may also help to discriminate between those MPs in centre-right/right-wing parties who hold relatively moderate or extreme economic opinions and policy positions. MPs in these parties who care most about acquiring social prestige, authority and resources (that is, Self-Enhancement values) seem, for example, to be considerably more right-wing in their economic positions than those who are less motivated by such goals. These relationships do not appear among MPs in parties on the Left.

MPs' basic values appear to share more consistent relationships with their social ideologies (Figure 4.3). For example, MPs in parties on the Left who attribute more importance to Self-Transcendence values are considerably more left-wing in their social ideology ($r = -0.41$, $p < 0.001$), as are MPs in parties on the Right who score higher for Openness to Change values ($r = -0.35$, $p < 0.05$). These results support comparative findings in the US and Denmark where politicians with psychological tendencies towards autonomy, creativity, social cooperation and inclusion tend to be more left-wing (Hanania, 2017; Nørgaard and Klemmensen, 2018). Conservation values also share moderate correlations with social ideology among MPs in parties on the Left ($r = 0.21$, $p < 0.05$) and Right ($r = 0.30$, $p < 0.05$). Therefore, regardless of partisanship, MPs with a greater need for social and individual stability and tradition appear to be more right-wing in their self-reported social ideology.

These results are interesting for a number of reasons. At a substantive level, they reveal a degree of interdependence between the basic values of national politicians in the UK and their self-reported ideological placement. In particular, MPs from across all parties are more right-wing where they also score highly for Conservation values. This adds to a long list of studies in political psychology that argue for identity-based approaches to political value systems (for early examples, see Lasswell, 1930). Such a claim appears to hold among UK politicians as well as mass publics. Put another way, Conservative or Labour MPs are not simply partisans of their respective party because they ascribe to conservative or liberal values (in the political sense), but because they have conservative or liberal personalities. Possibly of more interest to parliamentary scholars, these findings also have the potential to help us understand when and why MPs from different partisan groups may occasionally unite (either in the division lobby or in breakaway factions such as the Independent Group that formed as a cross-party coalition in the UK in 2019). There is, self-evidently, variation in the policy positions and ideological commitments of MPs in all political parties. As shown in Figures 4.2 and 4.3, these variations – in both ideology and basic values – may reflect or be the result of similarities between the fundamental social and human needs, as well the consequent ideological positioning, of MPs in different parties.

Methodologically, these results also highlight the benefits of (a) using a dual measure of ideology, and (b) looking at the partisan-specific associations between personality characteristics and ideology. In particular, the data presented above show that basic values and ideology appear to share different relationships among MPs in parties on the Left and Right. Self-Transcendence values, for example, correlate strongly with *economic* ideology for MPs in parties on the Right, but correlate with *social* ideology for MPs in parties on the Left. It is possible, again, that these variations reflect interesting ways in which the principles of instantiation – the cognitive and social links between general categories of values and specific behavioural examples (Hanel et al, 2017) – manifest in politics. The concept of instantiation suggests that the consistency of links between basic values and individual behaviours will depend upon how 'typical' a target (person, object, idea) is for a person (for examples, see Lord, 1994). In terms of politics, it is possible that politicians making policy-relevant judgements (such as those implicit in political ideologies) may overweight typical instances of a set category/target/object/idea (social group and so on) and ignore or underweight atypical cases. This is an argument in itself for a varied and diverse parliament, not only in terms of values and attitudes, but also in terms of a range of demographic and cultural variables that might affect the types of instantiations brought to bear on value-informed discussions. In the context of the findings presented above, it is possible that politicians socialized in parties on the Left necessarily associate Self-transcendence values, for example, with *social* actions and outcomes, whilst those socialized on the Right associate them with *economic* instantiations. Put another way, Self-Transcendence values (as a deep-seated and trans-situational set of human goals) may have been activated in response to different ideological questions (economic versus social) for MPs from different parties. Such a line of inquiry demands future research.

Leaders and followers

Research into principal–agent relations (that is, politician and voter) has long debated whether the principals' interests and preferences are cause or consequence of the political process (for a review, see Best and Vogel, 2018). In the former interpretation, principals select agents who appear the most able and trustworthy to convert their fixed and exogenous interests into policy. In the latter interpretation, elites enjoy wide autonomy from their principals and influence popular thought by offering competing political preferences (for an extended discussion, see Körösényi, 2018). The results presented in Chapters 2 and 3 have shown that (a) principals are driven by a different hierarchy of psychological motivations than their agents, and (b) that they are more similar to one another in these motivations than their corresponding sociodemographic groups in the general population. Therefore, whether one assumes a populist model in which democratic legitimacy is secured by agent responsiveness, or a trustee model in which it is exclusively assured by elite accountability, these findings have interesting implications. In the populist model, these data imply that elites may be forced to curtail their own psychological drives in order to tailor policies that fit, ex ante, a popular electoral mandate. In the trustee model, they suggest that MPs might be more inclined to anticipate citizens preferences and, ex post, mould and manipulate them to suit their own value valences when it comes to policy making. In either scenario, an organizing perspective is needed that mediates these potential differences and facilitates working democratic relationships between governor and governed. In most western democracies, political parties have grown to fill this gap. An important question to ask, then, is whether or not the basic values of a party's MPs correspond to those of the party's voters. In other words, do partisans in the general population elect MPs with similar personality characteristics who will, in turn, share their social and human motivational goals in the realm of representative politics?

In political psychology, the notion of personality similarity between voters and elites has been grounded in a powerful congruency principle that operates at various stages of democratic politics (Caprara and Zimbardo, 2004; Caprara and Vecchione, 2013). In the first instance, the congruency principle relates to common ideas and ideals, grounded in personality characteristics, that bind political elites together in partisan blocs. Evidence of this in the UK Parliament can be seen in earlier sections of this chapter. The same principle then functions in enabling voters to seek and identify congruency between their own values or psychological needs and those of candidates or groups of candidates (that is, political parties). In an evaluative sense, the congruency principle also relates to the ways in which voters use personality characteristics as yardsticks to appraise politicians' suitability for office and, in turn, their performance. Results from a study of Italian politicians and voters has corroborated this pattern. For example, both centre-left voters and MPs scored higher for Self-Transcendence values and centre-right voters and MPs attributed more importance to Conservation values (Caprara et al, 2010).

Whether or not UK politicians and voters are congruent in their basic values also matters in the context of growing evidence of links between character valence and satisfaction with democracy (Leiter et al, 2019). Initially developed by Donald Stokes (1992), character valence runs orthogonal to more traditional, instrumental notions of party evaluation in which voters support those parties or candidates most capable of handling a particular policy domain. Rather, character valence refers to issues 'on which parties or leaders are differentiated not by what they advocate but by the degree to which they are linked in the public's mind with conditions or goals or symbols of which almost everyone approves or disapproves' (Stokes, 1992, p 143). Put simply, character valence refers to those non-policy related characteristics such as honesty, loyalty, even ambition, that are psychological in nature and commonly associated with personality. The more that voters are able to perceive those same personal qualities in their political elites that they employ to guide their own behaviour or evaluate others positively, the more they will anticipate that their representatives will act like them and, ultimately, the more satisfied with, included in, and efficacious about politics they will feel (see also Leiter and Clark, 2015). Psychological congruency between voters and elites is, then, a crucial underpinning of representative democracy.

To test for psychological congruency between politicians and voters in the UK, a series of two-way ANOVA models were conducted to compare the higher order basic values of 168 MPs with their respective voters in the UK population (Figure 4.4). Data on the British public were again drawn from the eighth round of the European Social Survey and partisanship was derived from self-reported voting behaviour at the 2015 General Election. To maximize the statistical power of the comparisons, MPs and voters were once again grouped together on the left of centre and on the right of centre (see previous section), and any non-voters, voters for parties who did not win seats, or independent MPs (or voters thereof) were removed from the samples. The analysis shows that the main statistical effect of being an MP is,

Figure 4.4: Basic values by partisanship and status using ESS 8

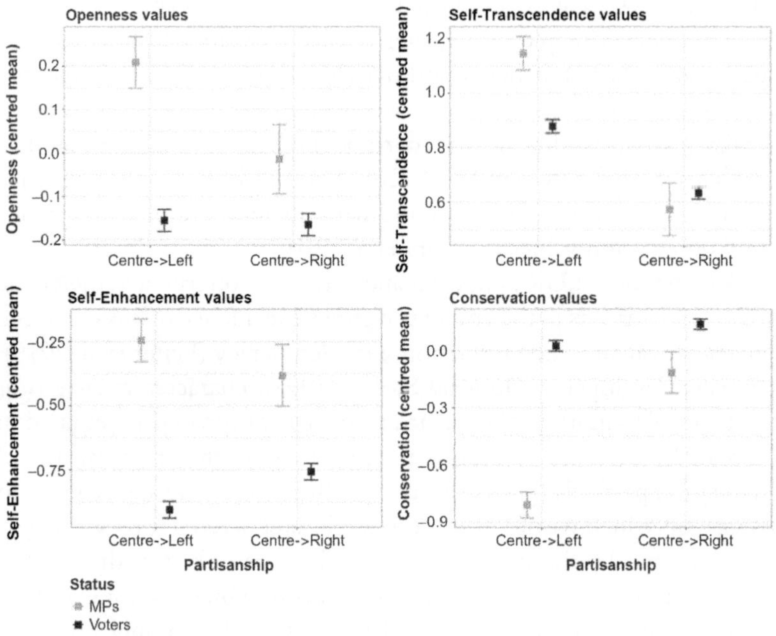

Note: Main effects of status: Openness to Change, $F(1, 1099) = 33.66$, $p < 0.001$; Self-Transcendence, $F(1, 1099) = 17.18$, $p < 0.001$; Self-Enhancement, $F(1, 1099) = 67.35$, $p < 0.001$; Conservation, $F(1, 1099) = 137.79$, $p < 0.001$). Main effects of partisanship: Openness to Change, $F(1, 1099) = 0.99$, $p < 0.31$; Self-Transcendence, $F(1, 1099) = 76.53$, $p < 0.001$; Self-Enhancement, $F(1, 1099) = 6.94$, $p < 0.01$; Conservation, $F(1, 1099) = 22.98$, $p < 0.001$). Significant interactions between partisanship and status: Openness to Change, $F(1, 1099) = 4.01$, $p < 0.05$; Self-Transcendence, $F(1, 1099) = 10.49$, $p < 0.01$; Self-Enhancement, $F(1, 1099) = 4.23$, $p < 0.05$; Conservation, $F(1, 1099) = 24.06$, $p < 0.001$. 95% confidence intervals for all estimates are shown by error bars.

as per discussions in Chapter 2, highly significant for all higher order values. Regardless of whether someone is an MP, partisanship also exerts a significant influence on three of the four higher order values. Of particular interest, the interactions between the two variables are also statistically significant in predicting all four higher order values, indicating differences in the effect of partisanship upon basic values in each status group. Together, these models account for 31% (adjusted partial $\eta^2 = 0.312$) of the overall variance in participants' higher order basic values. There are a number of highly relevant inferences to be made from these findings.

Firstly, the interactions between these variables show that there are not only substantive differences in basic values between MPs and the public, and between those on the Left and Right, but that those on

Table 4.1: Independent samples t-test of basic values by partisanship and status (centred mean scores)

Mean differences

Basic values	MPs Left versus Right	Voters Left versus Right	MPs (Left) versus voters (Left)	MPs (Right) versus voters (Right)
Openness to Change	0.22 ★	0.01	0.36 ★★★	0.15
Self-Transcendence	0.57 ★★★	0.24 ★★★	0.27 ★★★	−0.06
Self-Enhancement	0.13	−0.15 ★★	0.66 ★★★	0.37 ★★★
Conservation	−0.69 ★★★	−0.11 ★★	−0.84 ★★★	−0.25 ★★
N	92/46	483/482	92/483	46/482

Two-tailed significance: ★★★ $p < 0.001$, ★★ $p < 0.01$, ★ $p < 0.05$.

the Left and Right also display considerable psychological differences within each status group. Independent samples t-tests were conducted to investigate these differences further and to rule out sampling error (Table 4.1). The results confirm statistically significant differences across three out of four higher order values within each status group. For example, the Left are more committed to equality, care and support for others (Self-Transcendence values) and less motivated by preserving rules, traditions and stability (Conservation values). Whilst being wary of the difference in sample sizes, the data also show that differences in basic values are more exaggerated in the elite sample of MPs than the public, supporting prior research that has shown greater polarization among elites than publics around the western world (eg Jost, 2006; Sood and Iyengar, 2014). The interactions of the variables tested here also suggest that it makes a distinct psychological difference both to be on the Left and to be an MP. Whilst MPs on the Right in this sample only differ significantly from their supporters on two higher order value factors, MPs on the Left differ significantly from their supporters on all four factors and to much larger degrees.

Obviously voting records are just one, imperfect proxy of mass partisanship. Voters can switch their allegiances between elections or simply choose to vote in one election but not another as the strength of their partisan attachments increases or decreases. To assess the potential period effects that may influence the results presented above, these analyses were re-run using data from the seventh round of the European Social Survey published in 2014. Like the eighth round, the dataset includes results for the basic values of a mass sample in the UK along with their voting records for the previous 2010 General Election. Bringing to an end 13 years of Labour Government, the 2010 election resulted in a hung parliament without a majority for any of the main political parties. Those who did vote were, then, more likely to be longstanding partisans of parties on the Left or Right and thus provide a useful comparison. Non-voters, voters for parties that did not win seats, and independent MPs (or voters thereof) were once again removed from the samples before conducting a new series of two-way ANOVAs to test the effects of status and partisanship upon participants' higher order basic values. To limit confounding period and cohort effects related to, for example, the political climate in 2010 or subsequent changes to party selection mechanisms, MPs were also removed from the elite sample if they were elected after 2010. This produced comparative samples of 103 MPs and 1,342 voters. The results of these ANOVAs are illustrated in Figure 4.5.

As previously, close inspection of value differences at a between-groups level in Figure 4.5 shows that the congruency principle (Caprara and Zimbardo, 2004) appears to hold on the Right but not the Left in the samples used in this study. Whilst politicians and voters on the Right are congruent and statistically similar in their value orientations (only differing to levels of statistical significance on Self-Enhancement values), politicians and voters on the Left are statistically different. This provides a nuanced picture of the leader–follower match previously researched by scholars like David Winter (1987). On the ideological Right, it would seem that basic values, as part of a reflexive and purposive system of personality, help people to make political choices consistent with the basic principles that guide their lives. Thus, there is psychological congruence between leaders and followers. On the ideological Left, the leader–follower match fails in this study. This may reflect the broader ideological space on the Left and the challenge facing centre-left parties, particularly Labour, that must bridge support from small-c conservatives, cosmopolitan liberals and democratic socialists among the public.

Evaluating these findings and their implications for British politics is a daunting yet mouth-watering prospect. Subject to replication and future investigation, the unique data analysed here provide compelling evidence of a 'personality gap' between voters and political elites on the Left of British politics (mostly comprising Labour partisans). This makes a significant contribution to previous research on the congruence between personality factors and political ideology, vote choice, and theories of contemporary partisanship more generally (Caprara et al, 2006; De Neve, 2015). Whilst voters on the Left do appear to score

Figure 4.5: Basic values by partisanship and status using ESS 7

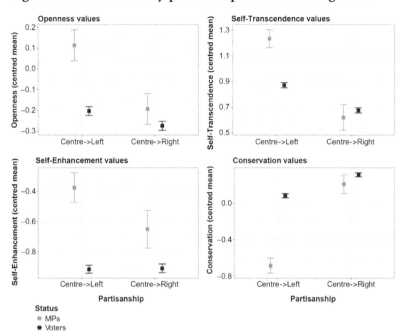

Note: main effects of partisanship: Openness to Change, $F(1, 1445) = 10.32$, $p < 0.001$; Self-Transcendence, $F(1, 1445) = 51.00$, $p < 0.001$; Conservation, $F(1, 1445) = 78.48$, $p < 0.001$). Significant interactions between partisanship and status: Openness to Change, $F(1, 1445) = 4.04$, $p < 0.05$; Self-Transcendence, $F(1, 1445) = 13.59$, $p < 0.001$; Conservation, $F(1, 1445) = 27.57$, $p < 0.001$. This model accounted for 21% (adjusted partial $\eta^2 = 0.21$) of the overall variance in participants' higher order basic values. 95% confidence intervals for all estimates are shown by error bars.

higher for Openness to Change and Self-Transcendence values, and those on the Right higher for Conservation values, these differences are relatively muted compared to differences in the elite sample of MPs collected for this book. On one hand, these findings corroborate previous measures of cognitive style, which affirm a more stable and tenacious link with political ideology among elites than in mass samples (eg Caprara et al, 2012). Put another way, the data presented in this book indicate that values may direct politicians towards certain career choices that encourage them to endorse particular ideologies and political programmes (via parties), which in turn reinforce their personal preferences. On the other hand, the data suggest that the basic values of voters on the Left are, if anything, more congruent with MPs on the Right than their own representatives. If voters do judge political candidates according to personality characteristics and vote for those they deem as similar to themselves (Caprara and Zimbardo, 2004;

Caprara et al, 2012; Bittner, 2014), then only indicative evidence is found of such a link between voters and representatives on the Right of British politics.

To make sense of this finding, there is profit to be found in returning to dual motivations theory (Groenendyk, 2018). The differences between voters and elites reported in this chapter show that partisanship may be more of an expressive identity on the Left and an instrumental choice on the Right (grounded in value congruence). Put another way, value congruence on the Right allows voters to make instrumental evaluations of the political environment and choose political parties (and their policies as well as politicians) that best suit their personal and political preferences. On the Left, social identity and motivated reasoning on the part of longstanding voters may override the effects of *in*congruence between their personal values and those expressed by a party's personnel or policy platforms (eg Mason, 2015; Huddy and Bankert, 2017). These findings need to be replicated in larger, longitudinal samples that can (a) account for interaction effects within the data, and (b) assess the stability of these results across multiple UK elections. However, if the results hold in those analyses, they pose a number of unanswered questions worthy of future research. For example, to what extent do basic values inform policy attitudes at the mass and elite level, and how far do these attitudes overlap between elites and voters on the Left and Right? What opportunities are there for voters to learn about party issues and ideological positions? And do these opportunities, as well as the attention paid to them, differ in the extent to which they predict vote choice on the Left and Right? In particular, these findings might inform future studies of party election campaigns and even electoral success.

If Labour Party MPs represent a comparatively conservative partisan bloc in the general public, whose support is a consequence of expressive social identity, then this also has clear implications for how the party may win or lose votes in general elections. For example, a rich literature on expressive partisanship (largely in the US) has demonstrated that social identification with a political party can be reinforced through 'negative partisanship' or negative campaigning (Abramowitz and Webster, 2016). In this scenario, animosity towards the out-group (that is, opposition party) becomes a more powerful driver of voting behaviour than positive affects about the in-group (that is, host party; eg Iyengar and Westwood, 2014). Based on the findings presented above, future research might therefore look for associations between negative campaigning by the Labour Party and its electoral success.

Whilst negative campaigning might reinforce the partisan sentiments of long-term supporters on the Left, the analyses conducted here also suggest that the Left (particularly the Labour Party) will have more difficulty in attracting new or floating voters than the Right. In line with notions of instrumental partisanship, the data indicate that the average British citizen will be more likely to vote for parties on the Right. It is on this side of politics that the personalities of potential representatives (and possibly policy platforms as well) appear to have greater resonance with citizens' own personal, social and human goals and motivations (that is, basic values). The Labour Party has only held a majority in the UK Parliament for 28 years during the last century and, to some extent, it is possible that this statistic reflects the political difficulties posed by a 'personality gap' between elites on the Left and the general British population.

In this respect, it is possible that studies such as this one can also add retrospective nuance to scholarship on the successes of New Labour under Tony Blair, which were elsewhere attributed in large part to the Party's move towards the ideological centre-ground (Turner, 2013; Hay and Farrell, 2014; Hindmoor, 2017). In 1997 Labour offered a modest yet unashamedly neoliberal policy agenda that included, for example, fast-track punishment for young offenders, caps on income tax, and the end of the Party's commitment to national ownership of public services. These are policies that drastically reduced the rile scores (policy differences) between Labour and Conservative campaign manifestos, and arguably made the former far more attractive to 'instrumental partisans' motivated by Conservation values. However, the New Labour movement simultaneously violated many of the norms associated with expressive social identification among its traditional support base. As the perceived differences between the two main parties decreased, it is possible that the cohesion of this support base dwindled (see Cruddas, 2006). The New Labour movement was, then, psychologically unsustainable, but by the same token strategists and leaders such as Jeremy Corbyn (who moved the Labour Party to the Left under his leadership) face a unique, Catch-22 style challenge. The inferences made here are deliberately broad in order to stimulate new discussions about, and future research into, the psychological determinants of partisanship and voting behaviour in British politics.

Partisans of nobody: non-voters and basic values

The data presented so far in this chapter have illustrated distinct differences between the basic values of those on the Left and the Right of politics; differences that are sustained to a greater extent among political elites. However, this study is also interested in understanding the role of personality, and specifically basic values, in contemporary political disengagement. Although voting is, to an extent, a rather minimal expression of partisanship specifically and political participation more generally, it is an important bellwether of the health of democracy. In line with the congruency principle discussed in the previous section, it makes sense that people will only vote if they perceive that action to serve or promote their own personal priorities (whether those be collectivist or individualist). Comparative research, again conducted in Italy, has shown that voters tend to assign more importance to Universalism or Security values (clear markers of Left–Right preferences) whereas non-voters assign more priority to 'apolitical' basic values like Stimulation and Hedonism (Caprara et al, 2012; Caprara and Vecchione, 2013). This extant research suggests that where citizens perceive political manifestos and politicians to be incongruent with their fundamental basic values, they are more likely to abstain from voting in election scenarios. It might be expected, therefore, that (a) non-voters also exhibit differences in their basic values to other voters in the UK, and that (b) non-voters are more different to MPs in terms of their basic values than voters.

To test the first of these assumptions, a series of 20 t-tests were conducted to assess differences in each of the lower order basic values between non-voters ($N = 492$) and Labour ($N = 371$)/Conservative ($N = 404$) voters in the 2015 General Election. The results show, firstly, that non-voters attribute more importance to Stimulation values than either Labour (t(821) = 2.12, $p < 0.05$) or Conservative voters (t(862) = 2.78, $p < 0.01$). This supports previous studies of non-voting in Italy, mentioned above. These analyses also reveal statistically significant differences between non-voters and Labour voters (but not Conservative voters) when it comes to Benevolence values (t(821) = −2.08, $p < 0.05$), Universalism values (t(821) = −5.57, $p < 0.001$), Achievement values (t(821) = 2.49, $p < 0.05$) and Power values (t(821) = 2.35, $p < 0.05$). At a holistic level, these results suggest, therefore, that non-voters in the UK may be more psychologically congruent with Conservative voters than Labour voters.

Having ascertained that non-voters differ from the majority of the voting public in terms of the relative importance they attribute to a variety of personal goals and motivations, binary logistic regressions were conducted to assess how these differences might predict (non-)voting intentions. In order to avoid multicollinearity between the lower order basic values, Achievement and Hedonism values were dropped as predictor variables.[3] Control variables were also included for sociodemographic factors such as age, gender, education (baseline = no qualifications), religion (baseline = Christian) and ethnicity (baseline = BAME). The AME for these models are presented in Figure 4.6. As expected, given the differences reported earlier in this chapter, Universalism values successfully predict voting intentions for the two major political parties in the UK. Those participants attributing most importance to equality, tolerance, out-group inclusion and the environment were, on average, 44% more likely to vote for Labour than any other political party or none at all in the 2015 General Election.

The data also suggest that Conformity, Tradition, Self-Direction and Stimulation values all shared statistically significant relationships with *not* voting in 2015. In particular, those participants most motivated by autonomy and individual thoughts and actions (Self-Direction values) were, on average, 25% more likely to stay at home than those least motivated by these values. It is possible that these citizens disengage when they cannot perceive their own influence in politics or, ironically, lack a sense of agency over their political fortunes. For such individuals, there needs to be a tangible benefit to their daily behaviours (Bardi and Schwartz, 2003). Thus, the inaccessibility of politics at a local or national level and the staid nature of political processes, let alone the sclerotic pace of political change, may antagonize a psychological need for individual control, creativity and innovation that is higher than in the average citizen. Citizens high in Self-Direction values may, therefore, be far less likely to engage in the act of voting if they perceive that act as being one in which they (a) give up control to others to make change on their behalf, or (b) confer a mandate on politicians who fail to deliver change.

The analyses presented in Figure 4.6 also suggest that those who ascribe most importance to excitement, novelty and variation in their lives (Stimulation values) were, on average, 22% more likely *not* to vote in 2015 than citizens who are least motivated by these values. In terms of making sense of political disengagement, it is possible that citizens high in Stimulation values are not sufficiently energized by contemporary politics to feel compelled by the act of voting. For people whose typical behaviours might necessarily depend upon the *extra*ordinary or involve more unconventional activities than the average citizen (Bardi and Schwartz, 2003), politics may seem anything but unconventional. This judgement may apply as much to the people *doing* politics as its conduct. A parliamentary population of disproportionately white, older, male figures in business attire is unlikely to inspire someone who is easily turned off by the mundane or stereotypical. It should be

Figure 4.6: Basic values and vote patterns in the 2015 General Election

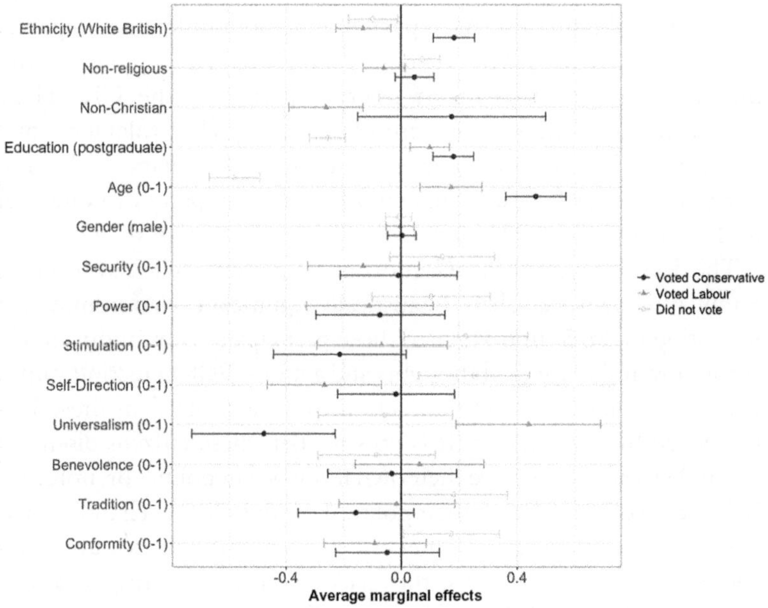

Note: voted Conservative (N = 404/1385), Cox & Snell R^2 = 0.134, AIC = 1512.3. Voted Labour (N = 371/1385), Cox & Snell R^2 = 0.112, AIC = 1482.6. Did not vote (N = 492/1385), Cox & Snell R^2 = 0.206, AIC = 1629.6. 95% confidence intervals for all estimates are shown by error bars.

noted that the R^2 scores for these regressions suggest that there is a lot of unexplained variance in the data that warrants additional research.

Both of these interpretations of voter disengagement point towards value incongruence between certain citizens and politicians who fail to meet the same psychological standards – or trans-situational goals – by which they govern their daily lives. These claims are hypothetical but may be supported by comparing non-voters to MPs (Table 4.2). A series of independent samples t-tests with Bonferroni corrections shows that non-voters differ from Labour MPs at high levels of statistical significance on all four higher order basic values. By contrast, only differences in Self-Enhancement values between non-voters and Conservative MPs reach statistical significance. If voters seek congruent personalities in elite politics and vote accordingly, these findings suggest that non-voters may be more likely to be *re-engaged* by politicians on the Right than the Left. These results paint a worrying picture for

Table 4.2: Independent samples t-test of basic values between MPs and non-voters in the 2015 UK General Election

Basic values	Centred mean					
	Labour Party MPs		Non-voters		Conservative Party MPs	
Openness to Change	0.17	★★★	−0.11	NS	−0.03	
Self-Transcendence	1.15	★★★	0.62	NS	−0.61	
Self-Enhancement	−0.22	★★★	−0.71	★★	−0.42	
Conservation	−0.78	★★★	−0.06	NS	−0.09	
N	68		492		45	

Two-tailed significance: ★★★ $p < 0.001$, ★★ $p < 0.01$, ★ $p < 0.05$.

politicians and parties on the Left – Labour in particular – that not only lack psychological congruency with their existing voters but also those who do not vote at all. It is these voters that political parties seek to attract in their bid to outdo one another in election campaigns, and it seems that Labour faces a far tougher challenge in this respect. Whilst previous chapters in this book have opened up the results of this study in terms of the descriptive and substantive representation of demographic group interests, this chapter has focused on the relationship between basic values and partisanship in British politics. In essence, it has shown that clear personality differences exist between partisans on the Left and Right in the UK; that these differences are exaggerated among political elites; and that congruency between elites and voters occurs to a much greater extent on the Right than on the Left (predominantly between Labour and Conservative MPs and their respective voters).

Parliamentary Behaviour: Personal Choices, Political Results

'I have no idea and I quite often wonder this, how people that are kind of 40 years my senior manage to do this because I regularly miss meals, I don't get nearly enough sleep, I do an incredible amount of travelling on aeroplanes, which are not the healthiest kind of way to travel. I don't understand how people who are much older than me can manage to put themselves through this, just even physically, if nothing else.'

Scottish National Party MP (Interviewee 7)

At the heart of imaginative and effective political science is a desire to comprehend the 'why' behind political behaviours and decision making. So far this book has analysed unique data on the basic values of UK politicians to demonstrate that they are psychologically distinct from one another, the general public and their electors. However, public dissatisfaction with British politics often reduces to internalized preconceptions about the immorality or corruption of MPs' political *behaviour* (Bowler and Karp, 2004; Allen and Birch, 2015b). In order to understand (a) how MPs interpret and respond to the formal and informal institutions of elite politics and (b) the extent of their personal agency in politics, this book now turns to examine the relationship between basic values and parliamentary behaviour. A rigorous extant literature has iterated the importance attached to values as central aspects of the self and as behavioural codebooks (eg Rokeach, 1973; Schwartz, 1992; Feather, 1995; Verplanken and Holland, 2002; Bardi and Schwartz, 2003). There is no reason, then, why this same logic should not help to illuminate the behavioural decisions and intentions of our political elites, especially those behaviours that are planned and temporally free from immediate constraint (see Eyal et al, 2009).

In addressing the second overarching 'problem' posed in this book – Do politicians' personal characteristics matter for their behaviour once they are elected to parliament? – this chapter makes a theoretical and an empirical contribution. It starts by reviewing the landscape of existing parliamentary studies in the UK and makes the case for a more holistic model of elite political behaviour that accounts for psychological as well as institutional explanations. In particular, it argues that the latter circumscribe, but do not eliminate, individual discretion. Data on MPs' basic values are then used to evaluate political agency in contexts of varying institutional constraint. The lion's share of the subsequent investigation is given over to examining MPs' voting behaviour in the House of Commons chamber, taking both a free or 'conscience' vote and a whipped vote as the substantive focus. The ensuing analysis explores whether or not basic values can help us to understand how and why MPs may vote with or against their party on any particular cause, and in doing so highlights the relative importance of MPs' basic values in [objectively] more or less autonomous parliamentary situations. Wherever possible, quantitative findings are complemented by the real, lived experiences of interviewees.

Away from traditional parliamentary studies

The majority of contemporary studies into the UK Parliament are etic in their attention to both process and policy space, and by implication the behaviour of our representatives. There is no doubt that existing research in this subfield is both rigorous and important, adding to our understanding of a range of developments such as legislative scrutiny (Kelso, 2009; Russell, 2016), free and whipped voting patterns (Cowley and Stuart, 2012), multilevel governance (Cairney, 2015; Mycock, 2016), or ministerial power and responsibility (Heffernan, 2003; Elgie, 2011). Where parliamentary studies have looked outside of Westminster, it has been to explore the functional relationships between policy makers and experts (Dommett and Flinders, 2015; Durose et al, 2014), the executive and the judiciary (Bradley, 2008; Gee et al, 2015), or peripheral and central government (Blunkett et al, 2016; Matthews, 2017). However, the result of such specialized and procedurally heavy literatures is that this subdiscipline remains, in line with the popular narrative of politics, rather parochial and distant to the uninitiated.

It would be difficult to talk of these studies into British politics and political behaviour in the UK Parliament without mentioning the Westminster Model (WM), what Andrew Gamble (1990, p 405) describes as the dominant 'organizing perspective' in British political studies. Born from the traditions of Whig historiography, the WM focuses on the institutions of politics and puts emphasis on the importance of continuity in the political system, punctuated by incremental change, since the Glorious Revolution of 1688 (Gamble, 1990, p 407; see also Judge, 1993). The WM (and scholars thereof) focus on principles of parliamentary sovereignty, ministerial responsibility and strong party government. These principles have become enduring realities in the literature on British politics. One may take Vernon Bogdanor's *The British Constitution in the Twentieth Century* (2003), Philip Norton's *Parliament in British Politics* (2013), or Michael Rush's *Parliament Today* (2005) as prime examples of the often descriptive, qualitative, overly technical and document-based analyses of the UK Parliament that work within the central tenets of the WM.

The WM and associated scholarship on the operation of the UK Parliament and other legislatures in the Anglosphere have been underpinned by the broader theoretical hook of Historical Institutionalism (HI). The logic of HI runs that certain intersubjectively present institutions direct people to act in particular ways at later stages. This relationship connecting constraints with action is commonly formulated within temporal sequences of causality, otherwise known as path dependency: institutional decisions taken at time t unintentionally direct subsequential action along certain historical paths (Mahoney and Schensul, 2006; cf Bell, 2017). As such, parliamentary change – as conceived in the HI tradition – is the product of 'critical junctures', which may include exogenous jolts to the political system, policy breakthroughs, or temporary institutional destabilization and ambiguity. These 'critical junctures' allow for the incremental evolution implicit in the WM and privilege institutional norms, rules and prior path dependencies over the agency of the individuals working within parliament. As Alexandra Kelso (2009, p 25) suggests: 'the structural institutional context of Parliament has a highly significant degree of influence over those actors who operate there, and […] Parliament's path dependency substantially constrain[s] the range of reform options that might be realistically contemplated' (for similar arguments, see Crick, 1962; Flinders, 2010).

The primary criticism of HI scholarship, for the purpose of this book, is that it focuses so exclusively on the macro dimensions of British politics and the top-down nature of principal–agent relations in British democracy that it elides the individuals who actually inhabit the system and make it work on an everyday basis. There is no room for the micro or even meso-level analysis that would enable scholars to engage with the extremely important and contested personal side of politics. Indeed, there has been surprisingly little deviance from unfavourable categorizations of the UK Parliament (as a collective of individuals) as 'reactive' (Martin and Vanberg, 2011) and even 'peripheral or totally irrelevant' (King and Crewe, 2013, p 361). At the same time, recent landmark studies by Meg Russell and colleagues (2016; see also Arter, 2006; Matthews, 2017) have challenged these preconceptions. Analyzing 4,361 amendments to 12 government bills and conducting over 120 interviews, Russell and colleagues (2016) add empirical weight to previous work on 'anticipated reactions' and 'preventative influence' (Blondel, 1970) in order to show that government success in the legislative process is often overstated, non-government failure is similarly exaggerated, and parliamentary influence before and after the formal passage of bills is often overlooked. These findings run in direct opposition to mainstream scholarship on the UK Parliament and they point to a more nuanced understanding of British government in which individual backbenchers and opposition party members may exert much more agency than previously assumed.

In terms of understanding politicians and their political behaviour *in vacuo* and as a causal influence on parliamentary outcomes, HI and the WM offer little explanatory purchase. It would appear naive to insist that simply because institutions create causal pressures and incentives, there is not a sustained element of contingency in each case that calls for the agency of actors within the institution. This may be seen as the mistake of the WM paradigm, in which HI scholars judge action in the UK Parliament in light of what *should* happen, according to the constitutional morality of sorts they see in the Westminster framework, and not actually what happens or how (see also Judge, 2005; Norton, 2013). To be clear, these criticisms are not wholly novel and have been iterated in recent years by a number of scholars who are more interested in *governance* than government (see, for example, Marsh, 2011; Rhodes, 2011; Bache et al, 2015). A reaction against the WM has attempted to redefine the study of British politics by moving from hierarchies to networks of self-organizing actors 'characterized by interdependence, resource exchange, rules of the game and significant autonomy from the state' (Marsh, 2011, pp 33–4). It is neither possible nor necessary to discuss the extant governance literature in detail, other than to highlight the premium it has placed on the role of individual actors within British politics. This development in studies of British politics is not only important for the renewed interest it has given to agency in parliamentary studies, but for opening up the intellectual space in which new (largely sociological) theories and methodological approaches to studying political behaviour, systems and reforms have gathered pace and pre-eminence (Table 5.1).

Whilst these emergent paradigms have given renewed attention to the people *doing* politics in parliaments and legislatures, they continue to prioritize *im*personal determinants of political events or change. Where individual action is prioritized, it is viewed in isolation from personal characteristics and there is a presumption that actors' behaviour, even if not explained in rational choice terms, can be deduced from the normative, historical or cultural logics of their parliamentary setting (see Simon, 1985). By contrast, this book is more interested in the unobservable psychological processes occurring in the minds of political actors and the impact these have on political behaviours in institutions like the UK Parliament. To answer this question, a number of political psychologists as well as political scientists have worked towards an institutional theory of political choice. In doing so, they have crossed epistemological divides to develop a complex picture of how institutions might channel but not dictate political behaviour (see, for example, Bendor et al, 2003; Sniderman and Bullock, 2004; Adams et al, 2005).

The central premise of this literature is that politics, or more precisely the institutions thereof, provide citizens and elites with a buffet of options; they 'do not get their choice of choices' (Sniderman and Levendusky, 2009, p 437). Thus by implication, an institutional theory of political choice demands multiple explanatory mechanisms that account for both citizens' internal preference formation and the external provision of choice.[1] As such, it offers a blueprint by which to unite the institutionalism of parliamentary studies in the UK with appropriate psychological theories to better understand the situated behavioural choices of our national representatives. At the same time, scholars in this subfield seeking to map political behaviours and institutional choice have been largely preoccupied with fitting MPs into certain parliamentary roles (see, for example, Müller and Saalfeld, 1997). Derived either deductively (Ilonszki and Edinger, 2007; Zittel, 2012) or inductively (Navarro, 2009; Jenny and Müller, 2012), these literatures are severely limited by their use and creation of static, trans-situational behavioural categories that can be applied to any single representative. However, beneath the varying approaches taken here, there is a fundamental and clearly appraisive desire to capture the way in which individual actors accommodate themselves to decision making

Table 5.1: Overview of prominent paradigms in parliamentary studies

Approach	Principal focus	Preferred research methods	Theoretical/methodological criticisms	Scholarship
Historical institutionalism	Emphasis on the continuity of British politics within the path dependency of the Westminster Model.	Descriptive, qualitative, largely technical and document-based analysis.	There is an exclusive focus on the macro-level of political structures and incremental change, as well as top–down principal–agent relations.	Gamble, 1990; Bogdanor, 2003; Flinders, 2010; Lijphart, 2012.
Interpretivism	Parliamentary studies become about decentred governance networks rather than hierarchical government.	Semi-structured interviews and participant observation.	Agency is reduced to aggregated social and cultural norms, whilst traditions are hypostasized at the expense of clear causality in behavioural explanation.	Bevir and Rhodes, 2006; Rhodes, 2011; Marsh, 2011; Geddes, 2020.
Neo-institutionalism	Agency defined according to the dialectic between career-driven rationality, emotional incentives, and institutional constraint.	Semi-structured interviews and transcription-based coding.	Personal or exogenous motivations are never truly understood; static role categories are created out of subjective analysis of self-reported images.	Payne et al, 1984; Searing, 1994; Tsebelis, 2002; Blomgren and Rozenberg, 2012.
Anthropology	Ethnographic perspectives on Parliament that take norms, ideas and beliefs as explanatory variables.	Interviews, participant and non-participant observation.	The methodological ambition is not matched by theoretical clarity and practical delivery. There is a blurred distinction between the ideational and institutional.	Abélès, 1988; Crewe and Müller, 2006; Crewe, 2014.

under institutional pressures (eg March and Olsen, 1989; Searing, 1994; Blomgren and Rozenberg, 2012).

Towards an integrated model of parliamentary political behaviour

In dissecting scholarship on institutional theories of political choice, it is possible to determine common lines of causality pertinent to the study of politicians' behaviours in parliaments and legislatures. As such, political behaviour is theorized here as a function of individual orientations (behavioural strategies arising from personality and attitudes) that form as the agent (for example, MP, councillor, President or Prime Minister) is subject to expectations exerted by role alters (for example, party whips, colleagues, voters, journalists) who interact with them on a regular basis. The expectations that UK MPs are subject to are wide-ranging and, as scholars like Rhodes (2011) and Crewe (2014) have demonstrated, largely normative. Other than the institutional code of conduct provided in Erskine May, being an MP in the UK Parliament is a job without a definitive description (Wright, 2010). Cues must be read off the culture of the workplace and responses developed with experience (Kwiatkowski, 2012). To the extent that such expectations in the House of Commons require interpretation, there is a premium on individual beliefs and value-driven behavioural responses. However, MPs *are* exposed to an extraordinarily wide selection of role alters, extending from their own colleagues (whether in the party, opposition, parliamentary staff or civil service departments) to the media and a national, even occasionally international, public audience. It is here, it seems, that the formal and *informal* institutions of politics do impinge on the individual behavioural choices of MPs. As explicated by theories of institutional choice, MPs must synthesize their own beliefs with the range of expectations they perceive from these role alters in order to reach behavioural choices within their occupational context. These decisions need to be not only desirable but the role occupant must also believe them to be the most appropriate. By delineating this process, it is possible to sharpen our understanding of the interaction between MPs' personality characteristics, such as basic values, and the institutions that circumscribe their professional lives.

In one of his more recent appraisals of the UK Parliament, Philip Norton (2017) comprehensively summarizes various advancing and retreating aspects of institutional constraint on individual MPs. Inside the Commons, Norton (2017, p 192) sees 'behavioural and institutional change on a remarkable scale'. Parliament is far stronger in its relation with the executive, wielding the capacity to scrutinize and influence government legislation through departmental select committees (Hindmoor et al, 2009); public bill committees have given MPs greater access to information previously monopolized by government (Thompson, 2016); MPs are (theoretically) secure from snap election defeat thanks to the Fixed Term Parliaments Act 2011; the Backbench Business Committee gives MPs the power to dictate 35 days of parliamentary business per year (for a nuanced discussion, see Norton, 2013); the party whips are increasingly unable to 'guarantee' votes (Cowley and Stuart, 2012, 2014); and there is more independent capacity for MPs to raise issues through ballot, on Opposition Days, or in parallel debates now held in Westminster Hall (Norton, 2013). Far from the 'Prussian discipline' talked of by Samuel Beer (1969, p 350), the UK Parliament is entering an era in which the independent member is given more institutional choice, faces fewer formal institutional constraints, and has more agency to 'make a difference' through diverse career paths (see Russell et al, 2016).

By contrast, the *informal* institutional constraints exerted by *external* role alters have intensified. Parliament has become more transparent than ever before and a greater proportion of the population can, and do, contact their MP. Indeed, the workload imposed on MPs to field the scale of public communication they receive may be one of the most restrictive aspects of their daily job (Rosenblatt, 2006; Norton, 2012). The public can watch MPs work in real time through the internet or the BBC Parliament channel, and in the process it is arguable that the expressive function of Parliament and its members has assumed heightened significance. Yet in spite of efforts to increase accountability, public opinions of MPs are more critical than ever (see Chapter 1). This raises an interesting paradox. Internal institutional reforms at Westminster have endowed MPs with a broader purview to act on individual motivations, whilst simultaneously making the House more transparent and thus contributing to a proliferation of external expectations from a (relatively) new, or at least expanded, set of role alters.

For rational choice theorists, this situation entails a zero-sum game in which politicians reconcile the expectations of external role alters and internal gatekeepers in order to maximize (a) their career agenda and (b) their chance of getting re-elected (see Strøm, 1997; Pierson, 2004; Hinterleitner and Sager, 2015). Employing agency strategies that shift responsibility to colleagues, presentational strategies that distort public perceptions, and depoliticization strategies that limit formal liability (Hood, 2002, 2007), this literature argues that politicians calculate every behavioural choice in order to maximize institutional advantage and minimize electoral fallout. In contrast, it is argued here that MPs may choose to engage in a particular behaviour because they hold it to be legitimate according to their personal trans-situational goals and cannot comprehend an alternative (that is, *proactive* behaviour), because they are able to unify their personal goals with formal and informal institutional expectations and pressures (that is, *interactive* behaviour), or because they are coerced to a greater or lesser extent by institutional pressures and the transaction costs associated with operating alone (that is, *reactive* behaviour). This explanation of parliamentary behaviour is thus far more fluid than other literatures reviewed in this section and allows for a more nuanced understanding of when, why and how so-called 'structure and agency' might operate in parliamentary politics.

At this point, it is worth explicating the causal mechanisms that might run between MPs' basic values and their parliamentary behaviours, and explaining how confounding variables might interfere with those mechanisms. In the first instance, it is assumed that parliamentary candidates will plan to reach value-associated goals through value-expressive behaviours, and that these abstract goals will remain constant once elected. Secondly, the likelihood of a value being activated in the first place depends on its accessibility. This is heightened in the case of each individual's most important values (Verplanken and Holland, 2002; Bardi and Schwartz, 2003). Activation experiments have shown, for example, that 'activating values *causes* behaviour' across diverse settings in daily life (Schwartz, 2005, p 24). MPs are faced with morally charged decisions on a daily basis and the task of discriminating between these options is likely to activate their basic values.

Schwartz and other political psychologists working in this field have, however, been accused of empirical bias in presuming direct relationships between basic values and political behaviours (Steenbergen and Leimgruber, 2010). As discussed in Chapter 4, individuals may require overarching, collective and/or organizational principles such as *political* values or ideologies through which to structure generalizable preferences into politically salient opinions and behaviours. As demonstrated in this book, the basic values of UK MPs share strong and nuanced relationships with their self-reported ideologies on both the Left and Right of British politics. Both Schwartz and colleagues (2010) and Leimgruber (2011) have also studied the effects of political and basic values upon public voting habits; in each case the effects of the latter have been fully mediated by the former. That said, the indirect effects of basic values on voting behaviour remained substantial and highly statistically significant. It is entirely possible, therefore, that MPs' basic values may require political translation via ideologies in order to have specific behavioural outcomes in the domain of parliamentary politics.

As discussed in Chapter 4, the party system is also extremely strong in UK parliamentary politics and political parties exert two central pressures on the representative behaviours of their members. The first is direct and is exerted through a range of disciplinary incentives and punishments. Party leaders and party whips have far-reaching powers to incentivize or punish legislators, whether it be exchanging the promise of promotion in return for loyalty or withholding reselection, career advancement, or financial resources. In his *Party Discipline and Parliamentary Politics*, Christopher Kam (2009) develops a game-theoretic model of legislator behaviour that builds on the policy-seeking, office-seeking and vote-seeking desires of MPs previously highlighted in this subfield (eg Müller and Strøm, 1999). Kam's LEADS model is based on the assumption that even when individual MPs differ ideologically, their 'Loyalty [can be] elicited through Advancement, Discipline, and Socialization' (Kam, 2009, p 15). Kam jumps to an epistemological position that MPs are motivated in essence by a desire for office, and that such motivation can be measured through proxy observations such as length of career, speed of promotion, or rate of dissent in the chamber (for a detailed empirical application, see Meserve, 2009). For Kam, the psychology of individual MPs is, then, merely epiphenomenal to the impact of institutional constraints on their behaviour.

The second link between political parties and parliamentary behaviour is indirect and operates through the socialization processes of party membership and selection. For the purposes of understanding abstract commitments to certain representative priorities, this explanation is far closer to the claims in this book. Parties are, in essence, coordination devices that provide a common platform for broad coalitions of interest. Meg Russell's (2014) research is a rare (and in this instance instructive) example of parliamentary studies in the UK adopting a psychological approach to understand cohesive partisan behaviour. Russell (2014, pp 716–19) finds evidence among members of the UK House of Lords that psychological or sociological motivations for party cohesion are far more important than instrumental rationality. Such findings are consistent with social identity theory that posit both informational reasons and normative reasons (eg Hornsey et al, 2003) for why group membership influences our sense of self and behaviour. Assuming that political candidates are attracted to the parties that align most closely with their basic values, it is expected in turn that membership of that group in parliament may subsequently mediate the effect of individual basic values on job-related attitudes and behaviours.

Having accepted that basic values may affect MPs' parliamentary behaviours *through* political values/ideology and in flux with formal and informal institutional constraints, but that neither of the latter is sufficient for explaining and understanding parliamentary behaviour at the micro-level, a more comprehensive theoretical model is offered (Figure 5.1). For want of a more refined name, this integrated model of parliamentary political behaviour combines the hypothetical causal factors for political behaviour explored within this chapter. The model presents a four-panel filter that shows how parliamentary political behaviour may be grounded in the psychological micro-level of basic values, whilst remaining flexible to account for a range of meso-level institutional constraints. The size of the arrows in the second half of the diagram indicates the theoretical causal primacy given to basic values – mediated by ideology – and/or institutional factors (for example, the party) for behaviours with high and low perceived choice, respectively.

This model is in no way offered as a definitive answer to studies of parliamentary behaviour in the UK or other legislatures. It is presented here, instead, as a first step towards a more holistic approach to parliamentary behaviour that incorporates the psychology of politicians. Equally, the model is simple, empirically reproducible and malleable. For example, it is to be expected that the effects of basic values on politicians' behaviour may bypass the second panel (ideology) when the individual is faced with a scenario that is highly moralized and/or crosses ideological boundaries. The model is also intended

Figure 5.1: An integrated model of parliamentary political behaviour (IMPPB)

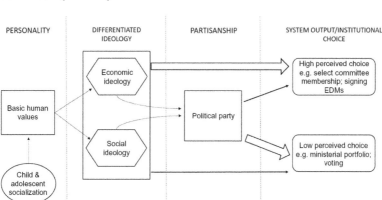

to work with, rather than against, existing research in parliamentary studies that currently privileges institutions. It is unlikely, for instance, that the institutional choices for action presented to elites in parliaments will always allow such neat delineations of personal and non-personal behaviour. Thus MPs might opt, in the majority of cases, for that choice which is simply most compatible with their personal values (interactive behavioural outcome). In many cases, this may be the ideologically charged option favoured or enforced by their party (Figure 5.1, panel 3/4). Existing research has shown, for example, that individuals are more likely to engage in ideologically dissonant behaviour in scenarios of low perceived choice (Kastenmüller et al, 2010; Nam et al, 2013). Hence, when perceived institutional choice is low in Westminster (for example, when voting under the party whip), then individual differences may be masked by collective compliance in counter-attitudinal behaviour. In these instances, behaviour is best explained by institutional constraint (Figure 5.1, panel 4). In contrast, where perceived institutional choice is high (for example, on the backbench and in the constituency), then individual differences such as basic values are likely to be more significant as causal factors for MPs' behaviour.

'Ayes to the right': basic values and voting behaviour in the House of Commons

Having theorized the link between basic values and parliamentary behaviours, these assumptions are now tested by analyzing the voting records of MPs who participated in this study. Vote records in the House of Commons have been the subject of a rich literature on the hierarchical nature, agenda-setting function and disciplinary powers of party organizations (cf Krehbiel, 1993, 1999; Hix et al, 2007; Kam, 2009). Peter Richards (1970, p 179) wrote of this: 'the average division list from the House of Commons is not an exciting or revealing document. It will faithfully reflect the size of a government's majority'. Even in the case of free or 'conscience' votes, when members are not obliged to follow party lines, there is evidence that party affiliation remains the largest predictor of vote choice (Cowley and Stuart, 2010). Philip Cowley (1998, p 188) concludes that free votes 'are more likely to cut down party lines than across them ... it is rare to find one vote where both of the major parties are significantly split'. This has been corroborated by a number of more recent studies (see, for example, Plumb, 2013). However, rebellions by backbench MPs have become more frequent in recent decades: the difficulties that plagued the premierships of John Major over European integration, Tony Blair over the invasion of Iraq and the introduction of tuition fees, and James Callaghan over devolution to Wales and Scotland are but a few examples that have intrigued scholars researching the UK Parliament (eg Norton, 1980; Cowley, 2002, 2005).

The mistake of scholars seeking to explain hiccups in the dominance of parties in the division lobbies has been to take 'the party' as both the explanation and the cause. Political scientists have drawn neat dividing lines between policy issues and parties on the Left or Right (eg Plumb, 2013). This type of analysis arguably fails to move beyond meso-level descriptions and assumptions about party political history and organization, and fails to interrogate differences in MPs' personal interests and motivations at the intra-party level. As such, this literature demonstrates that political parties act cohesively and divide in ways that are consistent, but it does not explain 'why' these patterns exist. Scholars attempting to explain rebellions in more depth have, for example, pointed to ideological heterogeneity, the level of personalization in the political system, and the style of party selection mechanisms as potential explanatory avenues for further research (for a review, see Benedetto and Hix, 2007). These explanations rely, however, on system-level and at-a-distance studies of vote records. By contrast, this chapter utilizes psychological data on MPs' basic values to discriminate between individual vote choices.

In the context of the IMPPB developed in the previous section, it is suggested that scholars of legislative voting must consider the level of institutional constraint exerted on the act of voting, the party political significance of the issue being voted upon, and the nature of the issue itself. For example, a highly politicized vote on boundary reform, in which the stakes are high for parties and the whip is strictly enforced, produces an extremely low-choice scenario in which the anticipated effect of individual personality characteristics will be small. In a free vote on a moral issue such as gay marriage where partisan pressure is only informal and institutional choice is relatively high (in a liberal western democracy), then the anticipated effect of personality characteristics will be larger. At the same time, popular access to 24-hour commercial media and the immediacy of the internet have, in recent years, greatly increased the transparency of Parliament and increased the external pressure on MPs to 'behave'. Nowhere is this pressure more acute than in the voting chamber, where every vote cast by an MP is recorded online, streamed live on the internet and television, or covered in the print media. Where particular pieces of legislation are the subject of public interest or anger, and thus receive heightened levels of scrutiny from *external* role alters such as voters, then institutional choice is reduced and the effect of personality may be diminished.

As a preliminary assessment of these assumptions, the voting records of MPs are analysed in three different contexts: a free or 'conscience' vote for both of the largest political parties (the 2013 Marriage (Same Sex Couples) Bill – third reading); a Public Bill on which only one of the largest parties gave its members a free vote (the 2015 vote to sanction 'UK Air Strikes Against Islamic State in Syria'); and a vote in which both of the largest parties enforced a three-line whip (the 2017 European Union (Notification of Withdrawal) Bill). As per the IMPPB, it is anticipated that basic values will explain more variation in MPs' voting patterns in a free vote scenario than a whipped one. In order to amplify the rigour of the analysis, votes were selected that maximized the number of participants who voted in each of these high/mixed/low *formal* institutional choice scenarios and could thus be selected.[2] At the same time, votes were selected that received higher than average attention in the media, thus accounting for maximum exposure to public scrutiny and, in turn, allowing the degree of agency exercised by each MP under the watch of external role alters (i.e. their electors) to be assessed. Full party summaries for these three votes are presented in Table 5.2.

For readers inside and outside the UK who are unfamiliar with the legislation chosen here, it is worth taking a moment to add a bit of context. The Marriage (Same Sex Couples) Bill of 2013 extended the Civil Partnership Act 2004 to allow same-sex couples to get married lawfully in England and Wales. The Bill provided that such marriages would be treated equally to those between a man and a woman; that same-sex marriages would be permitted religious rites in the process; that, at the same time, religious organizations or individual ministers of religion would not be obligated to conduct a same-sex marriage ceremony. Following the lead of a handful of other nations, this highly progressive Bill split MPs in both of the major political parties. As such, Labour leader Ed Miliband and Conservative leader David Cameron granted their MPs a free vote. Correlations between participants' basic values and their votes are reported in Table 5.3. Not surprizingly, Conformity and Tradition values are negatively associated with voting for same-sex marriage, whilst Universalism values are positively associated. Given that Conformity and Tradition values commonly express religiosity and commitment to social conventions, it is understandable that MPs scoring higher for these values would be less likely to endorse a major social and religious change.

Table 5.2: Summary of three high-profile votes in the UK House of Commons[9]

Party	EU (Notification of Withdrawal) Bill – Third Reading 8 Feb 2017		Marriage Same Sex Couples Bill – Third Reading 21 May 2013		UK Air Strikes Against ISIL in Syria 2 Dec 2015	
	Majority (Aye)	Minority (No)	Majority (Aye)	Minority (No)	Majority (Aye)	Minority (No)
Conservative	320 (+2 tell)	1	117 (+1 tell)	127 (+2 tell)	313 (+2 tell)	7
Democratic Unionist Party	8	0	0	8	8	0
Green	0	1	1	0	0	1
Independent	0	3	0	1	1	2
Labour	163	52	194	14	66	153
Liberal Democrat	0	7	43 (+1 tell)	4	6	2
Plaid Cymru	0	3	2	0	0	2 (+1 tell)
SDLP	0	3	2	0	0	5
Scottish National Party	0	52 (+2 tell)	-	-	0	53 (+1 tell)
UK Independence Party	1	0	-	-	1	0
Ulster Unionist Party	2	0	-	-	2	0
Total:	494	122	359	154	397	223
Turnout:	96.4%		82.4%		96.9%	

Table 5.3: Correlations between MPs' basic values and their voting records

Basic Values (Centred Means)	Marriage (Same Sex Couples) Bill – Third Reading	UK Air Strikes Against ISIL in Syria	European Union (Notification of Withdrawal) Bill – Third Reading
Conformity	−0.40 ★★	0.29 ★	0.31 ★★
Tradition	−0.49 ★★★	0.37 ★★	0.24 ★
Benevolence	0.19	−0.21	−0.25 ★
Universalism	0.43 ★★★	−0.47 ★★★	−0.38 ★★
Self-Direction	0.34 ★★	−0.18	−0.09
Stimulation	−0.12	0.10	0.05
Hedonism	0.28 ★	−0.06	−0.15
Achievement	0.11	−0.05	−0.01
Power	0.35 ★	−0.15	−0.04
Security	−0.31 ★	0.15	0.13
N	61	66	69

Note:$^*p < 0.05$; $^{**}p < 0.01$; $^{***}p < 0.001$.

The decision by UK MPs to support military action in Syria followed a United Nations Security Council Resolution (No 2249) in November 2015.[3] The motion acknowledged requests from France, the United States and regional allies for UK military assistance and recommended all necessary measures short of ground combat – specifically air strikes – to, in the words of the United Nations, 'eradicate the safe haven [ISIL] have established over significant parts of Iraq and Syria'.[4] Although the motion was carried, it deeply divided the Labour Party. Then newly elected leader Jeremy Corbyn unambiguously opposed military intervention, whilst a number of his shadow cabinet and backbenchers vehemently supported it. The Labour leader consequently granted his MPs a free vote on the motion, but the Conservative Party under Prime Minister David Cameron enforced the Whip. Strong negative correlations are reported here between MPs' Universalism values and voting for military action in Syria (Table 5.3). This would suggest that MPs who are particularly motivated by peace, tolerance and the welfare of all peoples were, understandably, less likely to endorse an act of war in 2015.

Following a politically charged referendum – in which UK citizens voted by a small majority to leave the European Union – and a protracted legal battle to allow Parliament a vote on the outcome, the 2017 EU (Notification of Withdrawal) Bill empowered Prime Minister Theresa May to trigger Article 50 of the Treaty on the European Union. This Bill was highly significant, not least because of the intra-party divides caused by the referendum campaign and the overwhelming majority of MPs who had supported Remain.[5] Both of the major parties enforced three-line whips to enact the referendum result: a decision that placed faith in the UK's ability to negotiate a deal with the EU and leave in a swift and orderly fashion – a somewhat nostalgic position for readers in the UK who have sat through the nation's subsequent Brexistential crisis and political turmoil. The positive correlations between MPs' Conformity and Tradition values and voting for the Bill (Table 5.3) indicate that MPs who are more attached to known cultures and customs were also more likely to vote to enact the referendum result.

To analyse the associations between MPs' basic values and their vote choices in greater depth, a series of sequential logistic regressions is now run for each of these votes. With a reduced number of participants in each model, only four lower order basic values are entered as predictors and robust standard errors are reported to account for heteroscedasticity in the data. Values are selected a priori for theoretical reasons and based upon correlations reported in Table 5.3. Controls are included in each case to account for the different facets of the IMPPB (ideology and partisanship) as well as other salient predictors. It is worth stressing, however, that this is far from a perfect test of the IMPPB. With such limited sample sizes, only indicative evidence can be provided of links between MPs' basic values and parliamentary behaviours in scenarios with different levels of institutional choice.

Marriage (Same Sex Couples) Bill 2013

The first of these analyses are reported in Table 5.4. Universalism and Power values are statistically significant predictors of whether an MP voted for same-sex marriage and these values remain statistically significant when controls are added for partisanship, ideology and gender. In model 1, basic values account for a substantial 41% of the variation in participants' voting behaviour. An additional 21% of the variation is explained when the control variables are added. These results suggest that MPs' basic values may have a substantial effect upon their legislative voting records when the whip is withdrawn (as predicted by the IMPPB). With freedom from formal party-political constraints, and facing a highly moralized decision, MPs' basic values

Table 5.4: Predictors of voting 'for' the Marriage (Same Sex Couples) Act 2013

	Dependent variable: vote cast (1 = FOR)	
	Model 1: values only	Model 2: IMPPB/ controls
Tradition (0–1)	−1.782	4.109
	(2.138)	(2.592)
Universalism (0–1)	8.912***	9.123*
	(3.049)	(5.252)
Self-Direction (0–1)	1.793	−0.939
	(1.321)	(1.870)
Power (0–1)	6.848**	15.146***
	(2.669)	(5.559)
Labour		−0.276
		(1.160)
Conservative		−1.470
		(2.395)
Economic ideology (0–1)		−3.603
		(3.477)
Social ideology (0–1)		−7.025*
		(3.719)
Gender (female)		4.528***
		(1.670)
Constant	−7.135**	−8.191
	(3.499)	(6.561)
Observations	61	59
Cox & Snell R^2	0.409	0.621
Log likelihood	−23.793	−11.262

Note: unstandardized regression coefficients and robust standard errors. *$p < 0.1$; **$p < 0.05$; ***$p < 0.01$.

appear to be activated and related to vote choices. These data run contrary to prior research, which argues that party affiliation remains the largest predictor of vote choice in free vote scenarios (Cowley and Stuart, 2010).

Even after controlling for partisanship, MPs scoring high for Universalism values were still significantly more likely to vote for same-sex marriage (albeit within 90% confidence intervals). The average marginal effects of these coefficients suggest that MPs who attribute most importance to equality and tolerance (Universalism values) were 51% more likely to support same-sex marriage. However, the positive relationship between Power values and voting for same-sex marriage is intuitively more problematic. The data analysed here suggest that those most motivated by the derivative goals of Power values were, on average, 85% more likely to vote for same-sex marriage. It is possible that this result is linked to public attitudes and, in turn, instrumental vote-seeking behaviour. Data from the British Social Attitudes Survey shows that more than 70% of the public supported same-sex marriage by the time of the 2010 Parliament, as opposed to less than 50% in the 1980s.[6] MPs high in Power values may, therefore, have seen this vote as a strategic way to get in line with public opinion and service future ambitions.

The value trade-offs reported here may also help to explain the split in the Conservative Party on this vote in 2013 (Table 5.2). As shown in Chapter 4, Conservative MPs score much higher than their Labour peers for Conservation values, but still attribute *relatively* high importance to Self-Transcendence values as well. Basic values tend to directly guide behaviour when they are (a) activated by the immediate scenario (Verplanken and Holland, 2002), and (b) accessible based on the importance attributed to them by the individual (Bardi and Schwartz, 2003). The Same Sex Marriage Bill likely activated both Conservation values and Self-Transcendence values in MPs; the split in the Conservative vote may, therefore, reveal a divide between MPs in that party who assign more or less importance to Universalism values. In contrast to the assumptions of the 'congruency principle' (Caprara et al, 2012), whereby political allegiance and values share a reciprocal relationship, these data suggest that free votes might reveal psychological differences within groups of partisan elites.

These findings are complemented by qualitative data from interviews with MPs. It was evident from each of the in-depth interviews that participants were aware of the trade-off between values and party loyalty that they engaged in on a daily basis. Some participants had made a conscious decision to ignore the whip upon their election but recognized, in turn, that they limited their career prospects in doing so:

'In answer to your question "Have I been able to be myself?", then yes, I made a special effort that I would always stick up for what I believed in. That's why I said in my maiden speech in Parliament that I would never accept a promotion. I would always stay on the backbenches so that I could actually always stand up and say what I thought rather than say what might help get me promoted.' (Interviewee 17)

Similar sentiments were echoed by other MPs in both of the major parties. There was, however, more of an attempt among Labour MPs to reconcile cognitive dissonance as a forgone aspect of representing citizens who had, ultimately, voted for a party. As one former frontbench MP (Interviewee 12) reflected: "what was best for my constituency was usually what the party wanted anyway. It made it easier". This justification was developed upon by a number of other interviewees who described party loyalty as a fundamental aspect of democratic politics:

'I think politics is about coalitions. In that each political party is a coalition and we live in a two-party country, pretty much, so you need to accept that and you know, work out which side you're on. And that there are good reasons for wanting your side to win, and then you need to be loyal.' (Interviewee 8)

In contrast, many interviewees circumvented the issue by talking of their personal and party values as one, and wherever possible reasserted this connection. Interviewee 15, for example, reflected on joining the Labour Party "[s]imply because that was the party that fitted most neatly or nearly to [their] views. Nothing more or less than that".

UK air strikes against so-called Islamic State (Daesh) in Syria

The vote to sanction military action against Daesh in Syria is equally revealing as a test of the IMPPB. Crucially the logit shows that basic values have meaningful relationships with MPs' voting behaviour even after controls have been added to account for internal party constraints and external public scrutiny (Table 5.5). However, the additional variation in the results explained by these variables increases by a larger margin (from 30% to 58%) than it did for the Same Sex Marriage Bill (from 41% to 62%). On this occasion, being a Conservative MP also exerts a strong and statistically significantly effect on voting 'yes' for the motion. Given that Conservative MPs voted under the influence of the Whip and Labour MPs did not, this testifies to the power of disciplinary sanctions/incentives to override psychological differences within the

Table 5.5: Predictors of voting 'for' UK Air Strikes against ISIL in Syria (2015)

	Dependent variable: vote cast (1 = FOR)	
	Model 1: values only	**Model 2: IMPPB/controls**
Conformity (0–1)	1.168	0.542
	(2.148)	(3.644)
Tradition (0–1)	1.521	–3.413
	(1.168)	(2.585)
Universalism (0–1)	–5.790***	–6.175**
	(2.089)	(2.509)
Power (0–1)	–2.556	–7.155**
	(2.021)	(2.936)
Labour		1.086
		(0.997)
Conservative		20.285***
		(1.467)
Economic ideology (0–1)		4.531
		(3.679)
Social ideology (0–1)		1.027
		(3.437)
Election margin (0–1)		–1.824
		(3.089)
Constant	3.227	4.946
	(2.811)	(3.626)
Observations	66	64
Cox & Snell R^2	0.301	0.578
Log likelihood	–33.667	–17.849

Note: unstandardized regression coefficients and robust standard errors. $^*p < 0.1$; $^{**}p < 0.05$; $^{***}p < 0.01$.

Conservative Party and unite them in the division lobbies. Put another way, the effect of Conservative MPs' personality characteristics is mitigated in a low-choice scenario by formal partisan constraints. This may be compared to the free vote on same-sex marriage, where intra-party differences in basic values appear to have split Conservative MPs.

After controlling for party affiliation, ideology and each MPs' electoral margin, Universalism and Power values remain statistically significant predictors of whether MPs voted for military action in Syria. Both values are negative predictors, indicating that those most motivated by Universalism and Power values were more likely to vote *against* air strikes than those less motivated by these values. This is a theoretically ambiguous result, given that Universalism and Power values sit opposite one another in the sinusoidal continuum of basic values and denote incongruent motivational goals (see Chapter 1). On the one hand, MPs highly motivated by Universalism values may have opposed military action to protect the welfare of Syrian civilians and to protest against British military involvement in *any* violent conflict. It is also possible that Universalism values interact with Labour Party membership here, given that the majority of Labour MPs score higher than Conservative MPs for these values (Chapter 4) and also voted against air strikes in greater numbers (Table 5.2). In the sample of MPs used in these models, 19 Labour MPs voted against air strikes and only 7 voted in favour.

By comparison, it is harder to explain the effect of Power values in this instance, given that the motivational goals of this value factor – such as authority, control and dominance – usually predict competitive and subordinating behaviour (Gandal et al, 2005) that one would associate with military conflict. There are three possible explanations that demand further consideration. Firstly, there may be confounding variables that are not included in this model. With a larger sample of participants, a more complicated model could unearth these effects using interaction and mediation analyses. Secondly, the ambiguity of this result may reflect differences proposed by the theory of instantiation discussed earlier in this book. It could be that military action does not, understandably, count as a 'typical' instantiation of Power values in terms of central tendency, ideals or familiarity for citizens who have grown up in the UK. Thirdly, this could be an instrumental decision. A decade previous, MPs had voted to engage in military action in Iraq and faced a steady backlash of public disapproval.[7] Only two years previous, in August 2013, MPs had overturned another government proposal to intervene in Syria, which had made David Cameron the first Prime Minister since Lord North in 1782 to lose a parliamentary vote on military action. For MPs who are highly motivated by Power values, and thus attribute great importance to the authority, recognition and influence accumulated via their parliamentary office, it is possible that supporting another potentially failed military campaign without clear public support would be a highly risky decision (see also Strong, 2015). It is neither possible nor necessary to explore these explanations in further depth here, but each warrants future investigation.

The power of party incentives and sanctions to override personal motivations in the Commons' chamber was also starkly revealed in interview data. Interviewee 1 – a Labour MP who had previously held ministerial office – not only recalled voting against their personal beliefs for the party but having done so to start a war, specifically the invasion of Iraq in 2003. Describing the period before the vote, this participant spoke of sustained pressure from the highest offices:

> 'Yes I did, and particularly if I can be specific, over Iraq and the invasion of Iraq … I was in interview after interview. I had a discussion with the Foreign Secretary, Prime Minister, three or four times, all about this issue and gradually they wore me down, in the sense of I had to balance my own individual point of view with what would be the impact on the Government and the future of the Labour party in government, should anything negative happen … Blair said he would have resigned, in fact he claimed he was going to. He said to me several times in private meetings that if he didn't get a majority of Labour members, he would resign … I eventually, reluctantly, came down on the side of trying to maintain the Government.'[8]

Whilst this is data are compelling as evidence of the extent to which MPs are manipulated to uphold the party directive in the Commons' chamber, the interview was even more telling for the way in which the participant went on to justify their actions. Rather than placing blame on the party leadership, the interviewee started to evoke value judgements in order to make sense of the invasion. Talking in terms indicative of Universalism values, the interviewee explained how they had attempted to soothe their own conscience:

> 'Iraq had gone through hell long before the invasion. They were subject to an embargo that embargoed critical medicines. Thousands upon thousands of children were dying. Others were dying as well. There was a no-fly zone, there was anarchy in the country. And I convinced myself while the invasion might be bad, it would bring some stability to the country. We'd get rid of a dictator

... [I] tried to justify it on the basis of the balance of probabilities. The people of Iraq would be in better shape with the invasion than without it. I have to say, looking back on that now, that was totally naive. The people of Iraq have suffered tremendously since the invasion ... Through heart-searching I still think I bear a responsibility for that.' (Interviewee 1)

These accounts add nuance to the statistics presented in Table 5.5. They add colour to narratives of party 'loyalty' and expose the degree to which party organizations can mask their internal differences to secure legislative victories. Taken together, the data presented here testify to the potential mitigating effect of party structures upon MPs' psychological agency as elected representatives in the UK Parliament.

European Union (Notification of Withdrawal) Bill 2017

The 2017 EU (Notification of Withdrawal) Bill is the only one of the three votes analysed in this book where both major political parties enforced a three-line whip. It is revealing, therefore, that this is the only one of the three votes where the statistically significant effects of MPs' basic values, in particular Universalism values, are eradicated after control variables for party affiliation are introduced (Table 5.6). By themselves, basic values account for just 21% of the variation in MPs' voting behaviour on this Bill, less than either of the other two votes studied above. The jump in variation explained by the model after controlling for each MP's party, ideology and electoral security is also considerable (a rise of 23%). In the values-only model (1), Universalism values are statistically significant predictors of *not* voting to trigger Article 50. Given that Universalism values denote an understanding and appreciation of all peoples, as well as a greater inclination towards social contact with out-group members, it makes sense that MPs particularly motivated by these values would not endorse risking the diverse social, cultural and even economic opportunities afforded by EU membership.

The results for model 2 are more compelling, indicating that MPs may accept cognitive dissonance in low perceived choice scenarios. Put another way, MPs are willing/coerced to vote against their personal preferences and goals when external constraints impinge on their freedom of choice (see Nam et al, 2013). In this instance, MPs were cajoled by both party Whips – including the prospect of disciplinary repercussions if they rebelled – and a fragile external environment in

Table 5.6: Predictors of voting 'for' the European Union (Notification of Withdrawal) Bill 2017

	Dependent variable: vote cast (1 = FOR)	
	Model 1: values only	Model 2: IMPPB/controls
Conformity (0–1)	2.533	3.069
	(1.624)	(2.341)
Tradition (0–1)	0.258	−0.652
	(1.445)	(1.966)
Benevolence (0–1)	−1.803	−0.852
	(1.667)	(1.620)
Universalism (0–1)	−3.397**	−1.006
	(1.659)	(2.312)
Labour		2.374***
		(0.826)
Conservative		19.244***
		(0.687)
Economic ideology (0–1)		1.837
		(2.343)
Social ideology (0–1)		2.908
		(3.674)
Election margin (0–1)		−1.195
		(1.713)
Constant	1.884	−3.194
	(1.688)	(2.799)
Observations	69	67
Cox & Snell R^2	0.212	0.443
Log likelihood	−35.700	−24.341

Note: unstandardized regression coefficients and robust standard errors. *$p < 0.1$; **$p < 0.05$; ***$p < 0.01$.

which the 'majority' of UK citizens (that is, their electors) had already chosen to leave the EU. In terms of Kam's (2009) LEADS model, there was no possible benefit for MPs to accrue from not following a public/party directive. As anticipated by the IMPPB, MPs' basic values become peripheral to behavioural outcomes in the context of such extreme formal and informal constraints. However, it is also possible that MPs' personality characteristics continue to influence these behaviours indirectly. The clear differences in the basic values of Labour and Conservative MPs reported in Chapter 4 reveal a powerful self-selection process in party recruitment to elite politics. It is possible, therefore, that MPs' values are merely mediated by party structures in low-choice scenarios (see Leimgruber, 2011). This contention requires a larger sample size for verification using mediation analyses such as structural equation modelling.

Whilst institutional constraints appear to mask the majority of individual differences between MPs in the context of the EU Withdrawal Bill, there were still some MPs on both sides of the House who defied the Whip. These MPs did not respond to the surveys issued by this study in sufficient numbers to pass quantitative judgements, but interview data reveal a number of key insights about the act of rebellion in general. A handful of participants admitted to being serial rebels. Some had rebelled against their party out of frustration and a sense of principle. As Interviewee 9 put it, "I was bored with them, I was fed up with them, I didn't like Blair, I thought the Labour Party stood for nothing". Others were compelled to rebel because of the strength of their local support base; Interviewee 15, for example, "never really got any sort of aggravation from the local party because of the times when [they] voted against [the Whip]. Local Party were very supportive". Yet for others still, the prospect of rebelling had become more attractive as they approached the end of their careers. Reflecting specifically on the 2017 EU (Notification of Withdrawal) Bill, Interviewee 3 said:

> 'I've seen Labour leaders make mistakes and I'm old enough, I'm not worried enough, and not on the career path enough to really give it more than a cursory thought. I absolutely feel I was in the right position on welfare in 2015 and I feel I'm absolutely in the right position on Brexit. I wasn't cavalier about it. I knew that I might be sacked. I didn't want to be but I love whichever role I've got, but had I been sacked, I would have said, "Well, that is fair dues since that is what normally happens."'

Whilst these participants were able to reconcile the act of rebellion, others could not. For many interviewees, the prospect of rebelling in the Commons' chamber was tantamount to treachery. These participants were quick to recognize that their colleagues may have genuine grievances with party policies but they advocated compromise and consensus behind closed doors.

'[M]y starting point is the importance of party loyalty – not just to the party to which you owe your seat, but also to the electorate that voted for that ticket. I do respect the fact that some of the times people either absent themselves or will vote against their party, but I think you've got to do a lot of soul-searching before you commit to that. There were quite a few of my colleagues who saw it as a badge of honour to vote against their party, and I rather despised that.' (Interviewee 16)

'I don't even like the use of the word "rebel". I prefer the use of the word "traitor". (Laughs) I never was attracted to the idea that there was something virtuous about rebelling against your party. I feel slightly different about it now, but actually, on the whole, the people I really respected were the ones who did support the party when they had difficulties with it, not the ones who bailed out at the first whiff of gun smoke.' (Interviewee 5)

The results reported in this chapter so far are compelling for a number of reasons. Firstly, the quantitative data analysed here show that MPs' personality characteristics such as basic values *do* matter for voting behaviour in the House of Commons. As anticipated by the IMPPB, it is also possible to discriminate between high- and low-choice scenarios. As a proxy for MPs' agency in the division lobbies, basic values may explain variation in MPs' voting behaviour when the whip is withdrawn. Contra to rational choice depictions of MPs as strategic and predictable party animals (Hazan, 2003; Kam, 2009), as well as rival studies that give pre-eminence to sociological unity within political parties (Russell, 2014; Daniel, 2015), the results of this study suggest that political elites diverge on legislation according to deep-seated personality characteristics. MPs in general, and the main political parties in particular, are not monolithic psychological groups. Internal party constraints (that is, the Whip) and external public expectations can, it seems, force a false image of unity that disguises more nuanced psychological cleavages at the intra-party level.

Outside the limelight: Early Day Motions (EDMs), written questions and select committee membership

The previous section of this chapter analysed three separate votes in the House of Commons to determine the potential causal influence of MPs' personality characteristics upon legislation in the UK. The results showed that even in the legislative chamber, where internal and external constraints upon politicians are greatest, MPs' basic values have a meaningful impact on their political choices. The final section of the chapter analyses three different parliamentary behaviours that are, by comparison to voting in the Commons' chamber, more distant from institutional constraints (formal or informal). In line with the propositions of the IMPPB, it is anticipated that basic values will have a significant effect on behaviours that are less visible to or understood by public role alters and, in turn, less important to party officials. This section starts by analyzing the number of Early Day Motions (EDMs) signed by participants in the parliamentary year 2015–2016. It then moves to examine the number of written questions asked by participants in that same year. Given that contextual factors are likely to impact on MPs' propensity to sign EDMs or ask written questions, a single parliamentary year was selected that maximized the subsample of participating MPs who were concurrently sitting and/ or for whom data were available. Future replication studies should, of course, seek to examine MPs' aggregate rates of signing EDMs or asking written questions across multiple parliamentary sessions. Finally,

Table 5.7: Correlations between MPs' basic values and moderate/ low-cost parliamentary behaviours

Basic values (centred means)	Number of Early Day Motions sponsored (2015–2016)	Number of written questions submitted (2015–2016)	Member of a select committee (at any point)
Conformity	0.08	0.12	**0.31 ★★**
Tradition	0.02	0.06	0.05
Benevolence	0.03	−0.03	**−0.21 ★**
Universalism	**0.33 ★★★**	0.03	−0.17
Self-Direction	0.01	−0.13	**−0.22 ★**
Stimulation	−0.01	−0.14	−0.17
Hedonism	−0.07	−0.07	**−0.21 ★**
Achievement	−0.15	−0.02	**0.25 ★★**
Power	**−0.29 ★★★**	−0.14	0.04
Security	0.01	**0.21 ★★**	0.02
N	81	73	94

Note: $^*p < 0.05$; $^{**}p < 0.01$; $^{***}p < 0.001$.

the impact of MPs' basic values upon their historic record of working on a select committee is assessed. Whilst parliamentary scholars and practitioners alike might argue that these three behaviours are only a small snapshot of what an MP does (and they would be correct!), the following analyses are simply offered as a preliminary investigation of the relationship between personality characteristics and low/moderate-cost parliamentary behaviours. Correlations between each lower order basic value and the three aforementioned parliamentary behaviours are reported in Table 5.7.

Early Day Motions (EDMs)

For readers who are unfamiliar with the more obscure processes and procedures in the UK House of Commons, EDMs offer one of many indicators by which scholars may assess MPs' preferences. Prior research on EDMs has examined these expressive acts as indicators of ideological blocs in political parties (Franklin and Tappin, 1977), proxies of elite opinions on specific legislative issues (Childs and Withey, 2004), measures of party cohesion (Bailey and Nason, 2008), and as signalling tools used by MPs in a competitive electoral climate (Kellermann, 2013). EDMs offer backbench MPs an outlet to cultivate a personal image by sponsoring non-binding internal motions that could hypothetically – though rarely – be debated in the chamber at an unspecified date in the future (House of Commons Information Office, 2010). EDMs can be used to offer support or criticism for government legislation; they can raise local issues that concern individual MPs; or they can be used as an additional arena for party political point scoring. To the extent that EDMs are of little parliamentary significance and are not tightly regulated by party whips, the costs of sponsoring them are small by comparison to other parliamentary behaviours. Within the small and under-developed literature on these peripheral legislative behaviours, there has not to date been any attempt to understand EDMs as a function of personal preferences or psychological differences within the legislative body.

As predicted by the IMPPB, basic values (specifically Universalism and Power values) are moderately correlated with how many EDMs each participant signed in 2015/16. The relative public anonymity of EDMs, as well as their political triviality in terms of party dynamics, arguably produces a 'high-choice perceived scenario' in which MPs' personal preferences may have a substantial direct impact on behaviour. In contrast to prior work that suggests peripheral parliamentary behaviours such as EDMs are, above all, expressive signals for party leaders or MPs' electors, and thus used strategically as a function of electoral pressure (see Kellermann, 2013), these correlations suggest that MPs might use EDMs to service personal motivations. The relationship between Universalism values and EDMs indicates that MPs with particularly strong commitments to furthering the interests and welfare of all electors equally may express that motivation through sponsorship of as many EDMs as possible. It is, however, impossible to know whether the increased frequency with which these MPs might sign EDMs is matched by their commensurate substantive focus.

These results deserve closer inspection. To account for the overdispersion of EDMs signed by each MP (median = 12, maximum = 918) as well as the number of participants who signed no EDMs (20% of the subsample), the effect of basic values upon MPs' sponsorship of EDMs is now tested in more detail using a zero-inflated negative binomial regression. To maximize the statistical power of the data with a limited pool of participants, only Universalism and Power values are included in the model along with controls for partisanship, economic and social ideology, tenure in parliament, and each participant's 2015 election margin. Even after controlling for different facets of the IMPPB, Power values exert an effect on EDM

Figure 5.2: EDM sponsorship as a function of MPs' power values

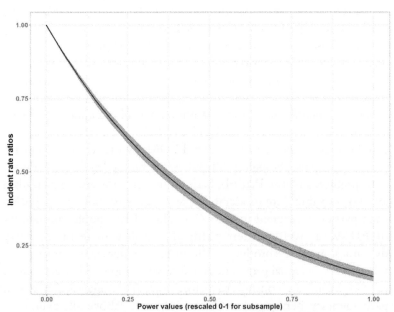

Note: 95% confidence intervals are shown in the shaded portion of the graph.

sponsorship (B = −2.149, $p < 0.001$). Incident rate ratios (IRR) – which compare the incidence of events happening at different times or across difference conditions – are illustrated in Figure 5.2 to show the relative rate of EDM sponsorship across the full range of scores for Power values in the working subsample (rescaled 0–1).

Figure 5.2 shows that even a small increase in MPs' Power values across the range of all scores in the current subsample produces a sharp decrease in the incident rate ratios of EDMs signed. For example, participants in the subsample with the highest scores for Power values signed just over a tenth as many EDMs as those MPs who attribute least importance to that value factor (IRR = 0.143). This result suggests that those MPs most concerned with their own authority, recognition and resource acquisition do not perceive EDMs as a way to further those goals. This is understandable, given that EDMs very rarely influence parliamentary debate or manifest in legislation. To the extent that they might accrue benefit to the signatory, EDMs are little more than a signal of support to party gatekeepers. The corollary of this finding is that those MPs least motivated by Power values will plough more time and energy into peripheral behaviours such as EDM sponsorship. Given the sinusoidal relationship of basic values – and the correlations found between Universalism values and EDM sponsorship – it is possible that parliamentary behaviours like EDM sponsorship (which occur under limited internal or external scrutiny) might delineate between MPs servicing very different types of ambition. Put another way, the results reported here help to distinguish between MPs who might sponsor an EDM for its broader intent or support for a specific cause and those MPs who will do so where they see instrumental utility. These inferences require future exploration.

Written parliamentary questions

Parliamentary questions are a common legislative tool used in the UK House of Commons. In recent decades, a typical session has involved more than 40,000 questions from MPs (United Kingdom House of Commons, 1998–2010). As such, written questions have become a topic of increasing academic scrutiny for their heuristic potential as a unit of analysis for legislative studies (see Martin, 2011). Yet in a parliamentary system where party organization and reputation tend to dominate legislative business and elections, political scientists have struggled to identify objective incentives for MPs to exert additional effort on constituency service (eg Norris, 1997; Margetts, 2011). Written parliamentary questions have proven one such puzzle. Typical explanations in both the UK and comparative systems split neatly between largely qualitative studies of MPs' preferences and constituency service (eg Saalfeld, 2011) and quantitative studies of legislators' rational vote-seeking behaviour (eg Rasch, 2009; Soroka et al, 2009).

The first of these two approaches uses the relative autonomy of parliamentary questions to map legislators' substantive interests. This literature has found that MPs often focus their questions on one key issue in any parliamentary session and that the nature of the questions often depends upon either the MP's demographic characteristics or those of their constituency. For example, there is evidence that women MPs ask more questions related to women's interests than male MPs (Bird, 2005). As formal and publicly recorded legislative acts that are not limited in number or tightly regulated by party officials, and which can force government responses that may receive media attention (Franklin and Norton, 1993), written parliamentary questions may also be used by legislators to build a personal vote. This electoral link has been demonstrated by Michael Kellermann (2016, p 91), who found that MPs in marginal constituencies asked 15% more questions on average than those in safe seats. However, existing scholarship is yet to utilize the correct psychological tools to discriminate between the potential validity of associated substantive arguments. For example, it is unknown whether MPs ask questions in order to explicitly pursue personal motivations linked to policy preferences, to pursue constituency interests because they are motivated to help those around them, or in order to appear successful according to standards of legislative productivity.

Participants in the subsample used in Table 5.7 asked an average of 86.6 written questions in 2015/16, with individual results ranging from 0 to 858 (median = 40). However, only 5% of the observations exceeded 300 questions, highlighting the effect of individual participant variation and overdispersion in the data. At the same time, the correlations reported in Table 5.7 suggest that there may be a relationship between MPs' scores for Security values and the number of written questions they submit. A poisson loglinear count model with robust standard errors was used to explore this result in more depth. Security values were included as a predictor alongside Self-Direction values (as an antithetical value factor) and the same control variables were included as with the analysis of EDMs. Even after controlling for important contextual factors such as electoral marginality and partisanship, MPs' Security values exert a statistically significant impact on the number of written questions they asked in 2015/16 (B = 1.576, $p < 0.05$).

Figure 5.3: Submission of written questions as a function of MPs' security values

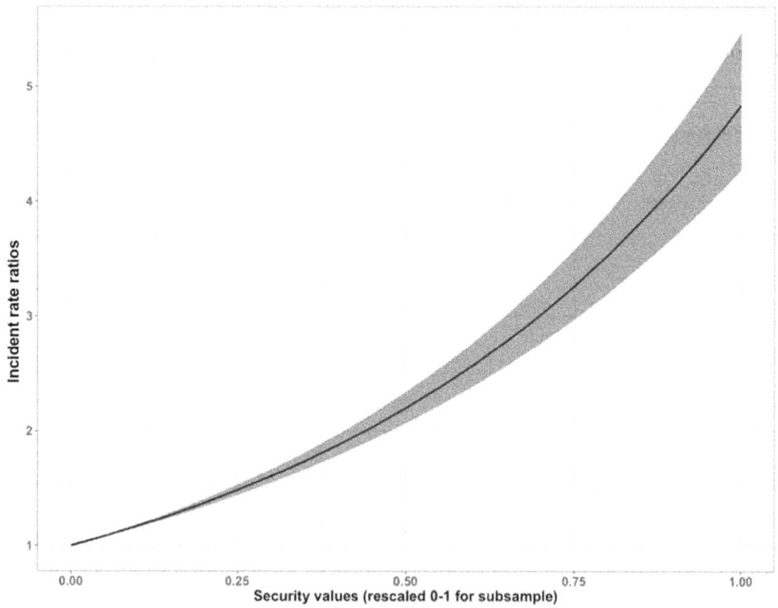

Note: 95% confidence intervals are shown in the shaded portion of the graph.

This result suggests that Security values have a positive effect on MPs' propensity to submit written questions in Parliament: participants scoring highest for these values asked almost five times more questions in one parliamentary year than those MPs who attributed least importance to Security values (IRR = 4.836: illustrated in Figure 5.3). Although electoral marginality was not a significant predictor in this model, these findings do add nuance to that body of work trying to explain personal vote-seeking behaviour. When viewed through the lens of MPs' personality characteristics, written questions become a strategic behavioural display by those MPs who are most motivated by stability in their own lives and thus may ask more parliamentary questions in order to attract positive support from their electors or party gatekeepers. From this perspective, the data imply that questions may be used as much to 'look busy' as they are to confer importance on any one representational issue, although such a conclusion relies on additional analyses of the relationship between each MP's basic values and the substance of their questions.

At the same time, these findings resonate with changes to the coverage of politics and reflect the pressures exerted by 24-hour news media that not only denigrate politicians' characters but use proxy metrics for legislator's productivity. The House of Commons now publishes online lists of the questions asked by each MP (Young et al, 2003) and the media have even used written questions as the basis for league tables that rank MPs on their (pro)activity (Leapman, 2005). Whilst composing and submitting written questions to the government takes time, it is therefore understandable that MPs who are psychologically sensitive to the lack of control inherent in a political career might try to ask as many questions as possible in order to signal their commitment to external role alters (who can keep them in office) and internal gatekeepers (who might open doors to promotion and/ or campaign support at the next election).

Select committee membership

Select committees have been a feature of the parliamentary landscape since 1979. Since the Wright reforms of 2010, they have become a high-profile adjunct to the House of Commons chamber in which MPs can scrutinize the business of government and influence policy. Described as 'the most significant change to the way that the House operates in 30 years' (Hagelund and Goddard, 2015), select committees are an 'empowered system' (Marsh, 2016, p 96) that receives increasingly frequent media coverage. Existing scholarship on select committees has sought to explain their power, autonomy and policy influence as well as the efficacy of the Wright Reforms (eg Kelso, 2009; Fisher, 2015; Bates et al, 2017). Meghan Benton and Meg Russell's (2012) study of the impact of select committees found that they exerted considerable influence, both measurable and non-measurable, upon government activity. For example, their carefully coded quantitative analysis of select committee recommendations from 1997–2010 found that departmental select committees were successful in securing more than 200 substantive changes to government policy every year (Benton and Russell, 2012, p 781).

The purpose of the final subsection in this chapter is not to augment this already established body of research on the efficacy of select committees' output and outcomes, but rather to add nuance to it by looking backwards at the types of people attracted to select committees that influence those outcomes. In the study mentioned above, Benton and Russell (2012, pp 782–3) argue that the success of select committees depends upon a combination of committee-, inquiry-, and recommendation-level factors. At the committee level,

Benton and Russell (2012, p 782) refer to 'the committee's style and reputation, the nature and culture of the department that it shadows, the personality and effectiveness of its chair, and the drafting style of its clerk'. The personal side of select committees has also been discussed by Marc Geddes (2020) in his interpretivist approach to role typologies among select committee chairs. Additional research has focused on the career paths of individual select committee members; as of 2016 11 of the 47 select committee chairs elected post-2010 were previously, or went on to, (shadow) cabinet positions (Democratic Audit, 2016). This would suggest that the increasing efficacy of select committees, as well as the emergence of the 'celebrity' chair (see Fisher, 2015), have transformed the career paths open to backbench MPs, especially those with aspirations to frontbench office. Equally intriguing, select committee chairs rebel against their party majority more frequently than their backbench colleagues (Democratic Audit, 2016). This maverick tendency among select committee chairs is suggestive of either the confidence endowed upon these individuals by internal parliamentary elections, or substantive personality differences in the types of MPs pursuing these positions.

In light of the above discussion, the decision to stand for select committee membership or chairmanship represents a potentially expressive behavioural decision that may reveal individual differences between backbench MPs. In utilizing the IMPPB to understand this, there are a number of competing explanations. Whilst it is evident that SCs have become increasingly autonomous of both party and government control – this would indicate high perceived choice for MPs considering a move onto the select committee 'circuit' – this has brought with it an increased public profile and reputational risks. Therefore, institutional constraint may be low in terms of internal and formal parliamentary and party structures, but the expectations of external role alters are growing. This may, in itself, limit the pool of potential applicants; MPs who place importance on security and stability, for instance, may be much less likely than other MPs to put themselves forward. Select committee membership also requires a level of cross-party collaboration and consensus rarely found in the UK Parliament. The ability to conceive of oneself working with, rather than against, political opponents may also filter potential applicants. Nevertheless, select committees allow MPs relatively high levels of institutional choice.

A binary logistic regression with robust standard errors was calculated to model the effect of basic values upon MPs' historic record of

Figure 5.4: Basic values and select committee membership

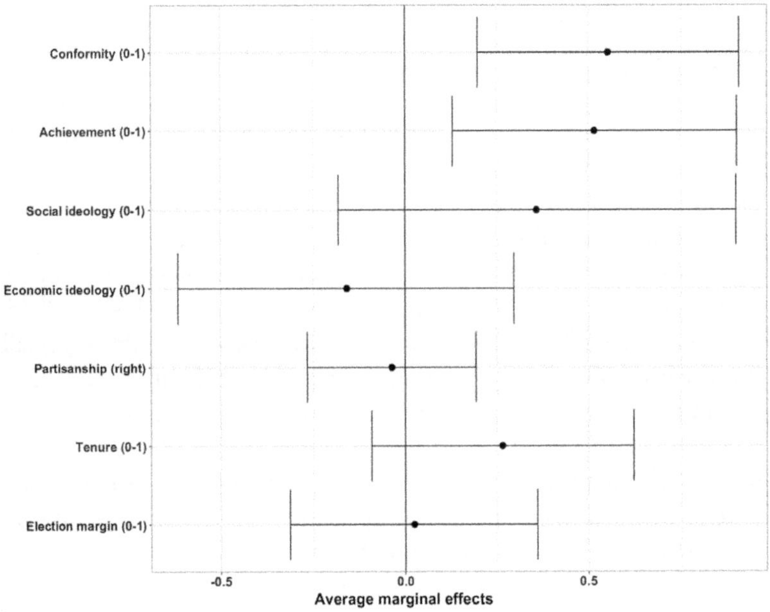

Note: AIC = 80.423; R^2 = 0.263; N = 94.
95% confidence intervals for all estimates are shown by error bars.

select committee membership. As with written questions and EDMs, only two moderately correlated basic values (Achievement and Conformity – see Table 5.7) were included along with controls for party affiliation (Left versus Right), tenure in Parliament and electoral marginality (as a percentage of all votes cast at the MP's last general election). The purpose of this analysis is not to differentiate within or between select committees per se, but rather to provide a preliminary perspective on 'who' puts themselves forward to these committees in the first place. Average marginal effects are reported in Figure 5.4.

The results of this regression show that Conformity and Achievement values are statistically significant predictors of select committee membership in the present subsample of MPs. The first of these results suggests that MPs who are most restrained in their actions and impulses, and thus prefer to avoid conflict with others, were 55% more likely to join select committees, on average, than those MPs who score lowest for Conformity values in the subsample. Individuals who are motivated by Conformity values tend to inhibit disruptive tendencies in order to facilitate successful social interaction (Schwartz, 1992). It is possible, therefore, that these MPs – who do not enjoy or do not want to engage in the competitive party-political sparring of the Commons' chamber – may see select committees as an alternative, collaborative forum in which to advance policy-specific goals. This finding supports previous observations that 'politicians who are less party-political tend to be selected, affording the committees greater independence from divisive, partisan politics' (Fisher, 2015, p 421). This is highly significant, since it suggests that the reputation of the select committee system for avoiding the adversarialism of the Commons' chamber is a product not only of their remit but also, crucially, of the personalities that comprise them. To move as one with a shared purpose, select committee members must be able to reach a consensus on, for example, the wording of a report. This requires diplomatic compromise with colleagues from all political parties. The success of select committees in achieving consensus, and thus presenting robust and unified scrutiny of the Executive, appears to be a function of the MPs who join them on the basis of these preliminary results.

The importance of Achievement values in predicting select committee membership also supports prior research on the career paths of MPs (Democratic Audit, 2016). The data indicate that the most ambitious MPs, those desirous of personal success and influence, were 51% more likely to join a select committee, on average, than those least motivated by Achievement values. As a member of a select committee, an MP has the potential not only to achieve measurable impact upon government policy (see Benton and Russell, 2012), but also avoids the protocols that bind ministers, for example, from commenting on issues beyond their portfolio. Ambitious MPs can thus use select committees to speak openly on contentious or sensitive topics and, in turn, seize opportunities to demonstrate their competence to party gatekeepers. At the same time, select committees command an increasingly high-profile media presence that gives MPs a platform to engage with, and impress, external role alters. Inquiries into, for example, phone hacking at News International, security at the 2012 London Olympics, or female genital mutilation have, in recent years, given MPs such as Tom Watson, Keith Vaz, Margaret Hodge and Sir Alan Beith a media presence akin to that of junior or even senior ministers in the government. The data presented here suggest that these changes might also have affected the type of politicians seeking to join select committees.

The findings presented here and throughout this chapter augment a comparative literature that has intensively researched the effects of institutions upon legislative behaviour (Shugart et al, 2005; Sieberer, 2006; André and Depauw, 2013) whilst mistakenly treating legislators as monolithic groups of rational actors with parallel behavioural incentives (see Fernandes et al, 2018). As André and colleagues (2015, p 468) argue, 'studies that focus on electoral institutions have largely ignored within-system differences in favour of differences across systems – as if legislators operating under the same set of rules all behave in a similar manner'. In an attempt to innovate the existing study of parliamentary behaviour (in the UK in particular), this chapter has added both theoretically and empirically to our collective understanding of agency in representative politics. Building upon psychological and institutional logics, it offers an integrated model of parliamentary political behaviour that eschews qualitative, structure-dominated and normatively charged generalizations about the 'organizing perspective' of the Westminster Model in British political studies (see Bogdanor, 2003; Rush, 2005; Norton, 2013). Employing unique quantitative data on MPs' basic values alongside qualitative accounts from the actors themselves, MPs' basic values are found to have a substantial effect upon legislative activities as diverse as voting in the Commons chamber, submitting written questions, and joining a select committee. Subject to more rigorous tests of the IMPPB – ideally using larger samples sizes and mediation analyses – these effects also appear to vary according to the institutional constraints exerted internally by party organizations and externally by a range of role alters such as the media and voters.

Perfect Politicians? Voting Preferences in the United Kingdom

'Then [Aneurin Bevan] realized he wasn't really very powerful as a backbench member of Parliament, so he eventually got into the Cabinet. Then he got into the Cabinet, and he wondered where on earth the power really lay and came to the conclusion, as I have done, that most of the power lies with the establishment. Parliament is just there to try and moderate the excesses of some parts of the establishment.'

Labour Party MP (Interviewee 12)

'My passion is helping local people.' In using this strapline on his campaign leaflets, Nick Palmer (Labour candidate for Broxtowe in 2017) was not alone in framing his appeal as a potential parliamentary representative in terms of his own core values. Indeed, it has become commonplace for MPs and candidates to talk on flyers and websites about their personal characteristics, likes and dislikes, far more than their political affiliations or opinions (Milazzo and Townsley, 2019). On his campaign flyer for the UK's 2017 General Election, for example, Vernon Coker (former Labour MP for Gedling) emphasized his commitment to care for and protect the interests of his nuclear family: 'like you [I] want the best for [my] children and grandchildren'. By contrast, David Lidington (Conservative MP for Aylesbury) used his website to stress his openness and motivation to help all peoples: '[David] believes that Britain at its best gives opportunity to all, regardless of background, race or religion.'

These anecdotal references are indicative of a phenomenon now universally current in democratic systems and touched upon in earlier chapters: specifically, the personalization of the political and the politicization of the personal in both media coverage of politics and political communication (for an extended review, see Cross et al, 2018). However, there has not been sufficient empirical research, in the UK especially, to demonstrate which 'personal' characteristics matter most in representative politics and how these might affect important political choices such as the public's voting preferences at the ballot box. So far this book has analysed unique data on the basic values of UK politicians, predominantly MPs, to show that personality characteristics can reveal important insights about who enters politics and why as well as how they represent us once they get there. This final chapter engages with the personalization phenomenon to address the third overarching problem posed in Chapter 1: *Do voters really get the 'wrong' politicians?* Regardless of the empirical data explored in the coming pages, this is a highly subjective question with subjective answers. Many of you may have already reached your conclusions based on what you've read in preceding chapters. Hopefully these conclusions challenge some of the preconceptions that you previously held and that may have motivated you to pick up this book in the first place. Please withhold your final judgement a little longer.

The pages that follow continue to synthesize conceptual and empirical insights from political science and psychology to understand the extent to which personality characteristics (specifically candidates' basic values) may improve our understanding of contemporary anti-politics when they characterize the choice set (that is, what voters see and select) rather than simply the participants (that is, politicians/candidates' self-report data that have been the subject of Chapters 2–5). Compared to studying other candidate-centric predictors of vote choice, it is argued that this endeavour matters profoundly for how we, as students of democracy, understand politics and how politicians themselves garner electoral support. In order to substantiate these theoretically informed propositions, a conjoint experiment is run with a diverse sample of the British public that combines images and text to assess the comparative influence of basic values on vote choice in the UK. The results of the conjoint experiment not only add to a small literature on the role of specific candidate characteristics in personalized voting behaviour in the UK (see Laustsen and Bor, 2017), but also reveal a striking overlap between the actual basic values of UK MPs and the ideal types of the British public. These data are used to suggest that public discontent with politics, founded upon cynical judgements about self-serving elites, may be grounded in a perception gap that says more about the consumption of politics in the UK than the 'quality' of its elected representatives.

Personalization and vote choice

A large corpus of research in recent decades has attested to the growing saliency of the personalization phenomenon across liberal democracies and, in particular, the accompanying stress on 'who' represents and 'how' in both political participation and communication (Cross et al, 2018). It is argued that, as a process in its own right, the personalization of politics revolves around changes to the way in which power is held and deployed, a veer towards public understandings of politics based upon the personal qualities of representatives, and a self-perpetuating politicization of the private and the personal (see, in particular, Poguntke and Webb, 2005). As such, the personalization of politics is treated as more than just the increasing importance attributed to mainstream political leaders – what is elsewhere referred to as *centralized* personalization (Balmas et al, 2014; Wauters et al, 2018). Modern types and styles of media have altered the public consumption of politics in an overtly agency-centred direction that heightens the critical reception of *all* candidates as humans as well as politicians (*de*centralized personalization) (Hayes, 2009; Teles, 2015).

In recent decades, this character-based model of political journalism in the print and visual media has created a false intimacy between voter and candidate and, in turn, perpetuated a mode of public appraisal based upon everyday cognitive judgements of representatives as *people*. This is discussed elsewhere as *behavioural* personalization, insofar as it refers to the increasing saliency of individual actors in journalistic and/ or popular political discourse (Rahat and Kenig, 2018). As early as the 1980s, Joshua Meyrowitz (1985, p 271) talked of the *lowering effect* of television on politicians, wherein 'the camera minimizes the distance between audience and performer ... [and] lowers politicians to the level of their audience'. Indeed, Rahn and colleagues (1990) suggest that this lowering effect facilitates public evaluations of politicians as 'common' people based on inferential strategies constantly employed in our everyday lives. The rest of this chapter seeks to understand how this lowering effect plays out empirically at the ballot box and, specifically, the relative importance that voters attribute to candidates' personal characteristics when selecting a representative.

As a tangential yet important caveat, the central arguments made here and in the wider personalization literature should not be taken as evidence that political *parties* no longer matter as a voting heuristic. These institutions have themselves undergone deep changes that are both cause and consequence of the personalization of politics (see Garzia, 2011; McAllister, 2007). Utility-maximizing parties, moving from class–mass to 'catch-all' profiles in an age of ideological dealignment, have focused more on presenting telegenic leaders than ideologically driven policy rhetoric (Farrell and Webb, 2000; Mughan, 2000). This has become particularly apparent as a campaign tactic, although arguably it has resulted in greater political power for individual politicians and a diminished role for parties themselves. As Rahat and Shaefer (2007, p 65) surmise, the personalization of politics reflects 'a process in which the political weight of the individual actor in the political process increases over time, while the centrality of the political group (i.e. political parties) declines'. At the same time, it has already been shown in Chapter 4 that powerful psychological divisions exist between voters on the Left and the Right that are replicated to an even greater extent among elites. If group identities are diminishing in politics, this is not reflected in the psychology of partisans as tested in this book.

In many ways, it is also possible to contend that the personalization phenomenon has changed the nature of political leadership (at all levels), insofar as contemporary politicians build authority 'not by being beyond the people … [but] by being of and like them' (Renshon, 1995, p 201). During times of systemic crisis when politics more broadly is deeply distrusted, new faces are even more likely to be judged by their symbolic proximity to the masses and their perceived similarity to each individual voter. Political parties and politicians alike are, however, aware of the power of political advertisement over modern voter perceptions, and thus package candidate images to match potential constituencies (see Campus, 2010). It is here that the distinction must be made between what the public are exposed to – that is, personality as perception – and those cognitive or motivational processes within that guide politicians' actual behaviour – that is, personality as functioning as analysed in Chapter 5. In this narrative, MPs are potentially obliged to focus on the public perception of their personalities, fuelling a self-fulfilling prophecy in which they honestly believe they must deceive in order to be trusted.

To theorize the connections above more clearly, this chapter draws upon perceptual-balance theory (Nimmo and Savage, 1976). Unlike cognitive realism, in which objects are perceived exactly as they are (eg Gibson, 1966), or cognitive constructivism, in which understanding comes entirely from inference (eg Neisser, 1967), perceptual-balance theory strikes a middle ground in which voters' perceptions of politicians are the product of both their subjective knowledge and the images projected by candidates (Cwalina et al, 2008). It is here that the dangers of personalization for the broader health of democracy arise. Political campaigns may well read public mood swings and attempt to construct affable images suitable for particular audiences in particular moments, but so long as voters are exposed simply to constructed personae, they can never truly judge the personality of those 'functioning' in politics on a daily basis. Therefore, public demand for personality politics is matched by a distorted supply that ultimately sets up public disappointment at the first sign of infidelity to that constructed image.

The validity of these theoretical concerns and hypothetical commentaries relies on the validity of connections between identifiable personality characteristics and political choices. Given the ubiquity of the personalization phenomenon in everyday political communication, it is extremely likely that citizens project from personal assessments of candidates to what kind of representative they might become or what kind of political system they symbolize (see Chapter 1 for an extended discussion). Yet whilst the literature on personalization has explicitly acknowledged the importance of politicians' personal qualities for vote choice, the role and relevance of specific characteristics have not received sufficient attention (see also Laustsen and Bor, 2017). What extant research there is in this area agrees that the 'common traits used to characterize politicians tend to fall into a limited number of categories: competence ("intelligent", "hard-working"), leadership ("inspiring", "[not] weak"), integrity ("honest", "moral"), and empathy ("compassionate", "cares about people")' (McGraw, 2011, p 190; for similar descriptions, see also Laustsen, 2016). The majority of studies collapse the first two factors and the latter two into a binary opposition of competence versus warmth (eg McAllister, 2016). Warmth is generally associated with morality, friendliness, trustworthiness, helpfulness and sincerity; competence is associated with knowledge, intelligence, confidence, skill and efficiency. Both of these dimensions are well established in social psychology as central aspects of social perception and unconscious categorization of others (Oosterhof and Todorov, 2008; Bor, 2017).

The political science literature on candidate evaluation has tended to play down the effects of warmth and focus on the apparent primacy of competence as a voting heuristic (eg McGraw, 2011; McAllister, 2016). Studies assume that voters care most about candidate competences in order to secure their preferred policy outcomes. However, these findings stand in stark contrast with a social psychology literature that consistently finds warmth to outperform competence in everyday social perceptions (eg Goodwin et al, 2014). Contrary to most political science studies in this area, Laustsen and Bor (2017) also find that warmth is a more significant predictor of candidate preferences in both a longitudinal analysis of the American National Election Study (ANES 1984–2008) and an experimental text-based study of 824 voting adults in the UK. They find that warmth outperforms competence across different methodological designs and cultural contexts, and their results held even after the authors controlled for the interaction effect between candidate party and participant partisanship.

Normatively, there is an evolutionary argument that suggests 'another person's intent for good or ill is more important to survival than whether the other person can act on those intentions' (Fiske et al, 2007, p 77). This principle is apposite in politics, where citizens must, in effect, relinquish their sovereign democratic liberty to another individual to act on their behalf (see Chapters 1 and 2). Coupled with the stylistic evolution of political discourse and communication encompassed by the personalization phenomenon, it becomes even more likely that voters will choose candidates with the 'right' or desired personal qualities. Given that personality characteristics such as basic values provide social justification for people's choices and behaviour (see Sagiv and Roccas, 2017), they offer a powerful tool for studying the personalization phenomenon and its repercussions at the ballot box. In particular, it is suggested that values matter for the ways in which politicians present themselves to voters, the ways in which they are in turn perceived by voters, and finally the candidate selections made in election scenarios.

Conjoint experiment of voting preferences: design

To assess the impact of candidate values upon political selections, a conjoint experiment is reported that asked voters in the UK to choose between hypothetical parliamentary representatives. A conjoint experiment is a multivariate choice-based survey technique that originates in marketing research. Typically, consumers are faced with an array of products that have a broad range of characteristics and must choose which of these they prefer. A conjoint experiment works on the premise of utility, which refers to each individual's unique subjective preference formation. Consumers can evaluate the objects offered as a whole, thus reducing the cognitive fatigue demanded of the participant. Conjoint experiments have been common in marketing research for over 40 years and their versatility has attracted the attention of scholars in other fields as diverse as transport management and financial services, oncology and taxation (Hundsdoerfer et al, 2013; Beusterien et al, 2014). In politics, conjoint experiments are yet to become a mainstream methodology (see Vivyan and Wagner, 2015).

In this instance, 1,637 UK adults were asked to choose between hypothetical MPs who varied in the following attributes: gender, age, ethnicity and disability; religion; family status; personality; education; prior occupation; accent (as a proxy for region); and political priority.[1] These variables were chosen in order to (a) capture a variety of factors that are current in empirical research into candidate selection and elections, and (b) to create an experimental scenario in which candidates appeared credible. The variable 'personal statement' underneath each candidate image drew on ten portraits of basic values as taken from the Twenty Item Values Inventory (see Chapter 1 for a discussion). In each case, the two portraits measuring each of the ten lower order values were collapsed into single portraits and rewritten in the first person. The variable 'political priority' constituted three statements related to the party, constituency and national policy objectives of the candidate. This variable was included to provide a direct comparison to prior survey work on public preferences for MPs (Campbell and Lovenduski, 2015; Vivyan and Wagner, 2015) and, again, to capture realistic information used by candidates on campaign literature and in television interviews. Figure 6.1 shows one random survey iteration.

Given that the number of potential combinations in a conjoint experiment grows exponentially with each additional attribute and level (that is, how many random options are used to populate, for example, the attribute 'Religion'), a fractional factorial design was used in which the participant was only ever presented with a selection of levels for each attribute at once. The number of attributes in the design was limited to eight, including the image, in keeping with received wisdom on the limits of this experimental design and its cognitive accessibility (Bradlow, 2005). The compensatory model underpinning conjoint surveys posits that participants evaluate an object in comparison to another object by combining the positive or negative value they assign to each of its different attributes. Where participants are presented with too many choices at once, they engage simplified criteria of selection (Hauser, 2014), whilst a large choice set also reduces the amount of data available for each attribute and therefore limits the accuracy and weight of statistical estimates (DeShazo and Fermo, 2002; Huertas-Garcia et al, 2016). To maximize the statistical power, efficiency and cognitive accessibility of this conjoint experiment, participants were asked to choose between three randomly populated profiles of MPs

Figure 6.1: Random iteration of a conjoint experiment testing personalized candidate selection

	Individual A	Individual B	Individual C
Accent	Liverpudlian accent	Welsh accent	Scottish accent
Family	Married with children	Married	Married
Occupation	Stock broker	Builder	Builder
Personal statement	I am curious and think that it is important to try to understand all sorts of things. I think up new creative ideas and like to do things in my own original way.	It is important to me that things around me are organized. I am concerned that the social order is protected and the government as well as society is stable.	I always show respect to older people and think that it is important to be obedient, to behave properly and to avoid doing anything people would say is wrong.
Education	Attended a State Grammar School	Attended a State Comprehensive School	Attended a Religious School
Religion	Buddhist	Atheist	Atheist
Political priority	Wherever possible I will prioritise the wants and needs of my constituents.	Wherever possible I will prioritise the common good of the nation.	Wherever possible I will stay loyal to my party and its manifesto.

with eight attributes each and to complete this process five times. Participants responded to the question: *Which of the following candidates would you elect to represent you as a Member of Parliament?* Apart from the image of each candidate, the order of attributes changed randomly between participants to control for order effects in the survey design.

It is worth stressing that conjoint experiments confer a number of advantages over more traditional ranking and rating survey techniques that are normally used to assess voting preferences. Given that the choice-based model creates a total utility value for each profile (or bundle of attributes), it is also possible to isolate the part-worth utility of individual attributes and their levels. This allows the researcher to capture not only the specific effect of certain attributes but also their effect when interacting with other combinations of attributes. For example, it might be that voters in highly professional occupations or social grades AB prefer MPs with a similar occupational background, but only when that MP is also committed to their party manifesto. This particular conjoint experiment allows conclusions to be drawn about the relative weight, if any, that citizens place on different basic values when asked to simultaneously judge other personal attributes such as gender, age and education. Faced with complex hypothetical profiles, participants are presented with realistic choices that make the findings more transferable to 'live' environments beyond the survey. Indeed, the profiles were purposefully designed to include the same types of personal information that appear on candidate flyers and websites.

Participants for this conjoint experiment were recruited by a polling agency, YouGov, and surveys were completed on 23 and 24 October 2017. Demographically, the sample was broadly representative of the UK population. The median age was 48 and participants resided in 11 different regions of the UK. No single region accounted for more than 13% of the sample (London). Although the number of participants who voted in the 2017 General Election was slightly higher than the national average (80% compared to 69%), it included a good mix of supporters from different political parties: 34% Conservative, 33% Labour, 6% Liberal Democrat, 1% UKIP, 1% Green and 4% Other. Approximately equal numbers of men and women completed the survey (51% of the sample is female) and participants were evenly spread across social grades: 28% categories AB, 29% category C1, 21% category C2 and 22% categories DE.[2] In the context of the highly contested Brexit vote in 2016, this sample was also split between those who voted Remain (38%), those who voted Leave (41%), and those who claimed they did not vote or could not remember voting (21%). In sum, the survey data reflected a representative mix of the UK population.

Conjoint experiment of voting preferences: analysis

The conjoint experiment reveals a number of important insights about the role of candidate personality in election scenarios. The average marginal (component) effects for all variables and levels are reported graphically in Figure 6.2. The data reveal distinct candidate preferences among the British public when it comes to selecting elected representatives. Each of these preferences will be briefly discussed in turn. Figure 6.2 shows, for example, that the public slightly prefer female candidates and older candidates to male or younger candidates. The first of these results presents somewhat of a paradox, given that the majority of MPs are male. It is possible, therefore, that public preferences in terms of gender are not translated into electoral choices due to a lack of female candidates rather than a lack of demand (see also Holman and Schneider, 2017). By contrast, it seems that public preferences for older politicians are successfully reproduced in a parliament comprised of MPs with an average age over 50.

The data also suggest that the British public moderately prefers candidates who went through state education as opposed to private schooling, reflecting the majority experience for members of the public (93% attend state schools) and, in turn, the disparity between public preferences and the composition of Parliament (29% of MPs elected in 2017 attended fee-paying schools). The public shows moderate preferences for MPs who have worked in the teaching or charity sectors over those who have already held elected office locally. This result echoes sentiments found in the political class literature, which highlights public dissatisfaction with the professionalization of career politics (see Chapter 3). In addition, participants moderately prefer candidates who are married with children; this possibly indicates greater trust in politicians who are perceived to be from stable, nuclear families.

Whilst the preferences reported above are all relatively marginal (and thus touched upon rather cursorily here), participants were more concerned about the religion, political priorities, and basic values of hypothetical candidates. Although the ethnicity of a candidate had no significant effect on vote choice, participants expressed strong preferences for Christian candidates over, in particular, Muslim ones. Muslim candidates were, in fact, more than 10% less likely to be selected than Christians. This may reflect public fears about radicalization, extremism and terrorism that have, in recent years, manifested in

Figure 6.2: Conjoint analysis of candidate preferences in the UK

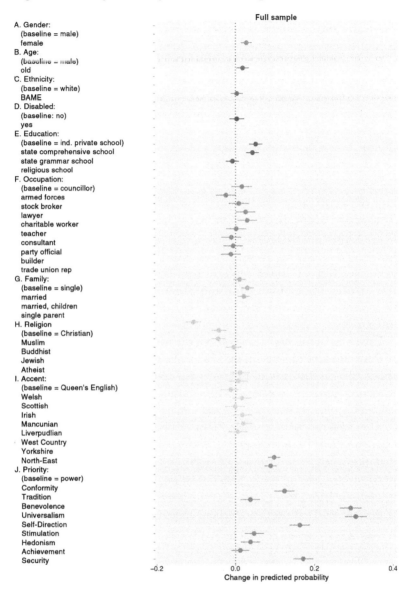

Note: 95% confidence intervals for all estimates are shown by error bars.

anti-Muslim, anti-immigration attitudes (see also Fisher et al, 2014). If these findings generalize to wider voting patterns, it suggests that Muslim candidates face a much more difficult task getting elected to the UK Parliament than their Christian peers. Considering that religious minorities are already underrepresented in British politics, this is a worrying finding.

Equally strong preferences were expressed for participants whose political message prioritized the good of the nation or their constituents over party interests. This extends a dense literature on attitudes to representative roles and confirms research indicating public preferences for constituency MPs (eg Campbell and Cowley, 2014). However, these data also support previous empirical studies that find surprizingly small differences between these 'local' inclinations and public support for other representative tasks (Campbell and Lovenduski, 2015). The Hansard's audit of political engagement in 2010, conducted at the height of the parliamentary expenses scandal, found that there was little difference between the number of citizens who preferred MPs to focus on local issues in the constituency (46%) and those who preferred MPs to focus on national interests (40%). Yet, as with that study, the results presented here show that the UK public prefers politicians to prioritize either of those interests over those of their political party. Put another way, public antipathy for partisan politicking appears to override individual preferences for traditional Burkean trustees or elegates.

The focus of this book is, however, the basic values of UK politicians. In this conjoint experiment, the UK public expressed strong preferences about the basic values of potential parliamentary representatives. In particular, participants wanted MPs who are high in Self-Transcendence values. Candidates with personal statements that reflected Universalism or Benevolence values were about 30% more likely to be chosen than candidates who expressed Power values.[3] This would suggest that, above all, voters are looking for MPs who are tolerant, broad-minded, honest and loyal. Self-Direction, Security and Conformity values also had a strong positive effect on vote choice. This implies that after Self-Transcendence values, citizens are most concerned about selecting representatives who are creative and independent but who, simultaneously, will apply themselves to protect the safety, stability and dominant character of society. For participants in this conjoint survey, basic values had a greater impact on vote choice than any other physical, socioeconomic or political variable.

At a subgroup level, it is possible to slice the data according to participants' self-reported partisanship. Chapter 4 of this book provided compelling evidence of psychological divisions between the Left and Right of British politics and potentially those who do not vote at all. These findings reproduce in the current conjoint experiment when participants are divided into partisan subgroups. For example,

Self-Transcendence values were more important for self-reported Labour voters (and to a lesser extent non-voters) than Conservative Party voters (Appendix D).[4] Labour voters were almost 40% more likely to choose candidates who prioritized Benevolence values, whereas this swing was only about 20% for Conservative voters. Accounting for the error terms in these results, Security and Conformity values were almost as important as Self-Transcendence values for Conservative voters. By contrast to both Labour and Conservative Party supporters, non-voters showed more distrust of hypothetical candidates who were characterized by Power values. Assuming that voters are discouraged from formal politics by specific evaluations of incumbent politicians, it makes sense that these citizens will also be most sensitive to those basic values that imply any hint of self-serving interest. In terms of sociodemographic characteristics, non-voters were more conservative in their selections. Though not statistically significant, non-voters showed preferences for non-disabled and white candidates that were not present in the results for the other two voting groups analysed here. However, Conservative voters were the most pro-Christian and anti-Muslim, and also preferred candidates who spoke 'the Queen's English' to all other accents.[5] The opposite was true for Labour voters.

The public's ideal types are now compared, as measured in the conjoint experiment, with the average value hierarchies of real MPs (Table 6.1). This comparison reveals a number of interesting trends. The fact that MPs, on average, attribute most importance to Self-transcendence values such as Universalism and Benevolence, and these are, at the same time, most important for citizens' candidate selections, implies that voters get the 'right' politicians. Put another way, citizens desire representatives with a particular set of personal characteristics and motivations and these are, to an extent, mirrored in reality. If a hypothetical line of causation is drawn between public preferences and candidate success, then these data suggest that either (a) voters correctly perceive the values of political candidates and fill the UK Parliament with MPs high in Self-Transcendence values, or (b) mediatized party political campaigns have adeptly manipulated the public's psychological preferences and/or perceptions of candidates. Either way this is a highly significant finding, given a large extant research base now pointing to the importance of leader evaluations for vote choice (Clarke et al, 2004; Garzia, 2013; Laustsen and Bor, 2017).

Beyond these aggregate similarities, MPs attribute more relative importance to Power values and less relative importance to Conservation values such as Security than the public would like in their ideal politicians. Whilst these value factors are relatively less important

Table 6.1: Value hierarchies for 'real' and 'ideal' MPs based on sample means (most important to least important)

Actual Members of Parliament	Ideal Members of Parliament
Benevolence	Universalism
Universalism	Benevolence
Self-Direction	Security
Stimulation	Self-Direction
Conformity	Conformity
Power	Stimulation
Security	Hedonism
Hedonism	Tradition
Achievement	Achievement
Tradition	Power
$N = 168$	$N = 1637$

to both MPs and voters than Self-Transcendence values, these differences may be crucial for understanding contemporary disaffection with political elites. It is on these personality characteristics (Power values in particular) that the media arguably concentrates, focusing public attention on the incongruence between public preferences and the values of their politicians. A preoccupation with finding fault in parliamentary representatives, as well as the constant impression management demanded of contemporary politicians, arguably distorts the public perception or projection of MPs' most important basic values. The public thus consumes a skewed and often homogenized set of political personae in the press that emphasize MPs' Self-Enhancement values and, consequently, undermine the personal trust judgements necessary to sustain political participation. More research is needed to understand the relative causal impact of media framing and candidate image projection on value-based voting behaviours.

Whilst these inferences require further research, they are also supported here by interview data with MPs. Comments reported in Chapter 2 testify to MPs' generally positive appraisals of one another – regardless of partisanship – but nearly all participants also spoke of the damage done to their reputations by a voyeuristic media and, in particular, the parliamentary expenses scandal of 2010. Interviewee 5 was overwhelmingly dismissive of the media and blamed a biased coverage of MPs' moral fibre for diminishing the transparency between politicians and the public:

> 'I think it's bollocks. The hardest-working, most virtuous [...] people that I've ever met have been fellow politicians. There's a certain hypocrisy amongst journalists in particular who claim to be disappointed about the fact that MPs aren't more open and free-thinking about what they say, when actually the thing that most shocked me about becoming Home Secretary was the way in which every single thing that I said was pored over, and dissected, and kept on record [...] To protect yourself, rightly or wrongly, you tend to be very careful about what you say.'

Other MPs were quick to point out the irony of a media profession that seeks to expose the worst traits in politicians without acknowledging the "small number of press barons who are mostly tax exiles and are just, in some cases, vile, and run campaigns against individuals that are disgraceful" (Interviewee 12). One senior Labour MP suggested that the media purposefully homogenizes its coverage of MPs in order to ingratiate itself to the public:

> 'So, it's nonsense to say we're all any one thing, but it makes the media more powerful if we're useless because then they are absolutely, amazingly clever and you can trust them to tell you what to think rather than trusting the politicians. That's really what they're after.' (Interviewee 14)

For more experienced MPs, it was the expenses scandal of 2010 that had sparked an intensification of the personalized pillorying of politicians. Interviewees expressed a sense of injustice at the fact that, for the sake of a few "who quite deliberately worked the system" (Interviewee 16), they could no longer instil trust in their electors:

> 'The expenses [scandal] did us a terrible amount of damage. There's always been this view that, "Oh, politicians are just in it for themselves. They don't represent us. They just think whatever they can achieve for themselves." That's always been there but I think the expenses stuff made that far, far worse. It didn't matter whether you were one of the people who were having fingers pointed at them in the press or not.' (Interviewee 15)

Basic values and voting: a perception gap?

Taken together, these findings represent a significant step forward in the academic understanding of personality in politics and specifically voting behaviour in Westminster parliamentary elections. Whilst democratic representation provides a solution to aggregating the diverse and contradictory demands of an electorate, it does not provide a manual by which constituents – with less power, resource and information – may evaluate the political fidelity of their representative in that role. In order to overcome this asymmetry of information and make decisions about those running for political office, it is argued that citizens rely on everyday evaluations of candidates' core values, and that the psychology of candidates has become increasingly salient with changes to the media coverage of politics as well as political communication. To test this thesis, the research questions or 'problems' guiding this book have been triangulated with an original conjoint experiment of public voting preferences. In doing so, it was found that:

- the basic values of parliamentary candidates have a greater effect on public voting habits than physical attributes such as age, gender, religion or ethnicity, socioeconomic attributes such as schooling and occupation, and candidates' political priorities;
- meaningful differences exist between the ideal candidates chosen by the British public according to voters' partisanship;
- on average, real MPs attribute most importance to Self-Transcendence values and these are, on average, the most desirable basic values in citizens' ideal candidates; but
- MPs still attribute more relative importance to Self-Enhancement values and less relative importance to Conservation values than the public would like to see in their ideal representatives.

These findings offer a range of new insights for the study of personality and vote choice in western democracies (eg Caprara et al, 2006; Barbaranelli et al, 2007). Simply observing congruence between the personality characteristics of voters and elites from partisan blocs (see Chapter 4) does not, for example, imply that voters on the Left or Right (or non-voters) *ideally* want their democratic representatives to be equally high or low in the same or other personality characteristics. This chapter has shown that the voting public does indeed have preferences for certain personality characteristics in politics and that these matter at the (hypothetical) ballot box. At the same time, these findings have additional substantive relevance in revealing a potential 'perception gap' in contemporary democratic politics. If voters are able to express clear psychological preferences for candidates in experimental scenarios, and these are at the same time reflective of real MPs, then we must ask why an extant literature in anti-politics routinely reports public disapprobation for the personal qualities of MPs.

In making sense of this paradox, meaning is found in the work of Ivar Kolstad and Arne Wiig (2018), whose study of voting habits in Tanzania shows that media coverage of elite tax evasion has a negative effect on participants' intention to vote. Moreover, this effect was accentuated among participants who received the information in a morally charged format. Whilst Kolstad and Wiig's study and this conjoint experiment need to be reproduced in a broad sample of comparative democracies, it is highly possible that charged media treatments of politicians, and specifically politicians' (mis)behaviour, not only undermines trust in politicians but also citizens' confidence in the existing social contract and broader political institutions and processes. Put another way, it is surmised that psychologically charged media coverage of individual, isolated or small-n cases of elite malfeasance may (a) heighten the salience of personal and psychological characteristics as a voting heuristic, (b) distort accurate evaluations of politicians, (c) compound distrust in political elites, and thus (d) lead citizens to disengage from formal politics altogether or vote for/with populist leaders who identify as anti-establishment. Whilst the substantive focus of this book is upon the UK, these findings, as well as the resulting methodological and theoretical lines of inquiry, are likely to be of significant interest to scholars researching elections, personalization, and the health of democracy worldwide.

The results presented in this chapter also have practical implications for prospective MPs and political parties. Whilst parties have, as discussed, become far more attuned to 'candidate packaging', the data presented in this chapter provide useful insights for party selection procedures and campaign tactics. In the first instance, party selectorates may make a more concerted effort to assess (implicitly or explicitly) the personal values of nominees and, in doing so, choose more electorally viable candidates. Similarly, parties may use the data in this chapter to construct personalized campaign adverts and candidate literature that speak directly to the psychological preferences of voters. On one hand, this may demote voters (even more) to the role of spectators in a 'managed' democratic process. On the other hand, it has the potential to refocus voters' attention on the political dynamics of their candidate selections as those candidates become equally preferable in terms of their visible psychological characteristics. Above all, these findings can carry intuitive lessons for candidates themselves. The proliferation of social media, for example, offers candidates an unprecedented opportunity to connect directly with voters and provide them with more, not less, information about their own core values. President Trump is both a shining and shocking example in this respect. Not only might candidates utilize these channels to improve their psychological appeal, but they can also circumvent the accusations of being anti-democratic or elitist current in the mainstream media.

Final thoughts

The research for this chapter and the entire book was embarked upon in order to expose and explain the role of personality characteristics, specifically basic values, in UK politics (and specifically parliamentary politics). On one hand, it is concluded that politics is a profession few 'ordinary' people care to enter. On account of the findings discussed and dissected throughout the book, it seems that MPs are individuals with an 'extraordinary' dedication to the welfare of others and an unusually high propensity for independent and creative thought and action. They exhibit much higher levels of personal ambition than those they govern, but we the voting public also appear to get the types of politicians we want if not always deserve. Former speaker of the House of Commons, John Bercow, puts this far more eloquently:

> This is a wonderful place, filled overwhelmingly by people who are motivated by their notion of the national interest, by their perception of the public good and by their duty— not as delegates, but as representatives—to do what they believe is right for our country. We degrade this Parliament at our peril. (HC Deb, 2019)

In this spirit, the empirical data in this book offer complementary evidence on the psychology of politicians, and specifically the psychological basis of what Fenno (1977) describes as the 'perception' of the principal–agent relationship. Put another way, MPs understand the mechanical rules of the game and the strategic choices that may or may not attract electoral benefits, but these 'facts' operate alongside or subordinate to a range of psychological beliefs or attitudes that affect the act of representation. At the same time, voters have clear psychological preferences when it comes to choosing their representatives, but they are unable to see these preferences reproduced in the body politic.

This book has also demonstrated that MPs' personalities, specifically their basic values, matter for studies of public policy and representation. MPs' basic values not only have the potential to influence their perceptions of what an elected politician on the national stage *should* be or do, but also have a substantial impact on a range of *actual* legislative behaviours. For the purpose of enriching future research, these findings offer a sharp rebuke to a long list of scholars who have prioritized behavioural economics and rational choice explanations of political agency (eg Downs, 1957; Strøm, 1990). That basic values share strong associations with significant representative activities such as legislative voting gives credence, in particular, to an institutional theory of political choice (eg Sniderman and Levendusky, 2009). Rather than assuming strategic and unitary desire on the part of *all* political elites and applying this same logic sequentially to all areas of representation in a democracy, it is suggested that MPs actually synthesize their own trans-situational goals and motivations within an extended climate of expectations from both internal and external role alters. In order to provide satisfactory accounts of politicians' behaviour, it is suggested that future studies must consider (a) the extent to which any representative behaviour is transparent to/of importance for a cynical media/electorate, (b) the extent to which the choice is affected by internal scrutiny and accountability procedures or party interests, and (c) the specific personality characteristics that inform each agent's interpretation of the choice itself as well as the constraints outlined in (a) and (b). Taken together and measured using appropriate variables, this triangulated approach to studies of elite political behaviour (summarized in the IMPPB in Chapter 5) may provide a much more accurate understanding of structure and agency in the UK Parliament and other representative chambers around the world.

It is hoped that readers of this book also take it as a fillip to question some of the major assumptions in parliamentary studies of party politics. To the extent that political parties still dominate the character and electoral outcomes of representative politics in the UK, competing psychological motivations are found among the MPs of different parties and those within them. If frameworks of accountability and delegation rely upon a consensus of support among political elites, it is suggested that such antagonistic cooperation relies as much upon broad coalitions of personality characteristics as it does upon party discipline, career incentives, or cost–benefit analysis. The fact that Labour MPs share heightened psychological commitments to Self-Transcendence values, whereas Conservative MPs do so for Conservation values, binds individuals who are otherwise competing contenders for vote, office and policy success. Kam's (2009) paradigmatic LEADs model, for example, no longer seems sufficient as an explanation of parliamentary political behaviour. When party representatives act as one, this solidarity may have as much basis in common personality characteristics as it does in their membership of a political movement. In fact, it is argued that the former may well facilitate the latter. Similarly, when MPs act against the grain of their party directive, it may be as much or more so about a divergence of their personal beliefs as any strategic decision related to electoral outcomes. To give weight to this preliminary observation, it is suggested that future studies should now draw, wherever possible, on the insights of psychological and preference-driven models of party politics in order to understand when and why political elites within and between parties compete or cooperate with one another, and in turn the impact this has upon representative outcomes.

At a practical level, this book has been used to raise a number of concerns about parliamentary representation that are apposite for those in control of party selectorates and political institutions. Whilst it may be that a small and psychologically unique section of the population puts themselves forward for office, it has been suggested throughout this book that such a phenomenon relies on supply-side factors as well as demand. Put another way, the contemporary conduct of politics, the character of its institutions and the rules that govern them, as well as the obscure internal machinations of dominant political parties, are likely to facilitate the political ambition of some to the detriment of the majority. Whether or not the basic values of elected politicians are objectively favourable, this psychological gap between governor and governed is worrying. Even when we divide politicians into socioeconomic or demographic groups, they are still more similar in their personality characteristics to one another than those same groups in the broader population (Chapter 3). This should also be of particular interest to party members and officials on the Left of British politics – those in the Labour Party especially – who continue to face an identity crisis at the time of writing. In order to win back the so-called 'Red Wall' in the North of England and appeal to a range of communities where the social identity of voting Labour is deteriorating, they will need to think carefully about how they close the personality gap reported in Chapter 4.

Finally, it is suggested that studies of personality in politics may also provide an empirical standard by which to measure politicians' integrity. In political theory, integrity is understood as a property of character exhibited 'in a person's resistance to sacrificing or compromising [their] convictions' (Scherkoske, 2013, p 29; see also Williams, 1981). From an external, anti-politics perspective (as discussed at the start of this book), it is this understanding of *integrity as propriety* that also underpins popular evaluations of political conduct (Jennings et al, 2016; Hall, 2018) and stands at odds with institutional or even elite conceptions of the term (Allen and Birch, 2015b). As such, official documents like the *Principles of Public Life* produced by the Committee on Standards in Public Life – designed to circumscribe official misconduct or malfeasance – do not satisfy unanswered questions about the integrity of our elected representatives. By studying the personalities of politicians, we not only gain a greater appreciation for their humanity, but we also acquire a yardstick by which to understand (and judge) their goals, motivations and, ultimately, their behaviours. With that in mind, the data presented and analysed throughout this book indicate that we may have grossly underestimated the integrity of *most* politicians. Not only do politicians' value hierarchies reveal a heightened psychological orientation to other- rather than self-enrichment (that is, Self-Transcendence values), but MPs' basic values – where they are activated – also appear to exert a sustained impact on MPs' elected behaviour in spite of the complex and contingent nature of democratic politics.

The aim in researching for and writing this book was not to build a sympathetic counternarrative about the political class or specifically politicians. Rather, the aim was to test unfounded psychological claims that underpin popular disillusionment with democratic politics and to clarify the contested and amorphous nature of related academic debates about parliamentary behaviour. In doing so, the findings in this book are presented as evidence that public understandings of politics and politicians – as well as academic accounts – can often be distorted and simplified versions of a complex truth. This book is, in sum, an attempt to provide theoretically driven empirical research that challenges ongoing debates about who enters politics and why. In turn, it is hoped that it will give life to future interdisciplinary research into the psychology of parliaments and politicians.

Notes

Chapter 1

[1] These trends are, admittedly, aggregate in nature and hide subtle variations within the population. Extant literature on the 'Youthquake' and young people's politics shows, for example, that Britain's young people are neither politically uninterested nor apathetic, even if they feel alienated from formal political representation (Ehsan, 2018; Sloam and Henn, 2018).

[2] The Mass Observation Project collects qualitative data from volunteer writers (often known as 'Observers'), who respond to 'Directives', or open-ended questionnaires, sent to them by post or email. The Directives contain a number of general themes related to extremely personal issues as well as broader political and social issues and events. More information about the project, as well as access to the archive, can be found online: www.massobs.org.uk/

[3] For a discussion of nature, nurture and the 'agentic person', see Sears and Brown (2013).

[4] Each of the ten basic values has its own central definition and value markers. Conformity captures a certain restraint of actions, inclinations and impulses likely to upset or harm others and violate social expectations or norms. Tradition refers to respect, commitment and acceptance of the customs and ideas that one's culture or religion provide. Benevolence is all about loyalty, honesty responsibility and caring for the welfare of the people with whom one is in frequent personal contact. Universalism leads to an understanding, appreciation, tolerance and protection for the welfare, equality and social justice of all people and for nature. Self-Direction centres upon independence in both thought and action – choosing, creating, exploring. Stimulation heightens the importance of excitement, novelty and challenge in life. Hedonism refers to pleasure, enjoyment in life and gratification of the senses. Achievement encapsulates one's ambition and in particular the desire for personal success through demonstrating competence in accordance with social standards. Power places importance on wealth, authority, social status and prestige, as well as control and dominance over people and resources. Security refers to the need for safety, harmony and stability of society, of relationships, and of self. For a full discussion of each of these values and their theoretical and empirical development, see Schwartz (1992, 2010).

[5] Gouveia and colleagues (2014, p 41) challenged the Schwartz taxonomy for its multiple configurations, which they believed to demonstrate a lack of 'parsimony and theoretical focus'. This criticism failed to acknowledge the theoretical core of basic human values, that (1) values sit on a motivational continuum and (2) values

are situated around the circle according to the congruency of their motivational goals (Schwartz, 2014). The circular continuum is in reality nothing more than a single curved dimension in the same manner as any theoretical circle and as such the orthogonals or partitioning of the circle should not be misconstrued as dimensions themselves. This unifying idea is extremely parsimonious and allows researchers (guided by the principle of congruency in the theory) to divide the circular continuum into the smallest or largest number of values required to explain the focus of their study.

[6] Email communications contained a secure personalized link to the survey, which was hosted via the online survey platform Qualtrics.

[7] Each portrait comprises an 'importance' statement and a 'feeling' statement. There has been some scepticism based on cognitive response theory that a respondent's answer will be weighted towards one of these statements rather than both (Neuman, 2000, p 508, Krosnick and Presser, 2010, p 264) but in a two-nation pilot Schwartz used Multi-Trait Multi-Method (MTMM) analysis to conclude that combining the two into one item neither increased nor harmed reliability and validity (Schwartz, 2006). Similar studies have since concurred that if a study is 'interested in the goodness-of-fit to Schwartz's two-dimensional structure then it doesn't matter whether the combined or split version is used' (de Wet et al, 2016, p 1583).

[8] Participants were identified through the Democracy Club database of political candidates, which contains details of all consenting individuals who have participated as a candidate in an election in the UK since 2010. More than 11,000 of these participants (total database = 70,000+) provided contact email addresses to the electoral commission. The database is free to use so long as Democracy Club are acknowledged in any research outputs that arise (CC-BY licence). The survey was fielded through the online platform Qualtrics to each political candidate that was contactable in this database. They received an email containing comprehensive information about the project, the survey and the security of their data, and all responses were gathered on Qualtrics anonymously.

[9] Data collected by the European Social Survey (2016) was accessed online and downloaded. Available at www.europeansocialsurvey.org/data/

[10] Data collected by the first survey of UK Members of Parliament ($N = 106$) are analysed in this book alongside data collected by a subsequent survey of political candidates (councillors = 415, MPs = 62, unsuccessful candidates = 503). All participants in both surveys completed the TwIVI – a 20-item version of the Portrait Values Questionnaire designed to measure basic values – but these surveys were completed at different times. Prior to comparing and combining the data, confirmatory factor analyses were used to assess measurement invariance between the sample. Measurement invariance evaluates the psychometric equivalence of a latent unobservable construct (such as a basic value) across groups or measurement occasions (such as each survey conducted above). For a full discussion of when and how to test for measurement invariance, refer to Putnik and Bornstein (2016). In this study, the survey data collected on the basic values of politicians achieves both metric and scalar invariance, suggesting that the items in the TwIVI have measured constructs equivalently across samples (Model 1: Configural invariance – $\chi 2$ (df) = 627.236 (250), CFI = 0.937, RMSEA = 0.056; Model 2: Metric invariance – $\chi 2$ (df) = 677.929 (260), CFI = 0.938, RMSEA = 0.055; Model 1/2 comparison – $\Delta\chi 2$ (Δdf) = 5.602 (10), $\Delta\chi 2$ significance = p < 0.848, ΔCFI = 0.001, ΔRMSEA = 0.001, Decision = ACCEPT; Model 3: Scalar invariance – $\chi 2$ (df) = 693.804 (270), CFI = 0.937, RMSEA = 0.054; Model 2/3

comparison − Δχ2 (Δdf) = 15.875 (10), Δχ2 significance = p < 0.103, ΔCFI = 0.001, ΔRMSEA = 0.001, Decision = ACCEPT).

[11] The diversity of the sample in terms of demographic, socioeconomic and partisan characteristics strongly suggests that the sample does not suffer from self-selection bias vis-à-vis overrepresentation of specific groups within the target population. More importantly, the variation in scores for the PVQ between participants (see Chapter 2) appeases potential criticisms of social desirability and self-selection by personality.

[12] Cronbach's alpha can underestimate the reliability of brief measures given that alpha is a function of average correlations among items on a scale. However, these scores meet acceptable levels for multivariate research with psychometric surveys (Hair et al, 2006).

Chapter 2

[1] The European Social Survey (ESS) has included a shortened measure of basic values (the PVQ-21) since the early 2000s. Although the PVQ-21 and the TwIVI used to collect data from politicians in this study are both derived from the same theoretical framework, ten of their item descriptors differ. Whilst this means that they still share extremely similar properties (see Sandy et al, 2017), it was not possible to use confirmatory factor analysis to assess measurement invariance between the data collected from politicians and the public. However, the ESS provides the only large-N source of data on the (Schwartz) basic values of the British population. Instead, a series of proxy tests are used to determine construct equivalence across these samples. Firstly, Cronbach alpha coefficients are compared to assess the relative internal reliability of the two measures. The alphas for the TwIVI (Conservation = 0.72, Self-Transcendence = 0.73, Self-Enhancement = 0.84, Openness to Change = 0.77) and the PVQ-21 (Conservation = 0.69, Self-transcendence = 0.67, Self-Enhancement = 0.72, Openness to Change = 0.72) are both reasonable. Secondly, exploratory factor analysis is conducted on both sets of data to assess relative construct validity. The data collected from politicians using the TwIVI produced a strong four-factor model (SS loadings = 2.436, 2.168, 2.159, 1.957; cumulative variance = 0.122, 0.230, 0.338, 0.436; χ2 = 881.44 (p < 0.001)) with an average uniqueness score of 0.564. The data collected from the public by the ESS using the PVQ-21 produced a moderate four-factor model (SS loadings = 2.123, 1.968, 1.869, 1.581; cumulative variance = 0.101, 0.195, 0.284, 0.359; χ2 = 749.25 ($p < 0.001$)) with an average uniqueness score of 0.641. In both cases, the chi-square statistic is statistically significant. This is expected, given that the data can also be partitioned into the lower order ten-factor model of basic values. Finally, the external validity of the two samples is tested by correlating the value scores in each with a series of external variables (age, gender and education). As shown in Appendix C, the data collected using the PVQ-21 and TwIVI share very similar relationships with the external variables. In total, 76% of correlations match in terms of direction and 53% match in terms of both direction and statistical significance. These three tests are taken as evidence that the PVQ-21 and the TwIVI have measured broadly equivalent latent constructs (that is, basic values) in each of the samples used in this book.

[2] In their conceptual model of value change, Bardi and Goodwin (2011) elaborate on the likelihood framework of persuasion (see Petty and Cacioppo, 1986) to argue that values may evolve by effortful cognitive or peripheral affective processes.

Drawing on this model, Arieli and colleagues (2014) have shown that short lab-based interventions can affect temporary value change. This research has direct applicability in politics, where the struggle between structure and agency is not only constant and acute, but also central to the operation of democracy.

[3] Binary logistic regression is an appropriate statistical analysis when the purpose of research is to evaluate the predictive effect of continuous and discrete independent variables upon a dichotomous dependent variable (in this case 'status'). More than ten participants per predictor are included in this equation to ensure that the statistical power of the model is retained. The items included in the model do not suffer from multicollinearity (see next section), which can skew logistic regression results, and both the classification accuracy of the model (80.4%) and the overall $\chi2$ omnibus test of model coefficients (45.847, $p < 0.001$) are acceptable.

[4] Robustness checks were conducted to rule out the effects of multicollinearity in each of the three regressions (M1–M3). Tolerance levels for all predictors were well above 0.25 and Variance Inflation Factors (VIF) for each value item were nearly all below 2 (all were well beneath the maximum accepted VIF scores of 5).

Chapter 3

[1] Data were retrieved online from the Inter-Parliamentary Union and were last updated February 2019 at the time of writing. Figures for parliaments around the world can be accessed here: http://archive.ipu.org/wmn-e/classif.htm

[2] Please note that politicians of different ethnicities are grouped together into a rather blunt binary opposition for the purposes of these analyses. It is entirely possible that additional variations might be discovered with more data and a more nuanced coding framework.

Chapter 4

[1] MPs in the Scottish National Party, Plaid Cymru and Irish Unionist Parties are dropped here on the basis that their attitudes to independence are contested on both the ideological Left and Right.

[2] For the sake of graphical simplicity and ease of interpretation, confidence intervals have been redacted. The statistical significance of the relationships between variables is reported in the text.

[3] This decision was made on the basis that differences between the Hedonism values of voters and non-voters were not statistically significant. Achievement values were dropped a priori on the basis that they share less of a theoretical connection to non-voting than other Self-Enhancement values (that is, Power). More than eight values in any one regression model risks skewing the results and producing inaccurate findings.

Chapter 5

[1] Research on internal mechanisms may include, for example, basic values (Vecchione et al, 2015), personality traits (Caprara and Vecchione, 2013), self-esteem (Gibson, 1981), and construal-level theory (Trope et al, 2007). Research on external

mechanisms may include, for example, information environments (Kuklinski et al, 2001), framing (Druckman, 2004) and task structuring (Saris, 2004).

[2] Not all participants were present in the House of Commons at the same time and many did not vote at the same time on specific legislation when they were.

[3] The UN Resolution can be downloaded at: www.un.org/en/ga/search/view_doc.asp?symbol=S/RES/2249%282015%29

[4] For full quotation, see UN Resolution 2249.

[5] MPs' declared stances were reported by the BBC the night before the referendum (22 June 2016): www.bbc.co.uk/news/uk-politics-eu-referendum-35616946

[6] Data are published online by NatCen and available publicly at: www.natcen.ac.uk/blog/charting-changing-attitudes-%E2%80%93-same-sex-relationships

[7] A YouGov poll in June 2015 showed that only 37% of the public ever believed that military action against Saddam Hussein was the correct decision (https://yougov.co.uk/news/2015/06/03/remembering-iraq/).

[8] Interviewer: "A number of other participants have talked about the kind of inner turmoil they felt when they had to vote with the party whip or act in a certain way against their conscience. I wondered whether you'd experienced that, and how you dealt with it?"

[9] These divisions were recovered online from The Public Whip (www.publicwhip.org.uk), a non-governmental, not-for-profit repository of parliamentary debate transcripts and voting records taken from Hansard. Records of participants' select committee memberships, as well as written questions and Early Day Motions for the parliamentary year 2015–2016, were retrieved online from TheyWorkForYou (www.theyworkforyou.com/). TheyWorkForYou is a repository of open data taken from the UK Parliament.

Chapter 6

[1] Gender, age, ethnicity and disability are represented in normed profile images of professionals obtained from the CIE Biometrics Poznan University of Technology (PUT) Face database. These images were supplemented with additional images of professionals and obscure foreign politicians selected and normed by researchers at the Sheffield Methods Institute.

[2] According to the National Readership Survey of the UK population in 2016, 27% of citizens fell into categories AB, 28% category C1, 20% category C2 and 25% categories DE. Social grades are calculated using interviews that ask about the occupation of the chief income earner in the household, qualifications and the number of dependants cared for by the participant.

[3] Power values were selected as a baseline because they are routinely rated as least important in representative samples around the world (Bardi and Schwartz, 2001).

[4] Participants were asked to self-report their voting record from the 2015 and 2017 General Elections. Given that the General Election of 2017 stood in stark contrast to elections over the last two decades – in terms of both turnout and vote shares – the data from 2015 were used to partition the participants. This is also in keeping with the data used earlier in this book to identify the partisanship of ESS participants.

[5] Accent was used here as a proxy for candidates' regional identity on the basis that voters have been proven to infer candidates' characteristics from biological and verbal cues (eg Antonakis and Eubanks, 2017).

Appendix A: Twenty Item Portrait Values Questionnaire (TwIVI)

Here I briefly describe some people. Please read each description and think about how much each person is or is not like you. Using a 6-point scale from 'not like me at all' to 'very much like me', choose how similar the person is to you.

1 = not like me at all; 2 = not like me; 3 = a little like me; 4 = somewhat like me; 5 = like me; 6 = very much like me

How much like you is this person?

1. S/he believes s/he should always show respect to his/her parents and to older people. It is important to him/her to be obedient
2. Religious belief is important to him/her. S/he tries hard to do what his religion requires.
3. It's very important to him/her to help the people around him/her. S/he wants to care for their well-being.
4. S/he thinks it is important that every person in the world be treated equally. S/he believes everyone should have equal opportunities in life.
5. S/he thinks it's important to be interested in things. S/he likes to be curious and to try to understand all sorts of things.
6. S/he likes to take risks. S/he is always looking for adventures.
7. S/he seeks every chance s/he can to have fun. It is important to him/her to do things that give him/her pleasure.
8. Getting ahead in life is important to him/her. S/he strives to do better than others.
9. S/he always wants to be the one who makes the decisions. S/he likes to be the leader.

10. It is important to him/her that things be organized and clean. S/he really does not like things to be a mess.
11. It is important to him/her to always behave properly. S/he wants to avoid doing anything people would say is wrong.
12. S/he thinks it is best to do things in traditional ways. It is important to him/her to keep up the customs s/he has learned.
13. It is important to him/her to respond to the needs of others. S/he tries to support those s/he knows.
14. S/he believes all the world's people should live in harmony. Promoting peace among all groups in the world is important to him/her.
15. Thinking up new ideas and being creative is important to him/her. S/he likes to do things in his/her own original way.
16. S/he thinks it is important to do lots of different things in life. S/he always looks for new things to try.
17. S/he really wants to enjoy life. Having a good time is very important to him/her.
18. Being very successful is important to him/her. S/he likes to impress other people.
19. It is important to him/her to be in charge and tell others what to do. S/he wants people to do what s/he says.
20. Having a stable government is important to him/her. S/he is concerned that the social order be protected.

TwIVI scale scoring: Conformity: 1, 11; Tradition: 2, 12; Benevolence: 3, 13; Universalism: 4, 14; Self-Direction: 5, 15; Stimulation: 6, 16; Hedonism: 7, 17; Achievement: 8, 18; Power: 9, 19; Security: 10, 20.

Appendix B: Confirmatory factor analysis of survey data on the basic values of politicians (UK Members of Parliament, *N* = 168)

Latent factor	Survey item	B	SE	Z	*p*-value	Beta
CON	Con1	1.000	0.000	NA	NA	0.590
CON	Con2	1.118	0.265	4.227	0.000	0.501
CON	Con3	0.384	0.212	1.814	0.000	0.220
CON	Con4	1.391	0.255	5.465	0.000	0.787
CON	Con5	0.897	0.216	4.156	0.000	0.558
CON	Con6	1.194	0.257	4.648	0.000	0.718
STR	Str1	1.000	0.000	NA	NA	0.734
STR	Str2	0.883	0.270	3.270	0.001	0.460
STR	Str3	1.113	0.188	5.927	0.000	0.719
STR	Str4	1.163	0.326	3.574	0.000	0.493
SEHN	Sehn1	1.000	0.000	NA	NA	0.863
SEHN	Sehn2	0.684	0.088	7.757	0.000	0.709
SEHN	Sehn3	0.965	0.086	11.222	0.000	0.875
SEHN	Sehn4	0.689	0.089	7.739	0.000	0.716
OPEN	Open1	1.000	0.000	NA	NA	0.591
OPEN	Open2	1.546	0.277	5.583	0.000	0.698
OPEN	Open3	1.609	0.302	5.328	0.000	0.725
OPEN	Open4	1.227	0.295	4.164	0.000	0.478
OPEN	Open5	1.985	0.355	5.588	0.000	0.719
OPEN	Open6	1.977	0.348	5.677	0.000	0.795

Note: maximum likelihood estimation was used to calculate the measurement model. All factor loadings are significant at $p < 0.05$. $N = 168$, AIC = 450.633, RMSEA = 0.09. OPEN – Openness to Change values; STR - Self-Transcendence values; SEHN – Self-Enhancement values; CON – Conservation values.

Appendix B: Confirmatory factor analysis of survey data on the basic values of politicians (UK Members of Parliament, N = 165)

Appendix C: External correlations across samples

	CO	TR	BE	UN	SD	ST	HD	AC	PO	SE
Politicians/Candidates (TwIVI, N = 1053)										
Age	0.11***	0.21***	−0.03	−0.01	0.06	−0.06*	−0.21***	−0.19***	−0.02	0.12***
Gender (male)	0.09*	0.08**	−0.17***	−0.08*	0.01	−0.06*	0.02	0.00	0.01	0.04
Education	−0.13***	−0.03	−0.03	0.00	0.08*	0.07*	−0.02	0.12***	0.06	−0.11***
Public/ESS Round 8 (PVQ-21, N = 1557)										
Age	0.22***	0.24***	0.03	0.12***	0.05	−0.20***	– 0.18***	– 0.28***	−0.13***	0.15***
Gender (male)	0.02	−0.02	−0.20***	−0.06*	0.00	0.06*	0.09***	0.10***	0.09***	−0.15***
Education	−0.13***	−0.13***	0.00	0.16***	0.14***	0.08**	−0.05	0.09***	−0.02	−0.18***

Note: CO = Conformity; TR = Tradition; BE = Benevolence; UN = Universalism; SD = Self-Direction; ST = Stimulation; HD = Hedonism; AC = Achievement; PO = Power; SE = Security; PVQ-21 = 21-item portrait values questionnaire; TwIVI = twenty item values inventory; education = factor with five levels (no qualifications, apprenticeship, A-Levels/vocational qualification, higher education degree, postgraduate degree). $* \; p < 0.05$, $** \; p < 0.01$, $*** \; p < 0.001$.

Appendix D: Conjoint experiment of candidate preferences by partisanship

Conjoint analysis of voting preferences among a representative sample of Labour Party voters ($n = 350$), Conservative Party voters ($n = 470$), and non-voters ($n = 432$) in the 2015 UK General Election. Graphs show the change in predicted probability of candidate selection by attribute.

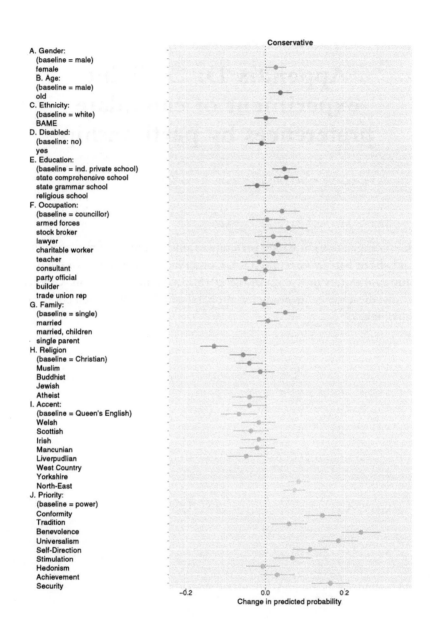

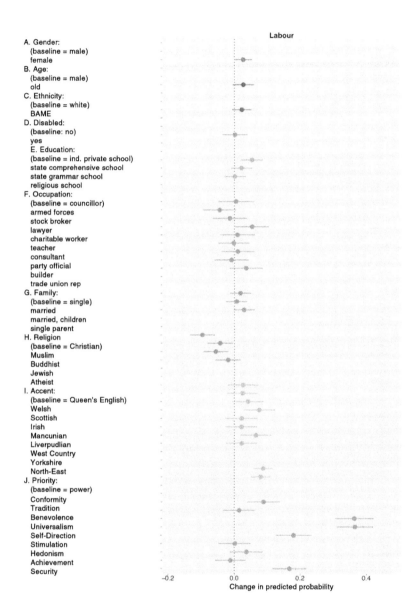

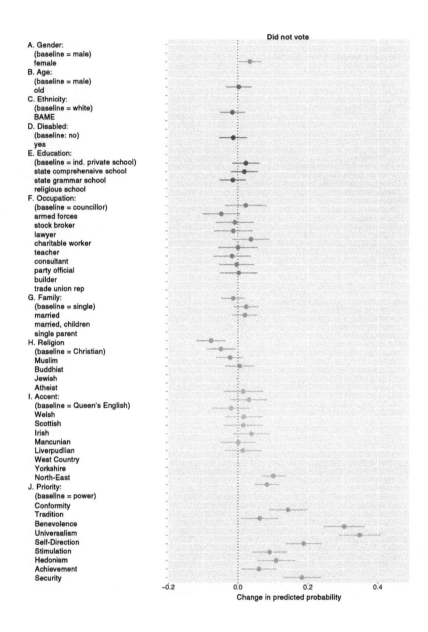

References

Abélès, M. (1988). Modern political ritual. *Current Anthropology*, 29(3): 391–99.

Abramowitz, A. I., and Webster, S. (2016). The rise of negative partisanship and the nationalization of U.S. elections in the 21st century. *Electoral Studies*, 41(2): 12–22.

Adams, J. F., Merrill, S., and Grofman, B. (2005). *A Unified Theory of Party Competition: A Cross-National Analysis Integrating Spatial and Behavioural Factors.* Cambridge: Cambridge University Press.

Adams, J., Ezrow, L., and Somer-Topcu, Z. (2011). Is anybody listening? Evidence that voters do not respond to European parties' policy statements during elections. *American Journal of Political Science*, 55(2): 370–82.

Allen, N. (2010). Keeping MPs honest? *Public Integrity*, 12(2): 105–23.

Allen, N., and Birch, S. (2015a). Process preferences and British public opinion: Citizens' judgements about government in an era of anti-politics. *Political Studies*, 63: 390–411.

Allen, N., and Birch, S. (2015b). *Ethics and Integrity in British Politics: How Citizens Judge their Politicians' Conduct and Why It Matters.* Cambridge: Cambridge University Press.

Allen, P. (2013). Linking pre-parliamentary political experience and the career trajectories of the 1997 General Election cohort. *Parliamentary Affairs*, 66(4): 685–707.

Allen, P. (2018). *The Political Class: Why It Matters Who Our Politicians Are.* Oxford: Oxford University Press.

Allen, P., and Cairney, P. (2015). What do we mean when we talk about the 'political class'? *Political Studies Review*, 15(1): 18–27, doi: 10.1111/1478-9302.12092.

Allen, P., and Cutts, D. (2018). An analysis of political ambition in Britain. *Political Quarterly*, 89(1): 73–81.

All Party Parliamentary Group for Women (2014). Improving parliament: creating a better and more representative house. http://appgimprovingparliamentreport.co.uk/download/APPG-Women-In-Parliament-Report-2014.pdf

André, A., and Depauw, S. (2013). District magnitude and home styles of representation in European democracies. *West European Politics*, 36(5): 986–1006.

André, A., Depauw, S., and Martin, S. (2015). Electoral systems and legislators' constituency effort: The mediating effect of electoral vulnerability. *Comparative Political Studies*, 48(4): 464–96.

André, A., and Depauw, S. (2017). The quality of representation and satisfaction with democracy: The consequences of citizen–elite policy and process congruence. *Political Behaviour*, 39: 377–97.

Antonakis, J., and Eubanks, D. L. (2017). Looking leadership in the face. *Current Directions in Psychological Science*, 26(3): 270–75.

Arieli, S., and Tenne-Gazit, O. (2017). Values and behaviour in a work environment: Taking a multi-level perspective. In S. Roccas and L. Sagiv (eds), *Values and Behaviour: Taking a Cross Cultural Perspective*. Switzerland AG: Springer International Publishing, pp 115–41.

Arieli, S., Grant, A. M., and Sagiv, L. (2014). Convincing yourself to care about others: An intervention for enhancing benevolence values. *Journal of Personality*, 82(1): 15–24.

Arieli, S., Sagiv, L., and Cohen-Shalem, E. (2016). Values in business schools: The role of self-selection and socialization. *Academy of Management Learning & Education*, 15(3): 493–507.

Arter, D. (2006). Questioning the Mezey question: An interrogatory framework for the comparative study of legislatures. *Journal of Legislative Studies*, 12: 462–82.

Atkeson, L. R. (2003). Not all cues are created equal: The conditional impact of female candidates on political engagement. *Journal of Politics*, 65(4): 1040–61.

Atkeson, L. R., and Carrillo, N. (2007). More is better: The influence of collective female descriptive representation on external efficacy. *Politics & Gender*, 3: 79–101.

Atkinson, M. M., and Bierling, G. (2005). Politicians, the public and political ethics: Worlds apart. *Canadian Journal of Political Science*, 38(4): 1003–28.

Audickas, L., and Kracknell, R. (2018). Social background of MPs 1979–2017. (CBP 7483). London: House of Commons Library.

Audickas, L., Dempsey, N., and Loft, P. (2019). Membership of UK political parties. (SN05125). London: House of Commons Library.

Bache, I., Bartle, I., Flinders, M., and Marsden, G. (2015). *Multi-level Governance and Climate Change: Insights from Transport Policy*. Lanham, MD: Rowman and Littlefield.

Bailey, D., and Nason, G. P. (2008). Cohesion of major political parties. *British Politics*, 3(3): 390–417.

Bakker, B. N., Klemmensen, R., Nørgaard, A. S., and Schumacher, G. (2016). Stay loyal or exit the party? How openness to experience and extroversion explain vote switching. *Political Psychology*, 37(3): 419–29.

Balmas, M., Rahat, G., Sheafer, T., and Shenhay, S. R. (2014) Two routes to personalized politics: Centralized and decentralized personalization. *Party Politics*, 20: 37–51.

Banducci, S. A., Donovan, T., and Karp, J. A. (2004). Minority representation, empowerment, and participation. *Journal of Politics*, 66(2): 534–56.

Bankert, A., Huddy, L., and Rosema, M. (2017). Measuring partisanship as a social identity in multi-party systems. *Political Behaviour*, 39(1): 103–32.

Barbaranelli, C., Caprara, G. V., Vecchione, M., and Fraley, C. R. (2007). Voters' personality traits in presidential elections. *Personality and Individual Differences*, 42: 1199–208.

Barber, S. (2014). Arise, careerless politician: The rise of the professional party leader. *Politics*, 34(1): 23–31.

Bardi, A., and Goodwin, R. (2011). The dual route to value change: Individual processes and cultural moderators. *Journal of Cross-Cultural Psychology*, 42(2): 271–87.

Bardi, A., and Schwartz, S. (2001). Value hierarchies across cultures: Taking a similarities perspective. *Journal of Cross-Cultural Psychology*, 32(3): 268–90.

Bardi, A., and Schwartz, S. H. (2003). Values and behaviour: Strength and structure of relations. *Personality and Social Psychology Bulletin*, 29(10): 1207–20.

Barenbaum, N. B., and Winter, D. G. (2008). History of modern personality theory and research. In O. P. John, R. W. Robins, and L. A. Pervin (eds), *Handbook of Personality: Theory and Research* (3rd edn). New York: Guilford Press, pp 3–26.

Barnea, M. F., and Schwartz, S. H. (1998). Values and voting. *Political Psychology*, 19(1): 17–40.

Barnes, T. D., and Burchard, S. M. (2013). 'Engendering' politics: The impact of descriptive representation on women's political engagement in sub-Saharan Africa. *Comparative Political Studies*, 46(7): 767–90.

Barreto, M. (2007). Si se puede! Latino candidates and the mobilization of Latino voters. *American Political Science Review*, 101(August): 425–41.

Bartle, J., and Bellucci, P. (2009). Introduction: Partisanship, social identity and individual attitudes. In J. Bartle and P. Bellucci (eds), *Political Parties and Partisanship: Social Identity and Individual Attitudes.* London: Routledge, pp 1–25.

Bates, S., Goodwin, M., and McKay, S. (2017). Do UK MPs engage more with select committees since the Wright reforms? An interrupted time series analysis, 1979–2016. *Parliamentary Affairs,* 70(4): 780-800.

Beer, S. H. (1969). *Modern British Politics.* London: Faber.

Bell, S. (2012). The power of ideas: The ideational shaping of the structural power of business. *International Studies Quarterly,* 56: 661–73.

Bell, S. (2017). Historical institutionalism and new dimensions of agency: Bankers, institutions and the 2008 financial crisis. *Political Studies,* 65(3): 724–39.

Bendor, J., Diermeier, D., and Ting, M. (2003). A behavioural model of turnout. *American Political Science Review,* 97(2): 261–80.

Benedetto, G., and Hix, S. (2007). The rejected, the ejected, and the dejected: Explaining government rebels in the 2001–2005 British House of Commons. *Comparative Political Studies,* 40(7): 755–81.

Bengtsson, A. and Wass, H. (2010). Styles of political representation: What do voters expect? *Journal of Elections, Public Opinion and Parties,* 20: 55–81.

Benton, M., and Russell, M. (2012). Assessing the impact of parliamentary oversight committees: The select committees in the British House of Commons. *Parliamentary Affairs,* 66: 772–97.

Berrington, H. (1985). MPs and their constituents in Britain: The history of a relationship. In V. Bogdanor (ed), *Representatives of the People?* Aldershot: Gower, pp 15–43.

Best, H. (2011). Does personality matter in politics? Personality factors as determinants of parliamentary recruitment and policy preferences. *Comparative Sociology,* 10: 928–48.

Best, H., and Vogel, L. (2018). Representative elites. In H. Best, J. P. Daloz, and U. Hoffman-Lange (eds), *Palgrave Handbook of Political Elites.* London, UK: Palgrave, pp 339–57.

Beusterien, K., Grinspan, J., Kuchuk, I., Mazzarello, S., Dent, S., Gertler, S., Bouganim, N., Vandermeer, L., and Clemens, M. (2014). Use of conjoint analysis to assess breast cancer patient preferences for chemotherapy side effects. *The Oncologist,* 19(2): 127–34.

Bevir, M., and Rhodes, R. A. W. (2006). *Governance Stories.* Abingdon: Routledge.

Biezen, I., and Poguntke, T. (2014). The decline of membership-based politics. *Party Politics,* 20(2): 205–16.

Biggs, M., and Knauss, S. (2011). Explaining membership in the British National Party: A multilevel analysis of contact and threat. *European Sociological Review*, 27(3): 1–14.

Bilsky, W., Janik, M., and Schwartz, S. H. (2011). The structural organization of human values: Evidence from three rounds of the European Social Survey (ESS). *Journal of Cross-Cultural Psychology*, 42(5): 759–76.

Bird, K. (2005). Gendering parliamentary questions. *British Journal of Politics & International Relations*, 7(3): 353–70.

Bird, K., Saalfeld, T., and Wust, A. (2010). *The Political Representation of Immigrants and Minorities: Voters, Parties and Parliaments in Liberal Democracies*. London: Routledge.

Bittner, A. (2014). Leader evaluations and partisan stereotypes: A comparative analysis. In M. C. Lobo, and J. Curtice (eds), *Personality Politics? The Role of Leader Evaluations in Democratic Elections*. Croydon: CPI Group, pp 17–37.

Blakeley, R. (2012). Elite interviews. In L. J. Shepherd (ed), *Critical Approaches to Security: An Introduction to Theories and Methods*. London: Routledge, pp 158–68.

Bloemraad, I., and Schönwälder, K. (2013). Immigrant and ethnic minority representation in Europe: Conceptual challenges and theoretical approaches, *West European Politics*, 36: 564–79.

Blomgren, M., and Rozenberg, O. (2012). Legislative roles and legislative studies. In M. Blomgren and O. Rozenberg (eds), *Parliamentary Roles in Modern Legislatures*. Routledge: Abingdon, pp 8–36.

Blondel, J. (1970). Legislative behaviour: Some steps towards a cross-national measurement. *Government and Opposition*, 5: 67–85.

Blunkett, D., Flinders, M., and Prosser, B. (2016). Devolution, evolution, revolution… democracy? What's really happening to English local governance? *Political Quarterly*, 87(4): 553–64.

Bogdanor, V. (2003). *The British Constitution in the Twentieth Century*. Oxford: Oxford University Press.

Bonotti, M. (2017). *Partisanship and Political Liberalism in Diverse Societies*. Oxford: Oxford University Press.

Bor, A. (2017). Spontaneous categorization along competence in partner and leader evaluations. *Evolution and Human Behaviour*, 38(4): 468–73.

Borchert, J., and Zeiss, J. (eds). (2003). *The Political Class in Advanced Democracies: A Comparative Handbook*. Oxford: Oxford University Press.

Borg, I. (2019). Age- and gender-related differences in the structure and the meaning of personal values. *Personality and Individual Differences*, 138: 336–43.

Borg, I., Bardi, A., and Schwartz, S. (2017). Does the values circle exist only within persons or across persons? *Journal of Personality*, 85: 151–62.

Bourne, H., and Jenkins, M. (2013). Organizational values: A dynamic perspective. *Organization Studies*, 34(4): 495–514.

Bowler, S., and Karp, J. A. (2004). Politicians, scandals, and trust in government. *Political Behaviour*, 26(3): 271–87.

Brader, T., and Tucker, J. A. (2012). Following the party's lead: Party cues, policy opinion, and the power of partisanship in three multiparty systems. *Comparative Politics*, 44(4): 403–20.

Bradley, A. W. (2008). Relations between the executive, judiciary and parliament: An evolving saga? *Public Law*, Autumn: 470–89.

Bradlow, E. T. (2005). Current issues and a 'wish list' for conjoint analysis. *Applied Stochastic Models in Business and Industry*, 21(4–5): 319–23.

Burns, N., Schlozman, K. L., and Verba, S. (2001). *The Private Roots of Public Action*. Cambridge, MA: Harvard University Press.

Cairney, P. (2007). The professionalization of MPs: Refining the 'politics-facilitating' explanation. *Parliamentary Affairs*, 60(2): 212–33.

Cairney, P. (2014) *What Is the Problem with the British Political Class?* https://paulcairney.wordpress.com/2014/06/30/what-is-the-problem-with-the-british-political-class/

Cairney, P. (2015). The Scottish Independence Referendum: What are the implications of a no vote? *Political Quarterly*, 80(2): 186–91.

Campbell, R., and Cowley, P. (2014). What voters want: Reactions to candidate characteristics in a survey experiment. *Political Studies*, 62: 745–65.

Campbell, R., and Lovenduski, J. (2015). What should MPs do? Public and parliamentarians' views compared. *Parliamentary Affairs*, 68: 690–708.

Campbell, D., and Wolbrecht, C. (2006). See Jane run: Women politicians as role models for adolescents. *Journal of Politics*, 68(2): 233–47.

Campbell, R., Childs, S., and Lovenduski, J. (2010). Do women need women representatives? *British Journal of Political Science*, 40(1): 171–94.

Campus, D. (2010). Mediatization and personalization of politics in Italy and France: The cases of Berlusconi and Sarkozy. *International Journal of Press/Politics*, 20: 1–17.

Caprara, G. V., and Cervone, D. (2000). *Personality: Determinants, Dynamics, and Potentials*. Cambridge: Cambridge University Press.

Caprara, G. V., and Silvester, J. (2018). Personality and political elites. In H. Best, J. P. Daloz, and U. Hoffman-Lange (eds), *Palgrave Handbook of Political Elites*. London: Palgrave, pp 476–488.

Caprara, G. V., and Vecchione, M. (2013). Personality approaches to political behaviour. In L. Huddy, D. Sears, and J. Levy (eds), *Oxford Handbook of Political Psychology*. Oxford: Oxford University Press, pp 23–58.

Caprara, G. V., and Zimbardo, P. (2004). Personalizing politics: A congruency model of political preference. *American Psychologist*, 59: 581–94.

Caprara, G. V., Barbaranelli, C., and Zimbardo, P. (1999). Personality profiles and political parties. *Political Psychology*, 20: 175–97.

Caprara, G. V., Schwartz, S., Capanna, C., Vecchione, M., and Barbaranelli, C. (2006). Personality and politics: Values, traits, and political choice source. *Political Psychology*, 27(1): 1–28.

Caprara, G.V., and Vecchione, M., and Schwartz, S. (2009). Mediational role of values in linking personality traits to political orientation. *Asian Journal of Social Psychology*, 12: 82–94.

Caprara, G. V., Francescato, D., Mebane, M., Sorace, R., and Vecchione, M. (2010). Personality foundations of ideological divide: A comparison of women Members of Parliament and women voters in Italy. *Political Psychology*, 31: 739–62.

Caprara, G. V., Alesandri, G., and Eisenberg, N. (2012). Prosociality: The contribution of traits, values, and self-efficacy beliefs. *Journal of Personality and Social Psychology*, 102: 1289–303.

Carlin, B., and Isaby, J. (2006). Senior Tory sacked in 'A-list' race row. *Telegraph*, 8 November.

Carman, C. (2003). *Public Preferences for Political Representation*. Paper presented at the Annual Meeting of the Midwest Political Science Association, Chicago, IL, 3–6 April 2003.

Carman, C. (2006). Public preferences for parliamentary representation in the UK: An overlooked link? *Political Studies*, 54(1): 103–22.

Celis, K. and Mügge, M. L. (2018). Whose equality? Measuring group representation. *Politics*, 38(2): 197–213.

Celis, K., Childs, S., and Kantola, J. (2014). Constituting women's interests through representative claims. *Politics and Gender*, 10(2): 149–74.

Cervone, D. (2005). Personality architecture: Within-person structures and processes. *Annual Review of Psychology*, 56: 423–52.

Childs, S. (2004). *New Labour's Women MPs: Women Representing Women*. London: Routledge.

Childs, S., and Cowley, P. (2011). The politics of local presence: Is there a case for descriptive representation? *Political Studies*, 59: 1–19.

Childs, S., and Krook. L. M. (2008). Critical mass theory and women's political representation. *Political Studies*, 56(3): 725–36.

Childs, S., and Withey, J. (2004). Women representatives acting for women: Sex and the signing of Early Day Motions in the 1997 British Parliament. *Political Studies*, 52(3): 552–64.

Chodorow, N. J. (1990). Gender, relation, and difference in psychoanalytic perspective. In C. Zanardi (ed), *Essential Papers in Psychoanalysis: Essential Papers on the Psychology of Women*. New York: New York University Press. pp 420–36.

Cieciuch, J., Schwartz, S. H., and Vecchione, M. (2013). Applying the refined values theory to past data: What can researchers gain? *Journal of Cross-Cultural Psychology*, 44(8): 1215–34.

Clarke, H., Sanders, D., Stewart, M., and Whiteley, P. (2004). *Political Choice in Britain*. Oxford: Oxford University Press.

Clarke, N., Jennings, W., Moss, J., and Stoker, G. (2018). *The Good Politician: Folk Theories, Political Interaction, and the Rise of Anti-Politics*. Cambridge: Cambridge University Press.

Conway, M. M. (2000). *Political Participation in the United States*. 3rd ed. Washington, DC: CQ Press.

Corbett, J. (2015). Diagnosing the problem of anti-politicians: A review and an agenda. *Political Studies Review*, 14(4): 534–43.

Cowley, P. (1998). Unbridled passions? Free votes, issues of conscience and the accountability of British Members of Parliament. *Journal of Legislative Studies*, 4(2): 70–88.

Cowley, P. (2002). *Revolts and Rebellions: Parliamentary Voting under Blair*. London: Politico's.

Cowley, P. (2005). *The Rebels: How Blair Mislaid His Majority*. London: Politico's.

Cowley, P. (2012). Arise, novice leader! The continuing rise of the career politician in Britain. *Politics*, 32(1): 31–8.

Cowley, P., and Stuart, M. (2010). Party rules, OK: Voting in the House of Commons on the Human Fertilisation and Embryology Bill. *Parliamentary Affairs*, 63(1): 173–81.

Cowley, P., and Stuart, M. (2012). A coalition with two wobbly wings: Backbench dissent in the House of Commons. *Political Insight*, 3: 8–11.

Cowley, P., and Stuart, M. (2014). In the brown stuff? Labour backbench dissent under Gordon Brown, 2007–2010. *Contemporary British History*, 28: 1–23.

Crewe, E. (2014). *The House of Commons: An Anthropology of MPs at Work*. London: Bloomsbury.

Crewe, E., and Müller, M. (eds). (2006). *Rituals in Parliament*. Frankfurt am Main: Peter Lang GmbH.

Crewe, I. (1985). MPs and their constituents in Britain: How strong are the links? In V. Bogdanor (ed), *Representatives of the People?* Aldershot: Gower, pp 44–65.

Crick, B. (1962). *In Defense of Politics*. London: Continuum.

Cross, W. P., Katz, R. S., and Pruysers, S. (eds). (2018). *The Personalization of Democratic Politics and the Challenge for Political Parties*. London: Rowman & Littlefield International, ECPR Press.

Cruddas, J. (2006). New Labour and the withering away of the working class? *Political Quarterly*, 77(1): 205–13.

Cwalina, W., Falkowski, A., and Newman, B. (2008). *A Cross-cultural Theory of Voter Behaviour*. New York: The Haworth Press.

Daniel, W. T. (2015). *Career Behaviour and the European Parliament: All Roads Lead Through Brussels?* Oxford: Oxford University Press.

Dahlerup, D. (2006). The story of the theory of critical mass. *Politics and Gender*, 2(4): 511–22.

Dalton, R. J., and Wattenberg, M. P. (2000). *Parties without Partisans: Political Change in Advanced Industrial Democracies, Comparative Politics*. Oxford: Oxford University Press.

Dalton, R. J., and Weldon, S. (2007). Partisanship and party system institutionalization. *Party Politics*, 13(2): 179–96.

Dean, J., and Maiguashca, B. (2020). Did somebody say populism? Towards a renewal and reorientation of populism studies, *Journal of Political Ideologies*, doi: 10.1080/13569317.2020.1699712.

Democratic Audit (2016). Elected Chairs do not seem to have brought a new kind of parliamentarian to Select Committee. www.democraticaudit.com/2016/07/06/elected-chairs-do-not-seem-to-have-brought-a-new-kind-of-parliamentarian-to-select-committees/

De Neve, J.-E. (2015). Personality, childhood experience and political ideology. *Political Psychology*, 36: 55–75.

DeShazo, J. R., and Fermo, G. (2002). Designing choice sets for stated preference methods: The effects of complexity on choice consistency. *Journal of Environmental Economics and Management*, 44(1): 123–143.

De Wet, J. P., Bacher, J., and Wetzelhütter, D. (2016). Towards greater validity in Schwartz's portrait values indicator using experimental research. *Quality and Quantity*, 50: 1567–87.

Dietrich, B. J., Lasley, S., Mondak, J. J., Remmel, M. L., and Turner, J. (2012). Personality and legislative politics: The Big Five trait dimensions among US state legislators. *Political Psychology*, 33(2): 195–210.

Dillman, D. A., Smyth, J. D., and Christian, L. M. (2014). *Internet, Phone, Mail, and Mixed Mode Surveys: The Tailored Design Method* (4th edn). Hoboken: Wiley Publishing.

Dodd, L. C. (1994). Political learning and political change: Understanding development across time. In L. Dodd and C. Jillson (eds), *The Dynamics of American Politics*. Boulder, CO: Westview, pp 331–64.

Dodson, D. E. (2006). *The Impact of Women in Congress*. Oxford: Oxford University Press.

Dolan, K. (2004). *Voting for Women: How the Public Evaluates Women Candidates*. Boulder, CO: Westview.

Domhoff, G. W. (2005). *Who Rules America? Power, Politics, and Social Change* (5th edn). California: McGraw-Hill.

Dommett, K., and Flinders, M. (2015). The Centre Strikes Back: Meta-Governance, Delegation, And The Core Executive In The United Kingdom, 2010–14. *Public Administration*, 93(1): 1–16.

Dorey, P. (2011). *British Conservatism: The Politics and Philosophy of Inequality*. London: I.B. Tauris.

Döring, A. K., Schwartz, S. H., Cieciuch, J., Groenen, P. J., Glatzel, V., Harasimczuk, J., Janowicz, N., Nyagolova, M., Scheefer, E. R., Allritz, M., Milfont, T. L. and Bilsky, W. (2015). Cross-cultural evidence of value structures and priorities in childhood. *British Journal of Psychology*, 106: 675–99.

Dovi, S. (2002). Preferable descriptive representatives: Will just any woman, Black or Latino do? *American Political Science Review*, 96(4): 729–43.

Downs, A. (1957). *An Economic Theory of Democracy*. New York: Macmillan.

Druckman, J. N. (2004). Political preference formation: Competition, deliberation, and the (ir)relevance of framing effects. *American Political Science Review*, 98(4): 671–86.

Dryzek, J. S. (2000). *Deliberative Democracy and Beyond: Liberals, Critics, Contestations*. Oxford: Oxford University Press.

Duckitt, J. (2001). A dual-process cognitive-motivational theory of ideology and prejudice. In M. P. Zanna (ed), *Advances in Experimental Social Psychology* (Vol 33). San Diego: Academic Press, pp 41–112.

Durose, C., Gains, F., Richardson, L., Combs, R., Broome, K., and Eason, C. (2011). *Pathways to Politics*. Manchester: Equality and Human Rights Commission.

Durose, C., Richardson, L., Combs, R., Eason, C., and Gains, F. (2013). Acceptable difference: Diversity, representation and pathways to UK politics. *Parliamentary Affairs*, 66: 246–67.

Durose, C., Justice, J., Skelcher, C. (2014). Governing at arm's length: Eroding or enhancing democracy? *Policy & Politics*, 43(1): 137–53.

Ehsan, M. R. (2018). What matters? Non-electoral youth political participation in austerity Britain, *Societies*, 8(101): 1–9.

Elgie, R. (2011). Core executive studies two decades on. *Public Administration*, 89(1): 64–77.

Elgot, J. (2017). Proposals to increase number of female MPs in Commons rejected. *The Guardian*, 7 September. www.theguardian.com/politics/2017/sep/07/uk-rejects-proposals-to-make-parliament-more-representative-of-women

Ellis, C., and Stimson, J. A. (2012). *Ideology in America*. New York: Cambridge University Press.

English, P. (2019a). Visible, elected, but effectively nominal: Visibility as a barrier maintaining the political underrepresentation of Britain's immigrant origin communities. *Parliamentary Affairs*, 72: 542–60.

English, P. (2019b). Visibly restricted: Public opinion and the representation of immigrant origin communities across Great Britain. *Ethnic and Racial Studies*, 42(9): 1437–55.

ESS Round 8: European Social Survey Round 8 Data (2016). Data file edition 2.1. NSD – Norwegian Centre for Research Data, Norway – Data Archive and distributor of ESS data for ESS ERIC. doi:10.21338/NSD-ESS8-2016.

Evans, E., and Kenny, M. (2016). Working for women? The emergence and impact of the Women's Equality Party. Paper presented at the American Political Sciences Association's Annual Meeting, Philadelphia, PA, 1–4 September.

Evans, G., and Tilley, J. (2015). The new class war: Excluding the working class in 21st-century Britain. *Juncture*, 21(4): 298–304.

Evans, G., and Tilley, J. (2017). *The New Politics of Class: The Political Exclusion of the British Working Class*. Oxford, Oxford University Press.

Evans, M., Stoker, G., and Nasir, J. (2013). *How Do Australians Imagine Their Democracy? Australian Survey of Political Engagement Findings 2013*. Canberra: Australian and New Zealand School of Government.

Evans, S. (2008). Consigning its past to history? David Cameron and the Conservative Party. *Parliamentary Affairs*, 61(2), 291–314.

Eyal, T., Sagristano, M. D., Trope, Y., Liberman, N., and Chaikene, S. (2009). When values matter: Expressing values in behavioural intentions for the near vs. distant future. *Journal of Experimental Social Psychology*, 45(1): 35–43.

Farrell, D., and Webb, P. (2000). Political parties as campaign organizations. In R. Dalton and M. Wattenberg (eds), *Parties without Partisans: Political Change in Advanced Industrial Democracies.* Oxford: Oxford University Press.

Fatke, M. (2016). Personality traits and political ideology: A first global assessment. *Political Psychology*, 38: 881–99.

Feather, N. T. (1995). Values, valences, and choice: The influence of values on the perceived attractiveness and choice of alternatives. *Journal of Personality and Social Psychology*, 68: 1135–51.

Feldman, S. (2003). Values, ideology, and structure of political attitudes. In D. O. Sears, L. Huddy, and R. Jervis (eds), *Oxford Handbook of Political Psychology*. New York: Oxford University Press, pp 477–508.

Feldman, S., and Johnston, C. (2013). Understanding political ideology. *Political Psychology*, 35: 337–58.

Fenno, R. (1977). U.S. House members in their constituencies: An exploration. *American Political Science Review*, 71: 883–917.

Fernandes, J. M., Geese, L., and Schwemmer, C. (2018). The impact of candidate selection rules and electoral vulnerability on legislative behaviour in comparative perspective. *European Journal of Political Research*, 58(1): 270–91.

Fernandez-Vazquez, P. (2014). And yet it moves the effect of election platforms on party policy images. *Comparative Political Studies*, 47(14): 1919–44.

Fisher, L. (2015). The growing power and autonomy of House of Commons select committees: Causes and effects. *Political Quarterly*, 86: 419–26.

Fisher, S. D., Heath, A. F., Sanders, D., and Sobolewska, M. (2014). Candidate ethnicity and vote choice in Britain. *British Journal of Political Science*, 45: 883–905.

Fiske, S. T., Cuddy, A. J. C., and Glick, P. (2007). Universal dimensions of social cognition: warmth and competence. *Trends in Cognitive Sciences*, 11(2): 77–83.

Flinders, M. (2010). In defence of politics. *Political Quarterly*, 81(3): 309–26.

Flinders, M. (2012). *Defending Politics: Why Democracy Matters in the Twenty-First Century*. Oxford: Oxford University Press.

Flinders, M., Weinberg, A., Weinberg, J., Geddes, M., and Kwiatkowski, R. (2018). Governing under pressure? The mental wellbeing of politicians. *Parliamentary Affairs*, 73(2): 253–273. doi:10.1093/pa/gsy046.

Ford, R., and Goodwin, M. (2010). Angry white men: Individual and contextual predictors of support for the British National Party. *Political Studies*, 58(1): 1–25.

Fox, R., and Korris, M. (2012). A fresh start? The orientation and induction of new MPs at Westminster following the 2010 General Election. *Parliamentary Affairs*, 65: 559–75.

Fox, R. L., and Lawless, J. (2004). Entering the arena? Gender and the decision to run for office. *American Journal of Political Science*, 48(2): 264–80.

Fox, R., and Lawless, J. (2014). Uncovering the origins of the gender gap in political ambition. *American Political Science Review*, 108(3): 499–519.

Franklin, M. N., and Norton, P. (1993). *Parliamentary Questions*. Oxford: Clarendon Press.

Franklin, M. N., and Tappin, M. (1977). Early Day Motions as unobtrusive measures of backbench opinion in Britain. *British Journal of Political Science*, 7(1): 49–69.

Fridkin, K., and Kenney, P. (2014). How the gender of US senators influences people's understanding and engagement in politics. *Journal of Politics*, 76(4): 1017–31.

Friedman, M. (1953). *Essays in Positive Economics*. Chicago, IL: University of Chicago Press.

Gamble, A. (1990). Theories of British government. *Political Studies*, 38(3): 404–20.

Gandal, N., Roccas, S., Sagiv, L., and Wrzesniewski, A. (2005). Personal value priorities of economists. *Human Relations*, 58(10): 1227–52.

Garzia, D. (2011). The personalization of politics in western democracies: Causes and consequences on leader–follower relationships. *Leadership Quarterly*, 22(4): 697–709.

Garzia, D. (2013). Party and leader effects in parliamentary elections: Towards a reassessment. *Politics*, 32(3): 175–85.

Geddes, M. (2020). *Dramas at Westminster: Select Committees and the Quest for Accountability*. Manchester: Manchester University Press.

Gee, G., Hazell, R., Malleson, K., and O'Brien, P. (2015). *The Politics of Judicial Independence in the UK's Changing Constitution*. Cambridge: Cambridge University Press.

Gerber, A. S., Huber, G. A., Doherty, D., Dowling, C. M., and Ha, S. (2010). Personality and political attitudes: Relationships across issue domains and political contexts. *American Political Science Review*, 104: 111–33.

Gibson, J. (1966). *The Senses Considered as Perceptual Systems*. Boston: Houghton Mifflin.

Gibson, J. L. (1981). Personality and elite political behaviour: The influence of self esteem on judicial decision making. *Journal of Politics*, 43(1): 104–25.

Goodwin, G. P., Piazza, J., and Rozin, P. (2014). Moral character predominates in person perception and evaluation. *Journal of Personality and Social Psychology*, 106(1): 148–68.

Gouveia, V. V., Milfont, T. L., and Guerra, V. M. (2014). Functional theory of human values: Testing its content and structure. *Personality and Individual Differences*, 60: 41–47.

Graham, J., Haidt, J., and Nosek, B. (2009). Liberals and Conservatives rely on different sets of moral foundations. *Journal of Personality and Social Psychology*, 96(5): 1029–46.

Griffin, J. D., and Keane, M. (2006). Descriptive representation and the composition of African American turnout. *American Journal of Political Science*, 50(4): 998–1012.

Groenendyk, E. (2018). Competing motives in a polarized electorate: Political responsiveness, identity defensiveness, and the rise of partisan antipathy. *Advances in Political Psychology*, 39(1): 159-171. doi: 10.1111/pops.12481.

Habermas, J. (1996). *Between Facts and Norms: Contributions to a Discourse Theory of Law and Democracy.* Cambridge, MA: MIT Press.

Hagelund, C., and Goddard, J. (2015). *How to Run a Country: A Parliament of Lawmakers.* London: Reform.

Haidt, J., Graham, J., and Joseph, C. (2009). Above and below left-right: Ideological narratives and moral foundations. *Psychological Inquiry*, 20: 110–119.

Hair, J. F., William C., Black, B., Babin, J., and Anderson, R. E. (2006). *Multivariate Data Analysis* (7th edn). New York: Pearson Education.

Hall, E. (2018). Integrity in democratic politics. *British Journal of Politics and International Relations*, 20(2): 395–408.

Hanania, R. (2017). The personalities of politicians: A Big Five study of American legislators. *Personality and Individual Differences*, 108: 164–67.

Hanel, H. P., Vione, K. C., Hahn, U., and Maio, G. R. (2017). Value instantiations: The missing link between values and behaviour? In S. Roccas and L. Sagiv (eds), *Values and Behaviour: Taking a Cross Cultural Perspective.* Switzerland AG: Springer International Publishing, pp 175–90.

Hansard Society (2019). *Audit of Political Engagement 16: The 2019 Report.* London: The Hansard Society.

Hardman, I. (2018). *Why We Get the Wrong Politicians.* London: Atlantic Books.

Hatier, C. (2012). 'Them' and 'us': Demonising politicians by moral double standards. *Contemporary Politics*, 18(4): 467–80.

Hauser, J. R. (2014). Considerations et heuristics. *Journal of Business Research*, 67(8): 1688–1699.

Hay, C. (2007). *Why We Hate Politics*. Cambridge: Polity Press.

Hay, C. (2009). Academic political science. *Political Quarterly*, 80(4): 545–52.

Hay, C., and Farrell, S. (eds) (2014). *The Legacy of Thatcherism: Assessing and Exploring Thatcherite Social and Economic Policies*. Oxford: Oxford University Press.

Hay, C., and Stoker, G. (2009). Revitalising politics: Have we lost the plot? *Representation,* 45(3): 225–236.

Hayes, D. (2009). Has television personalised voting behaviour? *Political Behaviour*, 31: 231–60.

Hazan, R. Y. (2003). Does cohesion equal discipline? Towards a conceptual delineation. *Journal of Legislative Studies*, 9(4): 1–11.

HC Deb (2019). Hansard, vol 664, col 497, 9 September. https://hansard.parliament.uk/Commons/2019-09-09/debates/11E8CA69-2C98-4F9B-B6AF-FCD403463BDD/Speaker'SStatement

Heath, A., Fisher, S., Rosenblatt, G., Sanders, D., and Sobolewska, M. (2013). *The Political Integration of Ethnic Minorities in Britain*. Oxford: Oxford University Press.

Heffernan, R. (2003). Prime ministerial predominance? Core executive politics in the UK. *British Journal of Politics and International Relations*, 5(2): 347–72.

Herman, L. E. (2017). Democratic partisanship: from theoretical ideal to empirical standard. *American Political Science Review*, 111(4): 1–17. doi: 10.1017/S0003055417000247.

Hindmoor, A. (2017). *What's Left Now? The History and Future of Social Democracy*. Oxford: Oxford University Press.

Hindmoor, A., Larkin, P., and Kennon, A. (2009). Assessing the influence of select committees in the UK: The Education and Skills Committee, 1997–2005. *Journal of Legislative Studies*, 15: 71–89.

Hinterleitner, M., and Sager, F. (2015). Avoiding blame: A comprehensive framework and the Australian Home Insulation Program fiasco. *Policy Studies Journal*, 43(1): 139–61.

Hitlin, S. (2003). Values as the core of personal identity: Drawing links between two theories of self. *Social Psychology Quarterly*, 66(2): 118–37.

Hix, S., Noury, A., and Roland, G. (2007). *Democratic Politics in the European Parliament*. Cambridge, MA: Cambridge University Press.

Holland, J. L. (1997). *Making Vocational Choices: A Theory of Vocational Personalities and Work Environments*. Odessa: PAR.

Holman, M., and Schneider, M. (2017). Gender, race, and political ambition: How intersectionality and frames influence interest in political office. *Politics, Groups, and Identities*, 6: 264–80.

Holmberg, S. (2007). Partisanship reconsidered. In R. Dalton and H.-D. Klingemann (eds), *The Oxford Handbook of Political Behaviour.* Oxford: Oxford University Press.

Hood, C. (2002). The risk game and the blame game. *Government and Opposition*, 37(1): 15–37.

Hood, C. (2007). What happens when transparency meets blame-avoidance? *Public Management Review*, 9(2): 191–210.

Hornsey, M. J., Majkut, L., Terry, D. J., and McKimmie, B. M. (2003). On being loud and proud: Non-conformity and counter conformity to group norms. *British Journal of Social Psychology*, 42(3): 319–35.

House of Commons Information Office (2010). Factsheet P3: Early Day Motions. Series P: No. 3.

Huddy, L. (2001). From social to political identity: A critical examination of social identity theory. *Political Psychology*, 22(1): 127–56.

Huddy, L., and Bankert, A. (2017). Political partisanship as a social identity. In W. Thompson (ed), *Oxford Research Encyclopaedia of Politics*. Oxford: Oxford University Press.

Huddy, L., and Terkildsen, N. (1993). Gender stereotypes and the perception of male and female candidates. *American Journal of Political Science*, 37(1): 119–47.

Huddy, L., Mason, L., and Aarøe, L. (2015). Expressive partisanship: Campaign involvement, political emotion, and partisan identity. *American Political Science Review*, 109(1): 1–17.

Huddy, L., Bankert, A., and Davies, C. (2018). Expressive versus instrumental partisanship in multiparty European systems. *Advances in Political Psychology*, 39(1): 173–199. doi: 10.1111/pops.12482.

Huertas-Garcia, R., Gázquez-Abad, J. C., and Forgas-Coll, S. (2016). A design strategy for improving adaptive conjoint analysis. *Journal of Business and Industrial Marketing*, 31(3): 328–38.

Huggins, C. (2014). Arranging and conducting elite interviews: Practical considerations. *SAGE Research Methods Cases.* https://methods.sagepub.com/case/arranging-and-conducting-elite-interviews-practical-considerations. doi:10.4135/978144627305013514687.

Hundsdoerfer, J., Sielaff, C., Blaufus, K., Kiesewetter, D., and Weimann, J. (2013). The influence of tax labeling and tax earmarking on the willingness to contribute – A conjoint analysis. *Schmalenbach Business Review*, 65: 359–77.

Hunt, K., Shlomo, N., and Addington-Hall, J. (2013). Participant recruitment in sensitive surveys: A comparative trial of 'opt in' versus 'opt out' approaches. *BMC Medical Research Methodology*, 13(3): 1–8.

Ignatieff, M. (2013). *Fire and Ashes: Success and Failure in Politics*. London: Harvard University Press.

Ilonszki, G., and Edinger, M. (2007). Members of Parliament in Central Eastern Europe: A parliamentary elite in the making. *Journal of Legislative Studies*, 13: 142–63.

Iyengar, S., and Westwood, S. (2014). Fear and loathing across party lines: New evidence on group polarization. *American Journal of Political Science*, 59(3): 690–707.

Jackson, M., and Smith, R. (1996). Inside moves and outside views: An Australian case study of elite and public perceptions of political corruption. *Governance: An International Journal of Policy and Administration*, 9(1): 23–41.

Jagers, J., and Walgrave, S. (2007). Populism as political communication style: An empirical study of political parties' discourse in Belgium. *European Journal of Political Research*, 46: 319–45.

Jennings, W., Stoker, G., and Twyman, J. (2016). The dimensions and impact of political discontent in Britain. *Parliamentary Affairs*, 69: 876–900.

Jenny, M., and Müller, W. C. (2012). Parliamentary roles of MPs. In M. Blomgren and O. Rozenberg (eds), *Parliamentary Roles in Modern Legislatures*. Abingdon: Routledge.

Johnston, R. (2006). Party identification: Unmoved mover or sum of preferences? *Annual Review of Political Science*, 9: 329–51.

Jonason, P. K. (2014). Personality and politics. *Personality and Individual Differences*, 71(1): 181–84.

Jost, J. T. (2006). The end of the end of ideology. *American Psychologist*, 61: 651–70.

Jost, J. T., Nosek, B. A., and Gosling, S. D. (2008). Ideology: Its resurgence in social, personality, and political psychology. *Perspectives on Psychological Science*, 3(2): 126–36.

Jost, J. T., Federico, C. M., and Napier, J. L. (2009). Political ideology: Its structure, functions, and elective affinities. *Annual Review of Psychology*, 60: 307–37.

Judge, D. (1993). *The Parliamentary State*. London: Sage.

Judge, D. (2005). *Representation: Theory and Practice in Britain*. London: Routledge.

Kahneman, D. (2011). *Thinking, Fast and Slow*. London: Penguin.

Kam, C. J. (2009). *Party Discipline and Parliamentary Politics*. Cambridge: Cambridge University Press.

Kane, J., and Patapan, H. (2012). *The Democratic Leader: How Democracy Defines, Empowers, and Limits Its Leaders*. Oxford: Oxford University Press.

Kant, I. (1991). *The Metaphysics of Morals* (1785). Cambridge: Cambridge University Press.

Kanthak, K., and Woon, J. (2015). Women don't run? Election aversion and candidate entry. *American Journal of Political Science*, 59(3): 595–612.

Karp, J. A., and Banducci, S. A. (2008). When politics is not just a man's game: Women's representative and political engagement. *Electoral Studies*, 27: 105–15.

Karpowitz, C., Monson, Q., and Preece, J. (2017). How to elect more women: Gender and candidate success in a field experiment. *American Journal of Political Science*, 61(4): 927–43.

Kastenmüller, A., Greitemeyer, T., Jonas, E., Fischer, P., and Frey, D. (2010). Selective exposure: The impact of collectivism and individualism. *British Journal of Social Psychology*, 49: 745–63.

Katz, R. S., and Mair, P. (2009). The cartel party thesis: A restatement. *Perspectives on Politics*, 7(4): 753–66.

Kazee, T. A. (1994). The emergence of congressional candidates. In T. Kazee (ed), *Who Runs for Congress? Ambition, Context, and Candidate Emergence*. Washington, DC: Congressional Quarterly.

Keane, J. (2009). *The Life and Death of Democracy*. London: Simon & Schuster.

Keane, J. (2011). Monitory democracy? In S. Alonso, J. Keane, and W. Merkel (eds), *The Future of Representative Democracy*. Cambridge: Cambridge University Press, pp 212–35.

Kellermann, M. (2013). Sponsoring Early Day Motions in the British House of Commons as a response to electoral vulnerability. *Political Science Research and Methods*, 1(2): 263–80.

Kellermann, M. (2016). Electoral vulnerability, constituency focus, and parliamentary questions in the House of Commons. *British Journal of Politics and International Relations*, 18(1): 90–106.

Kelley, K., Clark, B., Brown, V., and Sitzia, J. (2003). Good practice in the conduct and reporting of survey research. *International Journal of Qualitative Health Care*, 15: 261–66.

Kelso, A. (2009). *Parliamentary Reform at Westminster*. Manchester: Manchester University Press.

Kelsen, H. (1992). *Introduction to the Problems of Legal Theory*. Oxford: Clarendon Press.

Kelsen, H. (1999). *General Theory of Law and State*. Union, NJ: The Lawbook Exchange.

Kim, S., and Vandenabeele, W. (2010). A strategy for building public service motivation research internationally. *Public Administration Review*, 70: 701–9.

King, A. (1981). The rise of the career politician in Britain – And its consequences. *British Journal of Political Science*, 11: 249–85.

King, A., and Crewe, I. (2013). *The Blunders of Our Governments*. London: Oneworld Print.

Kirchheimer, O. (1966). The transformation of the western European party systems. In J. La Palombara and M. Weiner (eds), *Political Parties and Political Development*. Princeton, NJ: Princeton University Press, pp 177–200.

Kirkup, J. (2014). UKIP conference: Nigel Farage's damnation of Britain as a foreign land will do him no favours. *Telegraph*, 28 February. http://blogs.telegraph.co.uk/news/jameskirkup/100261717/ukip-conference-nigel-farages-damnation-of-britain-as-a-foreign-land-will-do-him-no-favours/

Kitschelt, H. (2006). Parties and political intermediation. In K. Nash and A. Scott (eds), *The Blackwell Companion to Political Sociology*. Oxford: Blackwell, pp 144–157.

Knafo, A., and Sagiv, L. (2004). Values and work environment: Mapping 32 occupations. *European Journal of Psychology of Education*, 19(3): 255–73.

Kolstad, I., and Wiig, A. (2018). How do voters respond to information on self-serving elite behaviour? UNU-WIDER 2018: WIDER Working Paper 2018/11.

Koplinskaya, E. (2017). Substantive representation in the UK Parliament: Examining parliamentary questions for written answers, 1997–2012. *Parliamentary Affairs*, 70: 111–31.

Körösényi, A. (2018). Political elites and democracy. In H. Best and J. Higley (eds), *The Palgrave Handbook of Political Elites*. London: Palgrave MacMillan, pp 41–52.

Krehbiel, K. (1993). Where's the party? *British Journal of Political Science*, 23: 235–66.

Krehbiel, K. (1999). Paradoxes of Parties in Congress. *Legislative Studies Quarterly*, 14: 31–64.

Krosnick, J. A., and Presser, S. (2010). *Question and Questionnaire Design*. https://web.stanford.edu/dept/communication/faculty/krosnick/docs/2009/2009_handbook_krosnick.pdf

Kuklinski, J. H., Quirk, P. J., Jerit, J., and Rich, R. R. (2001). The political environment and citizen decision making: Information, motivation and policy tradeoffs. *American Journal of Political Science*, 45: 410–24.

Kurz, T., Augoustinos, M., and Crabb, S. (2010). Contesting the 'national interest' and maintaining 'our lifestyle': A discursive analysis of political rhetoric around climate change. *British Journal of Social Psychology*, 49(3): 601–25.

Kwiatkowski, R. (2012). Politicians and power: MPs in the UK Parliament. In A. Weinberg (ed), *The Psychology of Politicians*. Cambridge: Cambridge University Press, pp 39–58.

Lakoff, G. (2004). *Don't Think of an Elephant! Know Your Values and Frame the Debate: The Essential Guide for Progressives.* White River Junction, VT: Chelsea Green.

Lamont, N. (2014). The people have spoken on mass immigration: So will the political class hear them? *Daily Mail*, 18 June. www.dailymail. co.uk/debate/article-2660839/NORMAN-LAMONT-The-people-spoken-mass-immigration-So-political-class-hear-them. html#ixzz35Baf35PP

Laustsen, L. (2016). Choosing the right candidate: Observational and experimental evidence that Conservatives and Liberals prefer powerful and warm candidate personalities, respectively. *Political Behaviour*, 39: 883–908. doi: 10.1007/s11109-016-9384-2.

Laustsen, L., and Bor, A. (2017). The relative weight of character traits in political candidate evaluations: Warmth is more important than competence, leadership and integrity, *Electoral Studies*, 49: 96–107. doi: 10.1016/j.electstud.2017.08.001.

Lasswell, H. D. (1930). *Psychopathology and Politics*. Chicago: University of Chicago Press.

Lawless, J. (2012). *Becoming a Candidate: Political Ambition and the Decision to Run for Office.* Cambridge: Cambridge University Press.

Lawless, J., and Richard L. Fox. (2005). *It Takes A Candidate: Why Women Don't Run for Office.* New York: Cambridge University Press.

Lawless, J., and Richard L. Fox. (2010). *It Still Takes A Candidate: Why Women Don't Run for Office.* New York: Cambridge University Press.

Layman, G. C., and Carsey, T. M. (2002). Party polarization and 'conflict extension' in the American electorate. *American Journal of Political Science*, 46(4): 786–802.

Leapman, B. (2005). *Is Your MP Good Value?* London: Evening Standard.

Leimgruber, P. (2011). Values and votes: The indirect effect of personal values on voting behaviour. *Swiss Political Science Review*, 17(2): 107–27.

Leiter, D., and Clark, M. (2015). Valence and satisfaction with democracy: A cross-national analysis of nine western European democracies. *European Journal of Political Research*, 54(3): 543–62.

Leiter, D., Clark, A., and Clark, M. (2019). Winners and losers reconsidered: party support, character valence, and satisfaction with democracy. *European Political Science Review*, 11(3): 285-300.

Lewis, G. J., and Bates, T. C. (2011). From left to right: How the personality system allows basic traits to influence politics via characteristic moral adaptations. *British Journal of Psychology*, 102(3): 546–58.

Li, Y., and Heath, A. (2010). Struggling onto the ladder, climbing the rungs: Employment status and class position by minority ethnic groups in Britain (1972–2005). In J. Stillwell, P. Norman, C. Thomas, and P. Surridge (eds), *Population, Employment, Health and Well-being.* London: Springer, pp 83–97.

Liberal Democrats (2013). Liberal Democrat Federal Constitution. http://www.libdems.org.uk/constitution.aspx

Lijphart, A. (2012). *Patterns of Democracy.* 2nd ed. New Haven, CT: Yale University Press.

Lovenduski, J. (2015). *Gendering Politics, Feminising Political Science.* Colchester: ECPR Press.

Lord, C. G., Desforges, D. M., Fein, S., Pugh, M. A., and Lepper, M. R. (1994). Typicality effects in attitudes toward social policies: A concept-mapping approach. *Journal of Personality and Social Psychology*, 66(4): 658–673.

Maestas, C., Fulton, S., Maisel, L. S., and Stone, W. J. (2006). When to risk it? Institutions, ambitions, and the decision to run for the U.S. House. *American Political Science Review*, 100(2): 195–208.

Mahoney, J., and Schensul, D. (2006). Historical context and path dependence. In R. Goodin and C. Tilly (eds). *Oxford Handbook of Contextual Political Analysis.* New York: Oxford University Press, pp 454–71.

Mair, P. (2003). Political parties and democracy: What sort of future. *Central European Political Science* Review, 4(13): 6–20.

Mansbridge, J. (1999). Should Blacks represent Blacks and women represent women? A contingent 'yes'. *Journal of Politics*, 61(3): 628–57.

Mansbridge, J. (2003). Rethinking representation. *American Political Science Review*, 97: 515–28.

March, J. G and Olsen, J. P. (1989). *Rediscovering Institutions: The Organisational Basis of Politics.* New York: Free Press.

Margetts, H. (2011). Single seat. In J. M. Colomer (ed), *Personal Representation: The Neglected Dimension of Electoral Systems.* Colchester: ECPR Press, pp 35–52.

Marsh, D. (2011). The new orthodoxy: The differentiated polity model. *Public Administration*, 89: 32–48.

Marsh, I. (2016). The Commons Select Committee system in the 2015–20 Parliament. *Political Quarterly*, 87: 96–103.

Martin, L. W., and Vanberg, G. (2011). *Parliaments and Coalitions: The Role of Legislative Institutions in Multiparty Governance.* Oxford: Oxford University Press.

Martin, S. (2011). Using parliamentary questions to measure constituency focus: An application to the Irish case. *Political Studies*, 59(2): 472–88.

Mason, L. (2015). 'I disrespectfully agree': The differential effects of partisan sorting on social and issue polarization. *American Journal of Political Science*, 59(1): 128–45.

Matthews, F. (2017). Majoritarianism reinterpreted: Effective representation and the quality of Westminster democracy. *Parliamentary Affairs*, 71(1): 50-72. doi: 10.1093/pa/gsx011.

Mazur, A. G., and Pollock, M. A. (2009). Gender and public policy in Europe: An introduction. *Comparative European Politics*, 7(1): 1–11.

McAdams, D. P., and Pals, J. L. (2006). A new Big Five: Fundamental principles for an integrative science of personality. *American Psychologist*, 61: 204–17.

McAllister, I. (2000). Keeping them honest: Public and elite perceptions of ethical conduct among Australian legislators. *Political Studies*, 48(1): 22–37.

McAllister, I. (2007). The personalization of politics. In R. J. Dalton and H. D. Klingemann (eds), *Oxford Handbook of Political Behaviour.* Oxford: Oxford University Press, pp 571–588.

McAllister, I. (2016). Candidates and voting choice. *Oxford Research Encyclopaedia of Politics.* https://oxfordre.com/politics/view/10.1093/acrefore/9780190228637.001.0001/acrefore-9780190228637-e-73?print=pdf

McGraw, K. M. (2011). Candidate impression and evaluations. In J. N. Druckman, D. P. Green, J. H. Kuklinski, and A. Lupia (eds), *Cambridge Handbook of Experimental Political Science.* Cambridge: Cambridge University Press, pp 338–364.

Meakin, A. (2017). Assault in the corridors of power: now can we talk seriously about rebuilding Westminster? https://theconversation.com/assault-in-the-corridors-of-power-now-can-we-talk-seriously-about-rebuilding-westminster-86863

Medvic, S. K. (2013). *In Defence of Politicians: The Expectations Trap and Its Threat to Democracy.* London: Routledge.

Mény, Y., and Surel, Y. (2002). *Democracies and the Populist Challenge.* London: Palgrave Macmillan UK.

Meserve, S., Pemstein, D., and Bernhard, W. T. (2009). Political ambition and legislative behaviour in the European Parliament. *Journal of Politics*, 71(3): 1015–32.

Meyrowitz, J. (1985). *No Sense of Place: The Impact of Electronic Media on Social Behaviour*. New York. Oxford University Press.

Milazzo, C., and Townsley, J. (2019). Conceived in Harlesden: Candidate-centred campaigning in British general elections. *Parliamentary Affairs*, 73(1): 127-146. https://doi.org/10.1093/pa/gsy040

Miller, S., and Gatta, J. (2006). The use of mixed methods models and designs in the human sciences: Problems and prospects. *Quality & Quantity*, 40(4): 595–610.

Mills, C. W. (1956). *The Power Elite*. Oxford: Oxford University Press.

Moncrief, G. F., Squire, P., and Jewell, M. E. (2001). *Who Runs for the Legislature?* Upper Saddle River, NJ: Prentice Hall.

Mondak, J. J. (2010). *Personality and the Foundations of Political Behaviour*. Cambridge: Cambridge University Press.

Montesquieu, C.-L. (2002). *The Spirit of Laws* [1798]. New York: Prometheus Books.

Mughan, A. (2000). *Media and the Presidentialisation of Parliamentary Elections*. London: Palgrave.

Müller, W. C., and Strøm, K. (1999). Political parties and hard choices. In W. C. Müller and K. Strøm (eds), *Policy, Office, or Votes? How Political Parties in Western Europe Make Hard Choices*. New York: Cambridge University Press, pp 1–35.

Murrary, H. A. (1968). Personality: contemporary viewpoints: Components of an evolving personological system. *International Encyclopaedia of the Social Sciences*. Vol. 12. New York: Macmillan, p 9

Mycock, A. (2016). The politics of England. *Political Quarterly*, 87(4): 534-545. doi: 10.1111/1467-923X.12283.

Naím, M. (2013). *The End of Power: From Boardrooms to Battlefields and Churches to States, Why Being In Charge Isn't What It Used to Be*. New York: Basic Books.

Nam, H. H., Jost, J. T., and Van Bavel, J. J. (2013). 'Not for all the tea in China!' Political ideology and the avoidance of dissonance-arousing situations. *PLoS ONE*, 8(4): PLoS ONE 8(4): e59837. doi:10.1371/journal.pone.0059837.

Näsström, S. (2015). Democratic representation beyond election. *Constellations*, 22(1): 1-12. doi: 10.1111/1467–8675.12123.

National Readership Survey (NRS). (2016). Social grade. www.nrs.co.uk/nrs-print/lifestyle-and-classification-data/social-grade/

Navarro, J. (2009). *Les Députés Européens et leur Rôle: Sociologie des Pratiques Parlementaires*. Brussels: Editions de l'Université de Bruxelles.

Neisser, U. (1967). *Cognitive Psychology*. New York: Appleton-Century-Crofts.

Nelson, K., Garcia, R. E., Brown, J., Mangione, C. M., Louis, T. A., Keelier, E., Cretin, S. (2002). Do patient consent procedures affect participation rates in health services research? *Medical Care*, 40: 283–88.

Neuman, W.L. (2000). *Social Research Methods. Qualitative and Quantitative Approaches*. Boston: Allyn & Bacon.

Nicholson, S. P. (2012). Polarizing cues. *American Journal of Political Science*, 56(1): 52–66.

Nimmo, D., and Savage, R. L. (1976). *Candidates and Their Images*. Santa Monica, CA: Goodyear.

Nørgaard, A. S., and Klemmensen R. (2018). The personalities of Danish MPs: Trait- and aspect- level differences. *Journal of Personality*, 87(2): 1–9.

Norris, P. (1997). The puzzle of constituency service. *Journal of Legislative Studies*. 3(2): 29–49.

Norris, P. (2011). *Democratic Deficits*. Cambridge: Cambridge University Press.

Norris, P., and Lovenduski, J. (1993). 'If only more candidates came forward': Supply-side explanations of candidate selection in Britain. *British Journal of Political Science*, 23(3): 373–408.

Norris, P., and Lovenduski, J. (1995). *Political Recruitment: Gender, Race and Class in the British Parliament*. Cambridge: Cambridge University Press.

Norton, P. (1980). *Dissension in the House of Commons, 1974–1979*. Oxford: Clarendon.

Norton, P. (2001). Playing by the rules: The constraining hand of parliamentary procedure. *Journal of Legislative Studies*, 7(3): 13–33.

Norton, P. (2012). Parliament and citizens in the United Kingdom. *Journal of Legislative Studies*, 18: 403–18.

Norton, P. (2013). *Parliament in British Politics*. London: Palgrave Macmillan.

Norton, P. (2017). Speaking for Parliament. *Parliamentary Affairs*, 70: 191–206.

Norton, P., and Wood, D. (1993). *Back from Westminster: British Members of Parliament and their Constituents*. Lexington: University Press of Kentucky.

Obstfeld, D. (2005). Social networks, the *tertius iungens* orientation, and involvement in innovation. *Administrative Science Quarterly*, 50(1): 100–30.

Oliver, D. (1995). The Committee on Standards in Public Life: Regulating the conduct of Members in Parliament. *Parliamentary Affairs*, 48: 590–601.

Oosterhof, N. N., and Todorov, A. (2008). The functional basis of face evaluation. *Proceedings of the National Academy of Sciences of the United States of America*, 105(32): 11087–92.

Operation Black Vote (2008). *How to Achieve Better BME Political Representation*. London: Government Equalities Office.

Operation Black Vote (2009). *Submission from Operation Black Vote*. Speaker's Conference on Parliamentary Representation. http://www.publications.parliament.uk/pa/spconf/167/167we03.htm

Pacheco, G., and Owen, B. (2015). Moving through the political participation hierarchy: A focus on personal values. *Applied Economics*, 47(3): 222–38.

Pager, D., and Quillian, L. (2005). Walking the talk? What employers say versus what they do. *American Sociological Review*, 70(3): 355–80.

Parks-Leduc, L., Feldman, G., and Bardi, A. (2015). Personality traits and personal values: A meta-analysis. *Personality and Social Psychology Review*, 19(1): 3–29.

Payne, J., Woshinsky, O., Veblen, E., Coogan, W., and Bigler, G. (1984). *The Motivation of Politicians*. Chicago: Nelson-Hall.

Perry, J. L. (2000). Bringing society in: Toward a theory of public-service motivation. *Journal of Public Administration Research and Theory*, 10(2): 471–88.

Perry, J. L., and Hondeghem, A. (2008). *Motivation in Public Management: The Call of Public Service*. Oxford: Oxford University Press.

Petty, R. E., and Cacioppo, J. T. (1986). The elaboration likelihood model of persuasion. In L. Berkowitz (ed), *Advances in Experimental Social Psychology*. New York: Academic Press, pp 123–205.

Phillips, A. (1995). *The Politics of Presence*. Oxford: Clarendon Press.

Pierson, P. (2004). *Politics in Time: History, Institutions, and Social Analysis*. Princeton, NJ: Princeton University Press.

Pitkin, H. F. (1967). *The Concept of Representation*. Berkeley CA: University of California Press.

Pitkin, H. F. (2004). Representation and democracy: an uneasy alliance. *Scandinavian Political Studies*, 27(3): 335–42.

Piurko, Y., Schwartz, S. H., and Davidov, E. (2011). Basic personal values and the meaning of left-right political orientations in 20 countries. *Political Psychology*, 32: 537–61.

Plumb, A. (2013). Research note: A comparison of free vote patterns in Westminster-style parliaments. *Commonwealth & Comparative Politics*, 51(2): 254–66.

Poguntke, T., and Webb, P. (2005). *The Presidentialisation of Politics: A Comparative Study of Modern Democracies*. Oxford: Oxford University Press.

Post, J. M. (ed). (2003). *The Psychological Assessment of Political Leaders*. Ann Arbor: University of Michigan Press.

Preece, J. (2016). Mind the gender gap: An experiment on the influence of self-efficacy on political interest. *Politics & Gender*, 12(1): 198–217.

Preece, J. and Stoddard, O. (2015). Why women don't run: Experimental evidence on gender differences in political competition aversion. *Journal of Economic Behavior & Organization*, 117: 296–308.

Prinz, T. S. (1993). The career paths of elected politicians: A review and prospectus. In S. Williams and E. Lascher (eds), *Ambition and Beyond: Career Paths of American Politicians*. Berkeley, CA: Institute of Governmental Studies, pp 11–63.

Putnik, D. L., and Bornstein, M. H. (2016). Measurement invariance conventions and reporting: The state of the art and future directions for psychological research, *Developmental Review*, 41: 71–90.

Radice, L., Vallance, E., and Willis, V. (1990). *Member of Parliament: The Job of a Backbencher*. Basingstoke: Macmillan.

Ragin, C. C. (2008). *Redesigning Social Inquiry: Fuzzy Sets and Beyond*. Chicago: University of Chicago Press.

Rahat, G. and Kenig, O. (2018). *From Party Politics to Personalized Politics? Party Change and Political Personalization in Democracies*. Oxford: Oxford University Press.

Rahat, G., and Shaefer, T. (2007). The personalization(s) of politics: Israel, 1949–2003. *Political Communication*, 24: 65–80.

Rahn, W., Aldrich, J., Borgida, E., and Sullivan, D. (1990). A social-cognitive model of candidate appraisal. In J. Ferejohn and J. Kuklinski (eds), *Citizens and Politics: Perspectives from Political Psychology*. Cambridge: Cambridge University Press, pp 136–159.

Rasch, B. E. (2009). Opposition parties, electoral incentives and the control of government ministers: Parliamentary questioning in Norway. In S. Ganghof, C. Hönnige and C. Stecker (eds), *Parlamente, Agendasetzung und Vetospieler: Festschrift für Herbert Döring*. Wiesbaden: VS Verlag für Sozialwissenschaften, pp 199–214.

Riemann, R., Grubich, C., Hempel, S., Mergl, S., and Richter, M. (1993). Personality and attitudes towards current political topics. *Personality and Individual Differences*, 15: 313–21.

Reeher, G. (2006). *First Person Political*. London: New York University Press.

Renshon, S. (1995). *The Clinton Presidency: Campaigning, Governing and the Psychology of Leadership*. Boulder, CO: Westview.

Rhodes, R. A. W. (2011). *Everyday Life in British Government*. Oxford: Oxford University Press.

Richards, P. G. (1970). *Parliament and Conscience*. London: George Allen and Unwin.

Riddell, P. (1993). *Honest Opportunism: The Rise of the Career Politician*. London: Hamish Hamilton.

Ritz, A., Brewer, G. A., and Neumann, O. (2016). Public service motivation: A systematic literature review and outlook. *Public Administration Review*, 76: 414–26.

Roccas, S., Sagiv, L., Oppenheim, S., Elster, A., and Gal, A. (2014). Integrating content and structure aspects of the self: Traits, values, and self-improvement. *Journal of Personality*, 82(2): 144–57.

Rocha, R. R., Tolbert, C. J., Bowen, D. C., and Clark, C. J. (2010). Race and turnout: Does descriptive representation in state legislatures increase minority voting? *Political Research Quarterly*, 63(August): 890–907.

Rokeach, M. (1973). *The Nature of Human Values*. New York: Free Press.

Roosevelt, T. (1910). Citizenship in a Republic. 23 April, Sorbonne, Paris. www.artofmanliness.com/citizenship-in-a-republic-by-theodore-roosevelt/

Rosanvallon, P. (2006). *La Contre-Démocratie: La Politique à l' Âge de la Défiance*. Paris: Editions du Seuil.

Rosenblatt, G. (2006). *A Year in the Life: From Member of Public to Member of Parliament*. London: The Hansard Society.

Runciman, D. (2008). *Political Hypocrisy: The Mask of Power, from Hobbes to Orwell and Beyond*. Princeton, NJ: Princeton University Press.

Rush, M. (1997). Damming the sleaze: The new code of conduct and the outside interests of MPs in the British House of Commons. *Journal of Legislative Studies*, 3: 10–28.

Rush, M. (2001). *The Role of the Member of Parliament since 1868*. Oxford: Oxford University Press.

Rush, M. (2005). *Parliament Today*. Manchester: Manchester University Press.

Rush, M., and Giddings, P. (2011). *Learning the Ropes or Determining Behaviour?* London: Palgrave Macmillan.

Russell, M. (2014). Parliamentary party cohesion: Some explanations from psychology. *Party Politics*, 20(5): 712–23.

Russell, M. (2016). Parliament: A significant constraint on government. In R. Heffernan, C. Hay, M. Russell, and P. Cowley (eds), *Developments in British Politics 10*. Basingstoke: Palgrave Macmillan, pp 99–121.

Russell, M., Gover, D., and Wollter, K. (2016). Does the executive dominate the Westminster legislative process? Six reasons for doubt. *Parliamentary Affairs*, 69(2): 286–308.

Saalfeld, T. (2011). Parliamentary questions as instruments of substantive representation: Visible minorities in the UK House of Commons, 2005–10. *Journal of Legislative Studies*, 17(3): 271–89.

Saalfeld, T., and Bischof, D. (2013). Minority-ethnic MPs and the substantive representation of minority interests in the House of Commons, 2005–2011. *Parliamentary Affairs*, 66: 305–28.

Saalfeld, T. and Müller, W. C. (1997). Roles in legislative studies: A theoretical introduction. In W. C. Muller and T. Saalfeld (eds), *Members of Parliament in Western Europe*. London: Frank Cass, pp 1–16.

Saggar, S., and Geddes, A. (2000). Negative and positive racialization: Re-examining ethnic minority political representation in the UK. *Journal of Ethnic and Migration Studies*, 26(1): 25–44.

Sagiv, L. (2002). Vocational interests and basic values. *Journal of Career Assessment*, 10(2): 233–57.

Sagiv, L., and Roccas, S. (2017). What personal values are and what they are not: Taking a cross-cultural perspective. In S. Roccas and L. Sagiv (eds), *Values and Behaviour: Taking a Cross Cultural Perspective*. Switzerland AG: Springer International Publishing, pp 3–13.

Sandy, C. J., Gosling, S. D., Schwartz, S. H., and Koelkebeck, T. (2017). The development and validation of brief and ultra-brief measures of values. *Journal of Personality Assessment*, 99: 545–55.

Saris, W. (2004). Different judgment models for policy questions: Competing or complementary? In W. Saris and P. Sniderman (ed), *Studies in Public Opinion*. Princeton, NJ: Princeton University Press, pp 17–36.

Saroglou, V., and Munoz-Garcia, A. (2008). Individual differences in religion and spirituality: An issue of personality traits and/or values. *Journal for the Scientific Study of Religion*, 43: 83–101.

Sartori, G. (1970). Concept misformation in comparative politics. *American Political Science Review*, 64: 1033–53.

Saward, M. (2006). The representative claim. *Contemporary Political Theory*, 5(3): 297–318.

Saward, M. (2010). *The Representative Claim*. Oxford: Oxford University Press.

Schattschneider, E. E. (2009). *Party Government, American Government in Action Series* [1942]. New Brunswick, NJ: Transaction.

Scherkoske, G. (2013). Whither integrity I: Recent faces of integrity. *Philosophy Compass*, 8(1): 28–39.

Schlesinger, J. A. (1966). *Ambition and Politics: Political Careers in the United States*. Chicago: Rand McNally.

Schmidt, V. (2008). Discursive institutionalism: The explanatory power of ideas and discourse. *Annual Review of Political Science*, 11(1): 303–26.

Schoen, H., and Schumann, S. (2007). Personality traits, partisan attitudes, and voting behaviour: Evidence from Germany. *Political Psychology*, 28: 471–98.

Schwartz, S. (1992). Universals in the content and structure of values: Theory and empirical tests in 20 countries. In M. Zanna (ed), *Advances in Experimental Social Psychology*. New York: Academic Press, pp 1–65.

Schwartz, S. (1994). Are there universal aspects in the structure and contents of human values? *Journal of Social Issues*, 50: 19–45.

Schwartz, S. H., and Boehnke, K. (2004). Evaluating the structure of human values with confirmatory factor analysis. *Journal of Research in Personality*, 38: 230–255.

Schwartz, S. H. (2005). Robustness and fruitfulness of a theory of universals in individual human values. In A. Tamayo and J. B. Porto (eds), *Values and Behaviour in Organizations*. Petrópolis: Vozes, pp 56–95.

Schwartz, S. H. (2006). Basic human values: Theory, measurement and applications. *Revue française de sociologie*, 47(4): 929–968.

Schwartz, S. (2014). Functional theories of human values: Comment on Gouveia, Milfont, and Guerra (2014). *Personality and Individual Differences*, 68: 247–49.

Schwartz, S. H., and Bilsky, W. (1990). Toward a theory of the universal content and structure of values: Extensions and cross-cultural replications. *Journal of Personality and Social Psychology*, 58: 878–91.

Schwartz, S. H., and Cieciuch, J. (2016). Values. In F. T. L. Leong, D. Bartram, F. Cheung, K. F. Geisinger, and D. Iliescu (eds), *The ITC International Handbook of Testing and Assessment*. New York: Oxford University Press, pp 950–51.

Schwartz, S. H., and Rubel, T. (2005). Sex differences in value priorities: Cross-cultural and multi-method studies. *Journal of Personality and Social Psychology*, 89: 1010–28.

Schwartz, S., Verkasalo, M., Antonovsky, A., and Sagiv, L. (1997). Value priorities and social desirability: Much substance, some style. *British Journal of Social Psychology*, 36(1): 3–18.

Schwartz, S., Caprara, G. V., and Vecchione, M. (2010). Basic personal values, core political values, and voting: A longitudinal analysis. *Political Psychology*, 31(3): 421–52.

Scott, C. and Medeiros, M. (2019). Personality and political careers: What personality types are likely to run for office and get elected? *Personality and Individual Differences*. https://doi.org/10.1016/j.paid.2019.109600.

Searing, D. (1994). *Westminster's World*. Cambridge, MA: Harvard University Press.

Sears, D. O., and Brown, C. (2013). Childhood and Adult Political Development. In L. Huddy, D. O. Sears, and J. S. Levy (eds), *The Oxford Handbook of Political Psychology* (2nd edn). Oxford: Oxford University Press, pp 59–95.

Shugart, M. S., Valdini, M. E., and Suominen, K. (2005). Looking for locals: Voter information demands and personal vote-earning attributes of legislators under proportional representation. *American Journal of Political Science*, 49(2): 437–49.

Sieberer, U. (2006). Party unity in parliamentary democracies: A comparative analysis. *Journal of Legislative Studies*, 12(2): 150–78.

Silbermann, R. (2015). Gender roles, work-life balance, and running for office. *Quarterly Journal of Political Science*, 10: 123–53.

Simon, H. A. (1985). Human nature in politics: The dialogue of psychology with political science. *American Political Science Review*, 79(2): 293–304.

Sloam, J., and Henn, M. (2018). *Youthquake 2017: The Rise of Young Cosmopolitans in Britain*. London: Palgrave.

Small, M. (2009). 'How many cases do I need?' On science and the logic of case selection in field-based research. *Ethnography*, 10(1): 5–38.

Sniderman, P. M., and Bullock, J. G. (2004). A consistency theory of public opinion and political choice: The hypothesis of menu dependence. In W. E. Saris and P. M. Sniderman (eds), *Studies in Public Opinion: Gauging Attitudes, Non-attitudes, Measurement Error, and Change*. Princeton, NJ: Princeton University Press, pp 337–57.

Sniderman, P. M., and Levendusky, M. S. (2009). An institutional theory of political choice. In R. J. Dalton and H-D. Klingemann (eds), *The Oxford Handbook of Political Behaviour*. Oxford: Oxford University Press, pp 437–56.

Sobolewska, M. (2013). Party strategies and the descriptive representation of ethnic minorities: The 2010 British general election. *West European Politics*, 36: 615–33.

Sood, G., and Iyengar, S. (2014). All in the eye of the beholder: Partisan affect and ideological accountability. Unpublished manuscript. www.gsood.com/research/papers/inNout.pdf

Soroka, S., Penner, E., and Blidook, K. (2009). Constituency influence in Parliament. *Canadian Journal of Political Science*, 42(3): 563–91.

Stafford, L. (2008). Social exchange theories. In L. A. Baster and D. O. Braithwaite (eds), *Engaging Theories in Interpersonal Communication: Multiple Perspectives*. Thousand Oaks, CA: Sage, pp 377–89.

Steenbergen, M. R., and Leimgruber, P. (2010). Values and value change: Theoretical approaches and empirical patterns. In S. Hug and H. Kriesi (eds), *Value Change in Switzerland*. Plymouth: Lexington, pp 3–22.

Stegmaier, M., Lewis-Beck, M. S., and Smets, K. (2013). Standing for Parliament: Do Black, Asian and minority ethnic candidates pay extra? *Parliamentary Affairs*, 66(2): 268–85.

Stoker, G. (2006). *Why Politics Matters: Making Democracy Work*. Basingstoke: Palgrave Macmillan.

Stoker, G., Hay, C., and Barr, M. (2016). Fast thinking: Implications for democratic politics. *European Journal of Political Research*, 55: 3–21.

Stokes, D. (1992), Valence politics. In D. Kavanagh (ed), *Electoral Politics*. Oxford: Oxford University Press, pp 141–64.

Strøm, K. (1990). A behavioural theory of competitive political parties. *American Journal of Political Science*, 34(2): 565–98.

Strøm, K. (1997). Rules, reasons and routines: Legislative roles in parliamentary democracies. *Journal of Legislative Studies*, 3(1): 155–74.

Strong, J. (2015). Interpreting the Syria vote: Parliament and British foreign policy. *International Affairs*, 91(5): 1123–39.

Tajfel, H. (1981). Human groups and social categories. *Human Groups and Social Categories*, 18(4): 127–42.

Tajfel, H., and Turner, J. C. (1979). An integrative theory of intergroup conflict. In W. G. Austin and S. Worchel (eds), *The Social Psychology of Intergroup Relations*. Monterey, CA: Brookes/Cole Publishing.

Teles, F. (2015). The distinctiveness of democratic political leadership. *Political Studies Review*, 13: 22–36.

The Electoral Commission (2016). Introduction to the Recall of MPs Act 2015. https://www.electoralcommission.org.uk/__data/assets/pdf_file/0004/184324/Recall-Act-Factsheet.pdf

Thomassen, J., and Rosema, M. (2009). Party identification revisited. In J. Bartle and P. Bellucci (eds), *Party Identification, Social Identity and Political Experience: Partisanship*. London: Routledge/ECPR Studies in European Political Science, pp 42–59.

Thompson, G., Staddon, A., and Stapenhurst, R. (2018). Motivation of legislators and political will. *Public Integrity*, 22(2): 134-153. doi: 10.1080/10999922.2018.1511669.

Thompson, L. (2016). Debunking the myths of Bill Committees in the British House of Commons. *Politics*, 36: 36–48.

Thorisdottir, H., Jost, J. T., Liviatan, I., and Shrout, P. E. (2007). Psychological needs and values underlying the left-right political orientation: Cross-national evidence from Eastern and Western Europe. *Public Opinion Quarterly*, 71: 175–203.

Tiernan, A., and Weller, P. (2010). *Learning to Be a Minister: Heroic Expectations, Practical Realities.* Melbourne: Melbourne University Press.

Treier, S., and Hillygus, D. S. (2009). The nature of political ideology in the contemporary electorate. *Public Opinion Quarterly*, 73(4): 679–703.

Trope, Y., Liberman, N., and Wakslak, C. (2007). Construal levels and psychological distance: Effects on representation, prediction, evaluation, and behaviour. *Journal of Consumer Psychology*, 17(2): 83–95.

Tsebelis, G. (2002). *Veto Players: How Political Institutions Work.* Princeton, NJ: Princeton University Press.

Turner, A. W. (2013). *A Classless Society: Britain in the 1990s.* London: Aurum Press.

Uhlaner, C. J., and Scola, B. (2016). Collective representation as a mobilizer: Race/ethnicity, gender, and their intersections at the state level. *State Politics & Policy Quarterly*, 16(2): 227–63.

United Kingdom House of Commons (1998–2010). *Sessional Returns.* London: The Stationery Office.

Van Deth, J. W. (1995). Introduction: The impact of values. In J. W. van Deth and E. Scarbrough (eds), *The Impact of Values.* Oxford: Oxford University Press, pp 1–18.

Van Hiel, A., Kossowska, M., and Mervielde, I. (2000). The relationship between openness to experience and political ideology. *Personality and Individual Differences*, 28, 741–51.

Vecchione, M., and Caprara, G. V. (2009). Personality determinants of political participation: The contribution of traits and self-efficacy beliefs. *Personality and Individual Differences*, 46(4): 487–92.

Vecchione, M., Schoen, H., González, C. J. L., Cieciuch, J., Pavlopoulos, V., and Caprara, G. V. (2011). Personality correlates of party preference: The big five in five big European countries. *Personality and Individual Differences*, 51(6): 737–742.

Vecchione, M., Schwartz, S., Caprara, G., Schoen, H., Cieciuch, J., Silvester, J., Bain, P., Bianchi, G., Kirmanoglu, H., Baslevent, C., Mamali, C., Manzi, J., Pavlopoulos, V., Posnova, T., Torres, C., Verkasalo, M., Lönnqvist, J., Vondráková, E., Welzel, C. and

Alessandri, G. (2015). Personal values and political activism: A cross-national study. *British Journal of Psychology*, 106(1): 84–106.

Vellinga, V., Cormican, M., Hanahoe, B., Bennett, K., and Murphy, A. W. (2011). Opt-out as an acceptable method of obtaining consent in medical research: A short report. *BMC Medical Research Methodology*, 11: 40–10.

Verba, S., Schlozman, K. L., and Brady, H. (1995). *Voice and Equality: Civic Voluntarism in American Politics*. Cambridge, MA: Harvard University Press.

Verplanken, B., and Holland, R. W. (2002). Motivated decision making: Effects of activation and self-centrality of values on choices and behaviour. *Journal of Personality and Social Psychology*, 82(3): 434–47.

Vivyan, N., and Wagner, M. (2015). What do voters want from their local MP? *The Political Quarterly*, 86(1): 33–40.

Volgy, T. J. (2001). *Politics in the Trenches: Citizens, Politicians, and the Fate of Democracy*. Tucson: University of Arizona Press.

Wauters, B., Thijssen, P., Van Aelst, P., and Pilet, J-B. (2018). Centralized personalization at the expense of decentralized personalization: the decline of preferential voting in Belgium (2003–2014). *Party Politics*, 24: 511–23.

Weinberg, J. (2019). The winner takes it all? A psychological study of political success among UK Members of Parliament. *Parliamentary Affairs*. doi.org/10.1093/pa/gsz017.

Weinberg, J. (2020). Who wants to be a politician? Basic values and candidate emergence in the United Kingdom. *British Journal of Political Science*. doi:10.1017/S0007123419000814.

Weller, P., and Grattan, M. (1981). *Can Ministers Cope?* Melbourne: Hutchinson Group.

Westen, D. (2007). *The Political Brain*. New York: Public Affairs.

White, J., and Ypi, L. (2016). *The Meaning of Partisanship*. Oxford: Oxford University Press.

Whiteley, P., and Seyd, P. (2002). *High Intensity Participation: The Dynamics of Party Activism in Britain*. Michigan: University of Michigan Press.

Williams, B. (1981). *Moral Luck: Philosophical Papers 1973–1980*. Cambridge: Cambridge University Press.

Wilson, D., and Game, C. (2011). Local Government in the United Kingdom (5th edn). London: Red Globe Press.

Winter, D. (1987). Leader appeal, leader performance, and the motive profiles of leaders and followers: A study of American presidents and elections. *Journal of Personality and Social Psychology*, 52(1): 196–202.

Wolbrecht, C., and Campbell, D. E. (2007). Leading by example: Female Members of Parliament as political role models. *American Journal of Political Science*, 51(October): 921–39.

Wolbrecht, C., and Campbell, D. (2017). Role models revisited: Youth, novelty, and the impact of female candidates. *Politics, Groups, and Identities*, 5(3): 418–34.

Wright, T. (2010). What are MPs for? *Political Quarterly*, 81(3): 298–308.

Wyatt, M., and Silvester, J. (2018). Do voters get it right? A test of the ascription–actuality trait theory of leadership with political elites. *Leadership Quarterly*, 29(5): 609-621. doi.org/10.1016/j.leaqua.2018.02.001.

YouGov (2017). Corbyn vs May: How the public sees the two leaders. https://yougov.co.uk/news/2017/06/06/corbyn-vs-may-how-public-sees-two-leaders/

Young, R., Cracknell, R., Tetteh, E., Griffin, G., and Brown, D. (2003). *Parliamentary Questions, Debate Contributions and Participation in Commons Divisions*. London: House of Commons.

Zaccaro, S. J. (2007). Trait-based perspectives of leadership. *American Psychologist*, 62(1): 6–16.

Zittel, T. (2012). Legislators and their representational roles. In M. Blomgren and O. Rozenberg (eds), *Parliamentary Roles in Modern Legislatures*. Abingdon: Routledge, pp 101–18.

Zumbrunnen, J., and Gangl, A. (2008). Conflict, fusion, or coexistence? The complexity of contemporary American conservatism. *Political Behaviour*, 30: 199–221.

Index

A

accents 157
accountability 1, 28, 71, 79, 114, 163
Achievement values 33, 40, 68, 86, 102, 142, 143
Adams, J 82
African Americans 55
age 17, 46, 86, 103, 151, 153, 160
aggression 36
Agreeableness 10, 29, 84, 85, 88
air strikes 122
Allen, Nicholas 28
Allen, Peter 6, 25, 42
  Why It Matters Who Our Politicians Are 5
allowances, MPs 27
  see also expenses scandal
All-Party Group on Women in Parliament 61
All-Party Parliamentary Group for Fair Representation 63
all-women shortlists 47, 61
  see also women
altruism 28, 33, 41
ambition 3, 37, 40, 41, 51, 72, 95
anti-politics 1, 3–8, 21, 23, 25, 61, 79, 80, 146, 161
apartheid 86
aristocrats 70–1
Atkeson, L.R 55
authoritarian 86

B

backbenchers 25, 110, 118, 126, 135, 141
  Backbench Business Committee 114
BAME groups 63–70
BBC Parliament channel 114
Beer, Samuel 114
behaviour *see* parliamentary political behaviour (IMPPB)
behavioural personalization 147
Beith, Sir Alan 143
beliefs 6, 11, 40, 87, 113, 164

Benevolence values 11, 30, 33, 46, 48, 156, 157
Benton, Meghan 140
Bercow, John 162
Best, Heinrich 29, 85
Big Five measure 10, 83, 84
Blair, Tony 101, 119, 129, 132
Blakeley, Ruth 19
blue-collar manual professions 54
Bogdanor, Vernon *British Constitution in the Twentieth Century* 109
Bor, A. 150
Borg, I. 12
boundary reform 119
Brexit 21, 153
  see also European Union
British Constitution in the Twentieth Century 109
British Psychological Society (BPS) 3
British Social Attitudes Survey 125
brokerage professions 47, 71, 72, 74, 76

C

Cairney, Paul 25, 71, 74
Callaghan, James 119
Cameron, David 64, 120, 122, 128
campaigns 79, 81, 100, 161
Campbell, R 14, 58
Canada 29
candidates 10, 149, 153, 158, 161
  emergence 3, 41–51, 65, 68, 71
  selection 9, 47, 64, 116, 151
Caprara, G. V. 88
careerism *see* professionalization
change, effect 12, 33
character valance 95
childcare 61
Christians 153–4
Citizen Political Ambition Panel Study (US) 42
civic voluntarism 42
Civil Partnership Act 2004 120
Clarke, H. 5

closed system 72
coalitions 87, 93
code of conduct 72, 113, 165
Coker, Vernon 145
collective representation 55, 56
Committee on Standards in Public Life 72, 165
'common good', perceptions of the 34, 80, 83
community connection 76
competence 149
ComRes 14
confidence 37, 57, 61
Conformity values 11, 33, 40, 103, 120, 142, 157
congruency, MP-voter 23, 68, 94–101, 98, 102, 104, 125, 158, 160
conjoint experiments 150–4, 154–9
connections 40
Conscientiousness 10, 29, 84, 85
consensus 142, 143
Conservation values 11–12, 16, 31, 40, 92, 95, 99
  and Conservative MPs 86, 125, 163
  and occupations 43, 47, 74
  and the public 30, 83, 160
Conservative Party 101, 104, 132, 145, 157
  and Conservation values 23, 86, 163
  and ethnicity 64
  and military action 122, 127
  and same-sex marriage 120, 125
  support for 81, 102, 153
  and women 57, 62
conservatives 83
continuity 109
Corbett, Jack 6
Corbyn, Jeremy 53, 83, 101, 122
core supporters 81
corruption 28, 107
councillors, local 30, 34, 46, 66, 71
Cowley, Philip 118
Crewe, E. 113
cross-party collaboration 141
custody sentence 27
cynicism 4, 5, 8, 42, 146, 163

D
Daesh 126
decision making 23, 41
demand-side explanation 4, 8
demand-side representation 56
democracy 9, 21, 22, 25, 54–6, 61, 80, 95, 149
Democrats 81, 84
demographic variables 11, 30, 46
demonization of politicians 4

Denmark 29, 84, 85, 88, 92
descriptive representation 22, 54–6, 61, 62, 70
desire for office 116
detachment of the political class 70
devolution 72, 119
Dietrich, B. J. 84
disabilities, people with 56, 151, 157
disadvantaged groups 56, 63
disciplinary incentives 116
diversity 15, 47, 56, 63, 87
dog-whistle politics 26
Dovi, Suzanne 56, 62
dual motivations theory 81, 100

E
Early Day Motions (EDMs) 133–7
economic ideology 89–93
education 55, 83, 103, 151, 153, 160
  higher education 46, 49, 54
elections 1, 5, 27, 48, 55, 114, 115
Electoral Commission 15, 16
electorate 19, 50, 160, 163
elites 1, 5, 12, 27, 70, 71, 72, 80, 94, 95, 163
Emotional Stability 29
England, North 164
English, Patrick 64
environment, the 34
equality 21, 48, 55, 63, 76, 83, 86, 97, 125
equal pay 69
ethical behaviour 5, 27, 74
ethnicity 22, 42, 44, 54–6, 63–70, 151, 153, 160
European Social Survey 16, 54, 88, 95, 97
European Union 1, 119
  referendum campaign 26
  Withdrawal Bill 130–3
expenses scandal 1, 2, 5, 21, 156, 158, 159
expressive partisanship 83
Extraversion 10, 29, 85

F
family 6, 42, 50, 62, 145, 151
female genital mutilation (FGM) 143
females see women
Fenno, R. 162
Fixed Term Parliaments Act 2011 114
Flinders, Matthew 4, 6
France 57, 122
Free Democratic Party (FDP) 85
free votes 118, 120, 124, 125, 127
frontbench MPs 38–9, 40
  see also leadership

G
Gamble, Andrew 109

Game, Chris 30
'gap' accounts 6, 7
Garzia, Diego 82
Geddes, Marc 141
gender 44, 46, 55, 56, 57–63, 103, 151, 153
General Elections (UK) 53, 54, 57, 63, 95, 98, 103, 145, 153
Germany 29, 82, 85
Giddings, P. 14
girls 58
Glorious Revolution 1688 109
government bills 110, 114
government policy 140
Green Party 153

H
Habermas, Jürgen 7
Haidt, Jonathan 84
Hall, Edward 28
Hanania, Richard 84, 88
Hansard Society 2, 14, 23, 156
Hardman, Isabel 2
Healey, Denis 76
Hedonism values 11, 33, 86, 102
helping people 76
Herman, Lisa 79
higher education 46, 49
Hindmoor, Andrew 54
Historical Institutionalism (HI) 109, 110, 112
Hodge, Margaret 143
Holman, M 153
homogeneity 53–4, 159
honesty 5, 95, 165
House of Commons 17, 63, 162
  conduct/procedures 27, 72, 113, 135–44
  ethnicity in the 63–4
  voting behaviours 108, 118–23
  women in the 47, 57, 61
House of Lords 57, 116
Huddy, L. 82

I
identity and partisanship 82
ideology 98, 117, 123, 128, 130
  and basic values 88–93
immigration 64, 155
Independent Group 93
Independent Parliamentary Standards Authority (IPSA) 27
inequality see equality
injustice 48
'in-role' success see success
Inside the Commons 113
instantiation 34, 93, 128

institutional pressures 57, 115, 119, 132
institutions of politics 109
instrumental jobs 71, 72, 74
integrity 27, 74, 149, 165
Ipsos MORI 2
Iraq 119, 122, 128, 129–30
Israel 83
Italy 29, 82, 83, 84, 85, 95, 102

J
Johnson, Boris 81

K
Kahneman, D. 4
Kam, Christopher 131, 164
  Party Discipline and Parliamentary Politics 116
Kane, J. 7
Katz, Richard 87
Keane, John Life and Death of Democracy 6
Kellerman, Michael 138
Kelsen, Hans 26, 27
Kelso, Alexandra 109
Kim, S. 28
King, Anthony 1
Klemmenson, R 29, 88
Kolstad, Ivar 161

L
Labour Party 38, 53, 83, 132, 145, 157, 159
  and candidates 47, 48, 49
  and military action 122, 126, 128, 129
  personality characteristics 23
  and same-sex marriage 120, 125
  and Self-Transcendence 85, 86, 163–4
  support for 17, 81, 100–1, 104
  and women 57, 62
Latinos 55
Lausten, L. 150
law 47, 71
Lawless, Jennifer 42
leader evaluations 157
leadership 9, 40, 69, 81, 82, 87, 94–101, 116, 148
LEADs model 116, 131, 164
left wing 62, 83, 97, 100
Leimgruber, P. 115
LGBTQ+ 56
Liberal Democrats 36, 37, 50, 81, 85, 153
Lidlington, David 145
Life and Death of Democracy 6
Likert scale 15
local issues 135, 156
local parties 47
London Mayoral elections 57
London Olympics 143

Lovenduski, J. 14
low income 55
loyalty 95, 116

M
Mair, Peter 87
Major, John 119
males *see* men
malfeasance 165
mandate, imperative 26
manifestos 79, 81, 82, 87
Mansbridge, Jane 55
manual occupations 54, 72
marginal constituencies 138
Marriage (Same Sex Couples) Bill 2013
    120, 123–30
Mass Observation 5
maternity leave 69
May, Erskine 113
May, Theresa 53, 57
media 7, 47, 114, 119, 140, 143, 163
    exposure to 38, 113
    and homogeneity of politicians 71, 74,
        158, 159
    and the personalization of politics 24,
        53, 146, 147, 148, 160, 161
Members of Parliament 2, 3, 13,
    14, 25, 72
    Recall Act 26–7
men 42, 54, 57, 58, 61, 103, 138
mental health and wellbeing 6, 15
Meyrowitz, Joshua 147
middle class 64
Miliband, Ed 120
military action in Syria 122, 126–30
Millbank House 20
ministerial power 108
minority groups 55, 56, 63, 64, 65
mirroring constituents 54
misconduct 8, 165
Montesquieu 26
morals 6, 8, 84, 119, 123
motivations 19, 28, 31, 44, 51, 59, 83,
    116, 165
Murray, Henry 9
Muslims 153–4

N
Näsström, Sofia 27
national interests 156
neoliberal reform agenda 7, 101
Netherlands 82
Neuroticism 10, 29, 85
New Labour 101
News International 143
Nolan, Lord 72
non-voters 101–5

Nørgaard, A. S 29, 88
North, Lord 128
Norton, Philip
    Inside the Commons 113
    Parliament in British Politics 109

O
occupational backgrounds 17, 22, 56, 73,
    75, 151, 153
    brokerage professions 47, 71, 72, 76
office, consider running for 42
Openness to Change values 12, 16, 29,
    30, 31, 43, 47, 88, 99
Openness to Experience 10, 84
opportunities from advancement 38
opportunity structures 44, 47, 51
Opposition Days 114
opposition party 110
Oxford/Cambridge 54

P
Palace of Westminster 19, 21
Palmer, Nick 145
parliament 27, 28, 61, 71, 109, 112
parliamentary political behaviour
    (IMPPB) 19, 107–11, 113–18, 119,
    131, 134–5, 141, 144
Parliament in British Politics 109
Parliament Today 109
participant observation 17
partisanship 13, 33, 79–84
Party Discipline and Party Politics 116
Party of Democratic Socialism (PDS) 85
peace, motivated by 122
perceptual-balance theory 148–9
personalities of politicians 13, 29–35,
    53–4, 84–7
personality characteristics 24, 95,
    158, 162–4
'personality gap' 98, 101
personality studies 9, 10, 13
personalization 24, 27, 145–50
personal success *see* success in politics
persuasion 40
petitions 27
Phillips, Anne 62
phone hacking 143
Pitkin, Hannah 26, 54
Piurko, Y. 88
polarization 81
policy decisions 10, 25, 38, 69, 82, 101
political behaviour *see* parliamentary
    political behaviour (IMPPB)
political career, choosing a 41
political choice 111, 113
political opportunity structures 44, 65
political parties 71, 79–80, 84, 87, 94, 163

membership 1, 10, 47, 81
  whips 114, 116, 130, 132
political psychology 9–12
Political Studies Association (PSA) 3
politicians and the public 29–35
politics, entering 25–9
polling agencies 2, 14, 153
popular disengagement 21, 79, 165
population subgroups 55
populism 1, 26, 94, 161
Portcullis House 20
Portrait Values Questionnaire (PVQ)
  15, 30, 35
post-communist 85
Power Achievement 11
Power values 22, 35–41, 48, 123, 125,
  128, 156
preferable descriptive representatives
  56, 65, 68
press barons 159
Prime Ministers 53, 57, 81, 119
  David Cameron 64, 120, 122, 128
  Tony Blair 101, 119, 129, 132
principal-agent relationship 162
Principles of Public Life 165
private education 153
problem-solving 47
professionalization 4, 6, 22, 54, 70–7, 153
psychological characteristics 8, 25, 27
psychological gap 164
public distrust and apathy 1–6, 29–33, 128
public profile 141
Public Service Motivation (PSM) 28–9

Q
qualitative and quantitative analyses
  2, 13, 16

R
racial groups 42, 55
  see also BAME groups
radicalisation 153
Rahat, G. 148
rebelling 132–3
Recall of MPs Act 2015 26–7
recruitment 57, 63, 71
'Red Wall' 164
referendum (EU) 1
religion 28, 103, 151, 153, 160
representation 3–9, 21, 26, 27, 80, 162
  types of 22, 54–6, 61, 62, 65, 70
reproduction 69
Republicans 81, 84
research 2, 13–15, 16–20, 19
  methodology 93, 151
Rhodes, R. A. W 6, 113
Richards, Peter 118

right wing 83, 85, 100
rile scores 101
Ritz, A. 28
Roccas, S. 12
role models 58
Roosevelt, President Theodore 25
Rush, Michael 14, 71
  Parliament Today 109
Russell, Meg 110, 116, 140

S
Sagiv, L. 12
same-sex marriage 119, 120, 123–30
Sartori, G. 10
Schlesinger, Joseph *Ambition and Politics* 41
Schneider, M. 153
Schwartz, Shalom 10, 11–12, 16, 51,
  88, 115
Scola, B. 55
Scotland 119
Scottish National Party (SNP) 33, 85, 107
scrutiny 140
Searing, Donald 14
seat, MP can lose their 27
Security values 11, 102, 138, 139, 157
select committees 72, 114, 135, 140–4
self-belief 38
Self-Direction values 11, 33, 103
Self-Enhancement values 11–12, 16, 37,
  40, 43, 49, 58, 74, 92, 160
Self-Transcendence values 11–12, 16, 21,
  36, 74, 83, 93, 125
  and the left 85, 95, 99, 163
  and occupations 43, 47
  and the public 156, 157, 160
  and women 58
Seyd, Pat 42
Shaefer, T. 148
social/environment welfare 48
social grades 153
social identity 82, 164
socialization experiences 44, 46, 49,
  57, 68, 82
socialization into politics 50, 116
social justice 21, 48
social media 162
social welfare policies 86
sociodemographic characteristics 80, 89,
  94, 103
socioeconomic characteristics 15, 28, 30,
  54, 64, 68, 160, 164
Spain 57
Speaker of the House of Commons 27,
  63, 162
stability 12, 97
state education 153
stereotypes 62

Stimulation values 11, 46, 86, 102, 103
Stoker, G. 4
Stokes, Donald 95
substantive representation 22, 61, 62, 65
success in politics 22, 70, 83, 100, 110
  candidates 43, 44, 61, 64, 65, 71
  in-role success 35–41
supply-side explanation 4, 8
support for others 97
Sweden 57
Syria 122, 126–30

T
tax evasion 161
television *see* media
tenure 17, 38
terrorism 153
Thompson, Gabriela 28
tolerance 103, 125
trade unions 45
Tradition values 11, 12, 31, 46, 67, 86,
  97, 103, 120
transfer of power 26
transparency 71, 72, 114, 119, 163
'trap' account 4, 7
Trump, President Donald 1, 162
trust 1, 5, 21, 54, 79, 158, 161
tuition fees 119
Twenty Item Values Inventory (TwIVI)
  15, 151

U
Uhlaner, C. J. 55
United Kingdom Independence Party
  (UKIP) 153
United Nations Security Council
  Resolution 122
United States 29, 41, 42, 53, 55, 81, 84,
  92, 122
  American National Election Study 150
Universalism values 11, 33, 48, 129, 130,
  136, 156
  and the Labour Party 128
  and same-sex marriage 120, 123
  and voters 102, 103, 157
university graduates 54

V
value hierarchies 31, 68, 165
values, basic 9, 10–13, 19, 21–4,
  29–35, 35–41
  and candidate emergence 41–51

and ethnicity 65–9
and ideology 88–94
and partisanship 79–84
of politicians 75, 84–7, 107–11, 112–18
and voting 101–5, 104–5, 118–23,
  123–30, 160–2
and women 58, 59
Vandenabeele, W. 28
Van Deth, J. W. 89
Vaz, Keith 143
Vecchione, M. 36
Verba, Sidney 70
vertical divisions 68
violating social norms 61
voter registration 55
voters, disillusioned 24
vote shares 81
voting (public) 10, 83, 84, 97, 100,
  104–5, 150–4, 160–2
voting behaviours (MPs) 13, 108,
  118–23, 124–33

W
Wales 119
warmth 149–50
Watson, Tom 143
wealth 72, 74, 76, 83, 87
welfare of people 34, 136
Westminster 3, 25, 61, 65, 114
  'bubble' 54, 75, 108
  Westminster Model (WM) 109,
  110, 144
whip/whipped votes 108, 114, 116, 119,
  120, 123, 130, 132
Whiteley, Paul 42
white people 54, 55, 64, 65, 103, 157
Why It Matters Who Our Politicians Are 5
Wiig, Arne 161
will of the people 26
Wilson, David 30
Winter, David 98
Wolbrecht, C. 58
women 42, 47, 55, 57–63, 69, 138, 153
Women's Equality Party 57, 58
working class 64, 72
working hours 61
work-life balance 57
Wright reforms 140
written questions 13, 65, 134, 137–40

Y
Yougov 153